Non-Persons

The Exclusion of Migrants in a Global Society

Alessandro Dal Lago

Translation by Marie Orton

IPOC
www.ipocpress.com

IPOC di Pietro Condemi
159, Viale Martesana
I – 20090 Vimodrone MI
Phone: +39-0236569954
Fax: +39-0236569954
ipoc@ipocpress.com
www.ipocpress.com

Translation by Marie Orton.
The moral rights of the translator have been asserted.

Original title: *Non-persone: l'esclusione dei migranti in una società globale*
First published by Giangiacomo Feltrinelli Editore, Milan, Italy, 1999
© Giangiacomo Feltrinelli Editore Milano, 1999, 2004, 2005

Printed in the United States and the United Kingdom on acid-free paper

ISBN: 978-88-95145-38-9

Front cover: Mario Digennaro, *L'uomo che pensa*, 2002.
www.mtartegallery.com

Contents

Acknowledgements

I could never have written this book without the help of friends, colleagues, and students. I owe a debt of gratitude to Salvatore Palidda, who has discussed migration, urban security, and the transformation of the social order with me for years, and who generously gave me advice, information, and material. Sandro Mezzadra provided me with a great deal of bibliographical information and carefully read the last version of the book, helping me to reduce the number of errors and inaccuracies. I would also like to thank Livio Quagliata because, among other things that connect us, his inquiry into the migrants lost at sea was extremely useful to me in organizing a chapter of this book. I thank Federico Boni, Francesco Carrer, Daniela Bruckner, Rocco De Biasi, Emilio Quadrelli, Stefano Padovano, Federico Rahola and Sabrina Vigna for their indispensable help in gathering materials and interviews. I am also grateful to Luca Guzzetti and Maria Teresa Torti for their advice and critiques. I thank Eleonoa Marletta for her suggestions regarding the interpretation of certain Biblical passages, and Serena Giordano and Paolo Rinaldi for putting their artistic skills at my disposal. Many ideas were given to me by the participants in the seminars held by the Department of Cognitive Science, Behavior, and Communication at the University of Genoa during the academic years 1995-6 and 1996-7. In addition to Sandro Mezzadra, Agostino Petrillo and Emilio Quadrelli, who were the directed the seminars, I would like to thank the following participants and speakers:

Flavio Baroncelli, Helmuth Dietrich, Marco d'Eramo, Marco Doria, Nando Fasce, Ferruccio Gambino, Renato Levrero, Yan Moulier-Boutang, Francesco Pivetta, Vincenzo Ruggiero, and Malek Sayad. With the deaths of Renato Levrero and Malek Sayad I not only lost two anchors in the research on migration, but also two dear friends. Norma Pozzi, Laura Tartarini, Antonello Petrillo and Marcello Maneri allowed me to use material from their masters' and doctoral theses. Antonello Petrillo, was especially generous in making available the original interviews used in his research. This study does not avoid a contestational tone, though it does try to keep within the limits of civil discussion. In every way, more than mere formal ritual, I assume complete responsibility for this, as well as for any errors that this study may contain.

Parts of this work were presented informally in my Sociology and Sociology of Cultural Processes courses at the University of Genoa over the last few years. I don't know if the students always shared my views, even in the erratic way in which I tend to expound them. But I do know that it was useful to me to discuss and collaborate in finding empirical and illustrative evidence. Among the friends, Italian and not, who helped me with this book directly and indirectly I would like to recognize Mouhcen Bendaoud; if we had never met years ago, perhaps I never would have become interested in the issues dealt with in this book, and Donatella Gorilla. She well knows, because she herself has lived it, the depths to which prejudice can reach. Kleves Jazxhi was a great help to me in analyzing the issue of Albania. My collaboration with friends from Città Aperta, Forum Antirazzista, and the Caritas di Genova have helped me to see the problems of migration through other eyes, and the same is true for the discussion group led by Bruno Murer from the EMASI in Milan. It is with great pleasure I remember a very difficult period while I was working on this book and Sister Maria Tarallo, Lucia Venini, Thiam and Serigne Sylla and other believers prayed for me, even though they knew (or because perhaps they knew) of my tenuous relationship with Heaven. Giovanna read and re-read several drafts of the book, helping me to give definite form to the text, and offering me her support, as always.

A final attempt at synthesizing the social construction of the migrant as enemy comes from my participation in a European research group on the impact of migration on the destination culture.[1] I thank the DGXII of the European Union for having permitted me to use excerpts from the interviews and other documentary materials gathered for that research.

[1] "Informal Economy, Deviance, and the Impact of Migration on Receiving Societies." Research completed for a grant from the European Union, DGXII, and submitted to the Universities of Genoa, Parma, Barcelona, Lisbon, and Atene, to the School of Higher Education in Political Sciences of Paris and to the Technical University of Berlin.

Introduction

He was mischievous, indeed, because he was wild; and he was wild because he was ugly. There was logic in his nature, as there is in ours.[2]

Originally I had conceived of this study as a treatise on the social stigmatization of migrants. But a treatise was not enough. Contrary to prevalent public opinion, the true victims of the clash between migrants and Italian society are the migrants. While the newspapers daily list the dozens of illegal "*clandestini*" who die at sea, and chart the continued violence, even lethal violence, against immigrants who live in Italy, a significant portion of the mass media relentlessly feeds the panic over "the invasion" of our country by "the poor immigrants" of the Third World. "Emergency: Illegal Migrants" is the monotonous leit-motif that resounded through the front pages of the Italian papers in the summer of 1998. Meanwhile, the protests and the attempted escapes by foreigners awaiting expulsion in the ironically named detention centers or "*campi di permanenza temporanea*," were put down only with violence.

While proceeding with this study, I became convinced that the immigration problem cannot be understood only as a modern myth fueled by the methods of mass information, rather it regards the limiting attitude of our society toward foreigners and the various social practices by which migrants are excluded and transformed into enemies of society.[3] According to a model now common in all

---

[2] Victor Hugo, *The Hunchback of Notre-Dame*, New York: Signet Classics, 2001, p. 151.
[3] As this study attempts to demonstrate, the various myths about migrants ("invasion," "criminals," etc.) have specific practical and symbolic functions. See Bell, D. *The End of Ideology: On the Exaustion of Polirical Ideas in the* Fifties, Glencoe, ILL.: The Free Press, 1960,

of Europe, migrants, real or imagined, are a danger to be opposed by every available means – from the militarization of borders to the proliferation of actual internment camps, from universal expulsion to the "economic assistance" offered to regimes from which the migrants are attempting to flee.[4] Refusing potential migrants corresponds to the social exclusion of current migrants. After 15 years of migration flows that show a certain degree of consistency, immigrants still do not have the civil rights (not to mention the social and political rights) enjoyed by Italians and other foreigners, European or Western, present in Italy.

The principal consequence of this double spiral of panic and exclusion has been an escalation of legal decrees and provisions with the purpose, more or less declared, of filtering foreigners, accepting a limited number of the "good ones," and closing the doors in the faces of those believed to be dangerous. According to the Dini decree of November, 1995, a foreigner suspected of disturbing public order or found guilty of misdemeanors could be removed from the jurisdiction of the judge and expelled from the country effectively without any form of appeal. This law represented a turning point in the political and juridical culture of Italy, in that it transferred to the police the responsibility of solving those microconflicts, both real and imagined, that are created by migration.[5] In February 1997, after different instantiations of the Dini decree, the center-left government put forth the proposal for a law that, together with certain measures aimed at the social integration of migrants, reaffirmed the politics of preventative expulsions and introduced the internment camps, modestly termed, *"campi di permanenza temporanea,"* for those foreigners awaiting expulsion. The bill was approved in February 1998,

---

a groundbreaking study on the social construction of "crime waves." See also Cohen, S. *Folk Devils and Moral Panics*, London: MacGibbon and Kee, 1972.

[4] The accords that Italy has stipulated or attempts to stipulate with authoritarian regimes such as those in Tunis or Morocco exemplify this viewpoint. At the beginning of August, 1998, the Italian goverment allocated millions to Tunis in an attempt to get rid of 1,200 migrants.

[5] The political significance of the decree and its practical consequences are discussed in Chapter One of this text.

with the abolition of the right to administrative vote for legalized foreigners.[6] That the center-left government continued with greater resolve along the path of previous governments in the stigmatization of migrants is evident in other legal provisions and administrative and police measures. Under the decree issued on March 20, 1997, when 15,000 Albanians arrived in Italy after the collapse of the Berisha regime, any migrant or refugee, whether Albanian or not, who was suspected of disturbing the peace could be expelled from Italy by the police prefects or commissioners.

The opinion of the educated public has played a decisive role in creating the climate of panic from which these legal measures have sprung. The opinion leaders who, without boasting any particular expertise in the area, have called for a "hard line" under various guises (such as closing the doors in the face of migrants and refugees, whether illegal or criminal or not), form a little local elite intellectual circle: philosophers, academics, noted journalists, and even supporters of radical culture. In other words, the intellectuals, who ought to have the moral obligation of critically examining the actions of the political system, and when necessary, to denounce its abuses, have shown themselves to be, at least in this case, the mouthpiece of the administrations and of the dominant public opinion.[7]

If the politics of immigration in Italy have shown how easy it is to ignore, circumvent or actually violate the universal principals granted by our own Constitution, it is also true that those principals are implicit, nebulous, or purely verbal. In this era of so-called globalization, and at a distance of more than 50 years from the downfall of Nazism, one would think that the equality of all human beings and their right to move freely on the earth to find a decent existence were obvious principles, even if those principles are without a

---

[6] See "Disciplina dell'immigrazione e norme sulla condizione dello straniero." *Il Sole 24 Ore*. 20 Feb. 1998.

[7] For a discussion of the role of intellectuals, see Said, E. *Representations of the Intellectuals: The 1993 Reith Lectures*, New York: Pantheon Books, 1994. Law and order, and the "war on crime" have become the rallying cry of influential university professors, philosophers, and moralists.

concise formulation.[8] However, this is not the case. Humanity is divided into majorities, citizens endowed with rights and formal guarantees, and minorities, illegitimate foreigners (not citizens, not nationals) for whom guarantees are negated.[9] Due to social mechanisms of labeling and implicit and explicit forms of exclusion, humanity is divided into *persons* and *non-persons*. Contributing to the maintenance of this distinction are those cultural movements that oppose universalism, or the political and moral notion that all human beings are equal by right. Rather than conceiving of diversity as plurality,[10] the articulation of a shared and egalitarian human condition, differentialism has often hypothesized cultural separation and has mythologized national and cultural roots. For all of these reasons, it was necessary to probe in-depth those processes that render foreigners second-class human beings. But it was also necessary to analyze those presuppositions in contemporary theory which have contributed to the exclusion of foreigners.

Thus, the original treatise transformed into a more complex study. It was necessary to understand how the appearance of foreigners seeking work or other social opportunities made certain clichés about humanity, tolerance, and rationality in our culture magically disappear. I don't refer only to overt manifestations of racism: acts of violence against defenseless foreigners, even children; uprisings that are clearly xenophobic in their methods and slogans

---

[8] In recent years in Italy, legal and political universalism have been progressively delegitimzed, and not only by the right. This trend concords perfectly with the re-invention of a nationalist culture that is now being opposed to the rights of migrants. For an examination of the revival of nationalisms in Europe, see Nguyen, E. *Les Nationlismes en Europe. Quête d'Identité ou tentation de repli.* Paris: Monde-Marabout, 1998.

[9] Noiriel, G. *La Tyrannie du national. Le droit d'asyle in Europe 1793-1993.* Paris: Calmann-Lévy, 1994. Noriel reconstructs events from the beginning of the twentieth century that essentially brought about the end of rights to asylum in the west.

[10] I refer here to the definition of the human condition described by Hannah Arendt in *The Life of the Mind,* New York: Harvest/HBJ, 1981. She offers compelling insights into the condition of foreigners and the connection between migration and citizenship in *The Human Condition* (1958), Chicago: University of Chicago Press, 1998 (2nd Edition) and *The Origins of Totalitarianism,* New York: Schocken Books, 1951 particularly in Part II.

against "criminal" immigrants; senseless proposals to blacklist immigrants in every way; deliberate or implicit falsification of information regarding foreigners. I refer instead to the decline in our political culture which could only conceive of expelling, containing, or confining migrants, and thus refuses to recognize them both as human beings and as an economic resource, which would seem obvious in a society the understands market exchange as a fundamental law. The left-wing government, preoccupied with maintaining political consensus at all costs, has refused to confront the issue of the rights of migrants. Similarly, so-called "liberal culture" has professed to resolve the problem of migration in purely police terms while simultaneously violating those principals to which they appeal to verbally, and thus revealing their true nature of *lassiez-faire* authoritarianism.[11] On the other hand, while Catholic volunteer services such the Caritas have proven that they, in the name of human universality claimed by monotheistic religions, understand the stakes in the public debate on immigration, the political expressions of Italian Catholicism have contributed, although with some embarrassment, to the raising of the legislative shields against foreigners.

It was therefore necessary to understand why many intellectuals and a large segment of the media, the political class, and "average citizens" formed a coalition that was hostile to migrants when confronted with a phenomenon of limited dimensions. The percentage of immigrants present in Italy today represents approximately 2% of the population, the lowest in any European country. It was necessary to bring to light and examine the scientific categories, politics, and popular beliefs that in Italy (and elsewhere) were employed in the debate on immigration, citizenship, and the rights of foreigners. A shocking chorus of clichés, of data based on hearsay, if not actually invented, of banalities passed off as realities, of vulgar prejudices, had in fact characterized the public debate on immigration from the past to the present. In the face of this, any opposition appeared paltry. The political right and the left, intellectuals and

---

[11] I refer of course to liberal culture in Italy. In other countries, the liberal position is more problematic.

politicians, journalists and citizens appeared extraordinarily jointly responsible and unified in their claims against granting Italian or European citizenship to "foreigners," "immigrants," "*clandestini*," and "criminals."

The rediscovery of the Nation-Italy and also of the Italian Homeland, i.e. a wide spread sentiment that forms the base for membership in the nation, is hardly extraneous to these developments.[12] In the Italian case, not only does this claim appear particularly weak, given the relatively short, conflictual, and dishonorable history of the Italian State (which in a little less than a century and a half was ruled by an authoritarian monarchy, a totalitarian regime, and a stymied and corrupt democracy). The main problem in this rediscovery of national sentiment of Italy as homeland is that it coincides with a process of rendering inferior other societies: poorer nations, backward regions in Italy itself, and the less wealthy areas in the dominant regions. A new kind of unity is affirming itself on the right and the left. In this rediscovery of the Nation, in this invention of new regional or sub-regional nationalisms, in the exaltation of local models of economic development (the "Northeast" as opposed not only to the "South" but also to the "Northwest"), the idea is reaffirmed that political society can only exist as a local community, bound in some exclusive way to a territory, and above all, in competition or conflict with other territorial communities.[13] The rediscovery of homelands obviously is not exclusive to our political culture, still less is it a consequence of the impact of those phenomena relative to migration. But these factors confer a particular emphasis to these new nationalisms and patriotisms.

---

[12] It is no coincidence that pleading for the nation ultimately arrives at the strategic problem of immigration, which is inevitably interpreted as a threat. See Viroli, M. *Per amore della patria. Patriottismo e nazionalismo nella storia.* Rome and Bari: Laterza, 1996, which contrasts "nationalism" with "patriotism." The latter is seen as the love of freedom and the institutions that support it. In this process of reinventing the nation, there is always the image of the "foreigner," sometimes seen as the enemy of "freedom." In fact, a sort of democratic xenophobia exists on the political left which sees immigrants as not yet ready to taste the delectable fruits of democracy, as we have.

[13] On the tendency to identify society with the nation as a manifestation of political and social decadence, see Elias, Norbert, *The Court Society*, Dublin: University College Dublin Press, 2006.

(1) la Bibbia

As I have endeavored to suggest in this book, migrants are an ideal public enemy for every claim to nation, local, or regional "identity." For urban patriotism, or neighborhood patriotism, migrants are criminals who threaten the security of daily life. For patriots of the region or canton, they are aliens who muddy ethnic purity. For national patriotism, they are foreigners who undermine social adhesion. For the patriot of class, they are "parasites" and "*clandestini*" who rob the working class of its successes, a *Lumpenproletariat* who compete with legitimate citizens in the workplace and take away their most recently bestowed benefits from the State. It seems almost superfluous to add that migrants are *symbolic* enemies (who absorb society's most disparate needs for expressing hostility) as well as *structural* enemies, which are necessary for the formation of identity by that "us" now required by both the right or the left.[14]

As with all social phenomena, hostility (with all of its motivations and practical manifestations) is a phenomenon incessantly constructed and reconstructed by daily life. Therefore, its content does not follow the logic of "rationality," (which a prevalent theory of action in the social sciences insists is dominant in democratic or "liberal" society). Rather its logic is that of social discourse, of *doxa* in the common usage, in the "so they say," of unverified public opinion, in short, of social mythology. Nearly all of the dominant affirmations regarding the threat that migration constitutes are debatable, if not simply false. It is not true that Italy, since the mid-1980s has been invaded by foreigners, that its extensive borders enables the entry of illegal immigrants more that in other Mediterranean countries, that migrants demonstrate a higher propensity to commit crimes, or that they tend to take jobs away from our youth. These are generic and unverifiable affirmations, essentially untrue. But it would be erroneous to think that they have been defeated once their absurdity has been discussed. They are socially "true" inasmuch as they move in lock step with the elaboration of a reactive identity[15] by those who use them. They

---

[14] See Schiffauer, W. *Fremde in der Stadt. Zehn Essays über Kultur und Differenz*. Frankfurt: Suhrkamp, 1997, whose thesis parallels my own.

[15] By "identity," I refer to the process of social construction in the definition of "we," however that is determined. Constructed identities, whether invented intentionally or not, contested or vindicated,

are true because they are tautological, necessary within a certain rhetorical economy, indispensable to a certain form of argumentation. They are included in the same methods of argumentation to which today the concepts of homeland or nation belong. It is perfectly evident that the concept of nation does not correspond to any objective entity in historical, constitutional, juridical, social or cultural terms. But if a consensus is created among scholars, politicians, and opinion makers regarding the homeland as something that objectively exists, then merely speaking of it, attributing to this verbal shell of "obvious" subject matter (which in turn refers to other subject matter and so on), confers objectivity to the existence of the homeland. In the same way, since migrants have become the favorite target of a certain public discourse, they are a "threat" independent of the fact that they threaten nothing, but simply that the relative cliché is reaffirmed in public opinion.[16]

The fact that we are dealing with social realities renders substantially ineffectual those critiques supported by data or analysis rather than common-places. The public discourse about the "immigration emergency" picks up deeply

but never the natural prerogative of any group. I agree with the work of Hobsbawm, E.J. *Nations and Nationalism since 1780: Programme, Myth, Reality*, New York: Cambridge University Press (2nd Edition), 1992, and Anderson, B. *Imagined Communities: Reflections on the Origin and Spread of Nationalism, London: Verso, 2006*, when they refer to "community" or "nation" as a contingent social and historical construct. Berezin, M. *Enacting Political Identity: Public Rituals as Arenas of the National Self.* Florence: Istituto Universitario Europeo, 1998 analyzes the nature of public ritual in the construction of collective identity. Weber, M. *Economy and Society: An Outline of Interpretive Sociology*, Berkeley, CA: University of California Press, 1978 noted how the concept of nation, although a vague idea, is a shell that can be filled with a variety of contents. This does not preclude, however, that identities are effective. The cultural history of the Northern League amply demonstrates the constructedness of identity which is effective at the same time. For a discussion of the conventional historical concept of identity see Hobsbawm, E.J. *On History*, New York: The New Press, 1998. On the construction of national mythologies, see Noiriel, G. *La Tyrannie du National. Le droit d'asyle in Europe 1793-1993*. Paris: Calmann-Lévy, 1994.

[16] When I say that hostility is socially and symbolically constructed, I mean that the existence of an enemy exceeds the conventional rationality of social action. An essential reference point for my work has been the Foucauldian theory of "state racism," in Foucault, M., *Security, Territory, Population*, Basingstoke, UK: Palgrave Macmillan, 2007, and in the writings of Pierre Bordieu on the logic of symbolic and social exclusion, particularly in Bourdieu, P., ed. *La misère du monde.* Paris: Seuil, 1993.

rooted commonplaces in contemporary society (much as anything associated with "security" in urban society).[17] At the same time, that discourse is reinforced and legitimized by "scientific" analysis that cloaks "what everyone knows" with pseudoconcepts taken from the social sciences. Consider for example all of the research about the inclination or propensity of foreigners to commit crime. "Inclination" is a term whose common usage could at the most indicate a certain distribution of data relative to a given "population," data whose meaning depends almost exclusively on categories employed by researchers. In reality, merely formulating research of this type means validating inherent prejudices about the population to be studied. No serious social scientist would ever dream of studying "the criminal tendencies of professors," regardless of the recent scandals that have emerged in Italy over the awarding of university positions. And no one, not even after Tangentopoli, would take seriously any examination of "the criminal tendencies" of the political class. If research of this type is considered legitimate in the case of immigrants, it is because they, as a category (and therefore as a cognitive group) are discredited in advance and stigmatized by public opinion and scientific *doxa*.

"Immigration" is therefore not only an economic, social, political, and legal issue, but is also a cognitive problem not only for social sciences but also for students of epistemology. A. Sayad summed up the role that immigrants play in producing social and scientific discourses with his concept of the "specular function of migration phenomena."[18] Simply by virtue of living among us, migrants are those who require us to reveal who we are: in the discourses we maintain, in the knowledge we produce, in the political identity that we claim.

---

[17] On the formation of public opinion obsessed with safety, see Palidda, S. *Devianza e criminalità tra gli immigrati*, Milan: Fondazione Cariplo/ISMU, 1994. For an excellent discussion of these issues in social theory, see Brion, F. *Contrôle de l'immigration, crime, et discrimination. Essai de criminologie réflexive à propos des propriétés et des usages politiques du crime, et de la science qui le prend pour objet*. Criminology Doctoral Thesis, Catholic University of Lovanio, 1995. See Palidda, S., Ed. *Délit d' immigration. La construction sociale de la deviance et de la criminalité parmi les immigrés*. Brussels: Cost A2/ Migrations, 1996.
[18] Sayad, A., *The Suffering of the Immigrant*, Cambridge: Polity, 2004.

Habitually we speak of "the specular function" of migration, the privileged site that it constitutes for rendering overt what is latent in the existence and functioning of the social order. It lays bare what is hidden in order to reveal that which would benefit from being ignored and maintaining a state of "innocence" and social ignorance, in order to bring to light or enlarge (thus the "specular effect") that which has habitually been hidden in the social unconscious and has therefore been elected to remain in the shadows, in a state of secrecy, and not considered socially.[19]

In other words, more than any other phenomenon, immigration reveals the nature of the so-called accepting society. When we speak of immigrants, we speak of ourselves in relation to the immigrants. And for this reason, any analysis that takes up the issue of immigration without considering who is speaking (and by what right, with what legitimacy, and with what cognitive, political, and national presuppositions) is already amputated in its construction, and is therefore false. Consequently, the work presented here does not address "immigration" as a phenomenon in itself, but as a mechanism that reveals the nature of our society. This study does not so much attempt to tell the social or existential truth about these foreigners, but rather attempts to speak to the relationship that is established between who is "inside" a society (with all of its acquired security), and who, coming from "outside" attempts to "enter within." A difficult, if not impossible task, because confronting the issue requires the re-evaluation of those scientific categories and knowledge that the analyst is inevitably entrenched in and which affords a position of security.

This book is thus a study of the social, political, and cognitive mechanisms that render immigration a (or perhaps "the") public enemy in contemporary society. Where does the author position himself? Although my training is in sociology, I have not conceived of this study as a mere sociological essay. First of all, I do not believe that the notion of "disinterested" social science is sustainable, particularly in the face of fundamental aspects of human co-

---

[19] Sayad, A. "La doppia pena del migrante. Riflessioni sul 'pensiero di stato'." *aut aut* 275 (1996): 10.

existence (such as equality and citizenship) that are not data, but the object of controversy and political struggle. Secondly, I believe that these issues go beyond the plane of mere scientific description, even from a theoretical point of view. They have to do with the basis of our existence, with the very definition of humanity, something that has no place in a social scientific approach that seeks operationalism and "objectivity."

I don't pretend to privilege quantitative, incontestable data. At least in Italy, the debate over immigration has demonstrated not only how statistics are debatable but also how statistics are produced and used according to preconceived notions and certain modes of argumentation, which have only the appearance of science, particularly regarding the number of foreigners and their antisocial, criminal tendencies. If a demographer stated that, based on formally consistent calculations, within twenty years, "a wave of migrations will crash against the West which is in full demographic decline," then he or she is not promoting science, but rhetoric. On one hand, those projections are pure rubbish, for they do not consider any of the unforeseeable political, cultural, or economic variables that alter such demographic projections.[20] On the other hand, the demographer would endow his or her data with a language that is complicitous with general public fears. Social scientists should know that, in this era of mass media, even scientific discourse creates, and thus contributes to the modification of reality. Frequently, there is a sort of pragmatic naivety, but at times there is a deliberate attempt to alter facts in the interest of an ideology that does not have the courage to openly admit that it exists.

This study, precisely because it does not wish to be merely a social critique but also a critique of the "science of immigration," must inevitably locate itself outside of that science. Wherein, then, does its legitimacy lie? And also, on what data, qualitative or quantitative, does it rely? The only legitimacy this study can claim is that which derives from its results. As for the data, this study locates itself in a transverse position. The problem here is not just that the data on

---

[20] Consider how the same social sciences that were unable to predict the demographic decline in Italy has untiringly predicted Italy's invasion by all the poor of the Third World.

immigration are frequently unreliable, but also that they are socially constructed. Statistics as such tell us very little, unless one reconstructs their input, i.e. the modalities by which they were collected and assembled, as well as their output, i.e. the interpretive modalities by which they became the images of reality. When I will use statistics here, I will endeavor to demonstrate their reliability regarding input and output. Let me add, while I am somewhat skeptical regarding the possibility that quantitative data represents the social reality of the phenomenon of migration, I nevertheless maintain that such data can frequently give us an idea of the dimensions of migration flows, which can be useful in unraveling the clichés about migratory "invasions."

A different line of discourse applies to the role of qualitative data. The extent of what we can know about the phenomenon of migration derives not only from statistics, but from secondary literature, from the newspapers and media in general, as well as the voice of those directly involved through interviews with migrants and native citizens who work with them daily as public functionaries, etc. Granted, even these materials are socially constructed and support different methodological objectives. The secondary literature is obviously an inexhaustible source of data and theoretical and analytical possibilities, a primary resource for a researcher. But in the social sciences, and above all in a field as controversial as migration studies, the secondary literature is subject to all of the distortions and prejudices of the dominant public opinion. It is necessary only to think of the highly common tendency to "ethnicize" any type of conflict or social problem, to speak of ethnicities, if not races, where one should only speak of individuals who interact with each other and with society. The "literature" therefore forces us to continually scrutinize and reflect upon its underlying categories and rhetoric which the social sciences sometimes uncritically inherit from public opinion.

A specific problem lies with an analysis of the media. Especially today, the media forms our *Umwelt*, the "skin" of our social world.[21] The written or

---

[21] Noelle-Neuman, E., *Die Schweigespirale: Öffentliche Meinung – Unsere soziale Haut*, München: Piper, 1980.

media as Umwelt

audiovisual information is of inestimable value for describing "what is going on." At the same time, it is that place where *"senso commune"* – common knowledge and discourses that form and perpetuate public opinion – is gathered, filtered, reproduced, and transformed into an objective version of reality. As privileged and yet deforming channels of the knowledge of social phenomena in formation, the mass media require continual analysis. The only way to utilize these materials without being captured by their socially constructed rhetoric is to contextualize them in terms of their production and signification. Thus, a journal article about an act of violence against a migrant tells us something about "racism," and "xenophobia," while the fact that in the same article, the journalist or the police officer who was interviewed excludes the racist roots of the violence tells us even more about the societal censorship which migrants face.

An aspect of the empirical materials utilized in this text that cannot be neglected is constituted by newspaper and journal articles, transcriptions of television programs, and iconographic evidence (leaflets, cartoons, photographs). It seems superfluous to add that these materials, drawn from the sea of information that is transmitted daily, are the result of the choice and subjective editing on the part of the writer. I don't know if the reader will experience my same dismay in the face of the documents presented here. Following the information transmitted daily regarding immigrants was a voyage through the grotesque for me. Perhaps this sensation was purely subjective, like the selection of the materials presented here. But I wish to assure the reader that this material is a small part of that which seems to be growing in the recesses of the common political usage in the media and locally. If I have juxtaposed a sampling of daily examples of falsehood and racism with news stories and even-handed political positions, that is not out of a personal preference for extremes, but merely because this cross-section seems representative, and as such, speaks eloquently. It is possible that anyone devoted to statistics or quantitative content analysis will be disappointed by my moderate use of percentages. However, it seemed to me that a front-page headline like, "Who

Will Halt the Invasion of Illegal Immigrants?" or "The Macedonian Were-Wolf Confesses," tells us something that no percentage or table could capture.[22]

The interviews and the personal stories are the privileged instrument of any qualitative analysis of reality. These constitute the sole access to the voices of those who, by definition, are excluded from public discourse; the daily actors (and this is even more the case for those who are "illegitimate" actors, either marginal or excluded as migrants). Yet they cannot help but have an exemplary value. Exempla, therefore, that are significant, more than objective representations of facts, experiences, or existence. The sociological quality of such interviews depends on subjective factors, such as the availability of the interviewees, and the capabilities or experiences of the interviewers. At the same time, we have to admit that it is practically impossible to prescribe a uniform method of conducting and transcribing interviews. Above all, even when interviews faithfully reproduce the accounts of the social actors, they also elaborate subjective points of view, and are windows on heterogeneous experiences that by definition echo the moment and context of the interview.

However, they constitute an invaluable documentary instrument for elaboration and verification. This is true for personal testimonies (of foreigners and citizens alike) as well as the "privileged" testimonies of the experts, the social actors assigned specific social and practical duties. For this reason, the interviews of police officers, magistrates, lawyers, social operations, and witnesses of various types find ample space in this study: although subjective, these accounts describe the institutional practices that often become obscured in our pluralistic complex world due to the division of social work, practices subject to unintentional but inevitable secrecy.[23] For obvious reasons, the names and qualifications of the interviewees has not been reported here, except in a very few cases, and with the express permission of the interviewee. I did not adopt any particular system for the transcription of interviews, but

---

[22] My methodology in this regard owes much to the work of E. Goffman, particularly in *Frame Analysis: An Essay on the Social Organization of Experience*. Harmondsworth: Penguin, 1975.
[23] See the chapter on "secrecy," in Simmel, G., *The Sociology of Georg Simmel*, Tampa, FL: Free Press, 1964.

restricted myself to respecting as much as possible the original, spoken discourse and introducing punctuation and paragraph breaks to render the reading smoother. When it seemed opportune to me, I referred to the written accounts by migrants, such as published biographies, and so forth. Even more than in the case of interviews, caution when using these documents is critical. Once again, the use and editing of qualitative materials are the fruit of a subjective choice that can be justifiable in the arguments put forth in the comprehensive complexity of a book.

A word of warning regarding terminology: definitions in common usage such as "immigrants" not to mention the pseudo-juridical neologism "*extra-comunitari*" or the generic "foreigners," can not possibly define the complex condition of migrants in the wealthy North of the world and in Italy. An "immigrant" is certainly a foreigner who does not belong to the European Union, but an "immigrant" is above all a citizen in search of an occupation, someone who comes from a subordinated country in the international division – both economic and political – of labor. The terms "immigrant" and "immigration," likewise carry with them the scientific legitimacy of a given point of view, namely, from the common usage in the migrant's destination culture. Furthermore, the two terms, precisely because of their common usage, recall the image that our world has created of migrants. Therefore, in this study, I will use the terms "migrants" to describe the condition of those who abandon their national space and the term "immigrant" to refer to the ways in which our wealthy society treats and labels them. Analogically, I will not make use of the terms "host society" or "welcoming society," but rather "destination society," which seems less hypocritical to me (the Albanians who were held in the stadium at Bari in 1991 and others who have been detained in the "*campi di permanenza temporanea*" could comment on the welcome they received from this society). This choice is not dictated by political correctness, but from basic linguistic caution necessary in order maintain distance from a *langue de bois* that dominates the writings about migration. Frequently the debates criticizing the extremes born of political correctness also hide the desire to discriminate against those social agents who are the weakest or most defenseless, beginning with language.

Finally, I dedicate this work to the true protagonists, both implicit and explicit: the foreigners who are treated as "non-persons" when they attempt to live in another society, and nevertheless, they endeavor to live as human beings. And then, to all those who, like Dragan, a friend from a now distant summer, desert the "ethnic" wars and refuse to be conditioned by racism or the nationalistic stupidities. They could say, paraphrasing Dr. Johnson: "Nationalism is the final refuge of scoundrels."

I Public Enemies

You're not from the castle, you're not from the village, you're nothing. Unfortunately there's one thing you are, though, namely a stranger, an outsider, someone who's superfluous to requirements and in everybody's way, someone who creates a great deal of head-scratching, makes us dismiss the servants, and no one really knows what intentions you have...[24]

1 Facing Migrants

In the summer of 1967, after the riots in the ghettos of Detroit, a leader of the American Civil Rights Movement observed, "The black man is an intelligence test for the white man."[25] In that period, there was still hope that those in the ghettos would become integrated into the great society of Kennedy and Johnson. Looking back nearly 30 years, the tensions that culminated in the quelled riots of South Central Los Angeles, the revanchism against the blacks, the campaigns against migrants and the systematic demolition of government programs that support minorities have dissolved any hope that white America has passed the test.[26] However, limiting this discourse to the United States would be unjust and closed-minded. Here in Europe and in Italy, if we substituted "African-

---

[24] F. Kafka, *The Castle*, New York: The Modern Library, 1969.

[25] Statement attributed to Reverend Albert Cleage, cited in Davis, M. *Ecology of Fear: Los Angeles and the Imagination of Disaster*, New York: Vintage, 1999.

[26] For an analysis of these developments, see West, C. *La razza conta*. Milan: Feltrinelli, 1995, and Cartosio, B. *L'autunno degli Stati Uniti: Neoliberismo e declino sociale da Reagan a Clinton*. Milan: ShaKe, 1998. See also Davis, M. *City of Quartz: Excavating the Future of Los Angeles*. London: Verso, 1991. "Who Killed Los Angeles? A Political Autopsy." *New Left Review* 197 (1993): 23-28 and 198 (1993): 29-542; and "Who Killed Los Angeles, Part Two: The Verdict is Given." *New Left Review* 199 (1993). For current politics on migration in the United States, see Ocasio, L. "The Year of the Immigrant as Scapegoat." *NACLA: Report on the Americas* 3 (1995).

American" with foreigners, migrants, and refugees, white men here have shown themselves to be vastly unprepared for the same intelligence test.

During the 1990s, the governments of countries with long histories of immigration, France, Germany, and England, adopted measures that were increasingly more restrictive toward migrants and refugees. In 1993, the German government effectively abolished the right to asylum, which had been the condition that made Germany one of the countries most open to foreigners after World War II (though migrants and refugees have always been considered "guests" in the Federal Republic of Germany, and thus deprived of any political rights or the possibility of obtaining citizenship).[27] Consequently, tens of thousands of foreigners are sent back to their countries of origin and more than 40,000 are rejected at the borders.[28] The German government has made accords with the governments of Romania, Poland, and the Ukraine regarding the detention of migrants in camps organized inside and outside of German territory, and detention can last months in the absence of any intervention by international organizations.[29] Even the British government has drastically reduced the number of asylums granted and has held thousands of foreigners in

[27] Roos, A. "Staatliche Politik gegenüber Flüchtingen." *Migration und Ausländerfeindlichkeit.* Ed. G. Böhme, R. Chakreborty, and F. Weiler. Darmstadt: Wissenschaftliche Buchgesellschaft, 1994. 191.
[28] See "Forschungsgesellschaft Flucht und Migration." *Gegen die Festung Europa*, Heft 1: *Polen vor den Toren der Festung Europa.* Berlin and Göttingen: Verlag der Buchladen Schwarze Risse-Rote Strasse, 1995, and *Gegen die Festung Europa*, Heft 2:*Rumanien vor den Toren der Festung Europa.* Berlin and Göttingen: Verlag der Buchladen Schwarze Risse-Rote Strasse, 1996. For a reconstruction of the migration debate in Germany see Bade, K.J. *Homo Migrans. Wanderungen aus und nach Deutschland.* Essen: Klartext, 1994. For a discussion of xenophobia in Germany during the 1990s, see Nirumand, B., ed. *Angst vor den Deutschen. Terror gegen Aüslander und der Zerfall des Rechsstaates.* Reinbek bei Hamburg: Rowohlt, 1992.
[29] Dietrich, H. "La fortezza Europa." Unpublished paper, Department of Cognitive Science, Behavior and Communication, University of Genoa, May 1997, and "Feindbild 'Illegale': Eine Skizze zu Sozialtechnik und Grenzregime." *Mittelwig36* 3 (1998), and Toller, L. "Gli sbarchi dei migranti senza documenti al sud: modelli di differenzialismo nella fortezza Europa." *Altreragioni* 6 (1997): 47-61. For information on the increasing number of controls migrants are subject to in Germany, see "Forschungsgesellschaft Flucht und Migration." *Gegen die Festung Europa*, Heft 4: *"Sie Behandeln uns wie Tiere". Rassismus bei Polizei und Justiz in Deutschland*, Berlin and Göttingen: Verlag der Buchladen Schwarze Risse-Rote Strasse, 1997.

internment camps, while thousands more live in the country illegally as they wait for their asylum requests to be granted. In France, the Easter law of 1994 limited the rights of citizenship for the children of migrants. The war on immigration in the summer of 1996, instigated by the administration of Chirac-Juppé, which culminated in the expulsion of those took refuge in the Church of St. Bernard in Paris, has not spared the legal migrants. The proposed Debré law from early 1997 provided for a requirement that French citizens denounce their foreign guests who were without residence permits (*permessi di soggiorno*), an openly totalitarian measure that promotes secret accusations among the general public. The provision was abandoned after intellectuals and artists mobilized in February of 1997.[30] In April of 1998, the Socialist government of Jospin launched a law against immigration that fundamentally confirmed a hard line against illegal immigrants, similar to the barbed wire politics common in all European countries today.[31]

An eloquent illustration of the closing of Europe to foreigners is evident in the migration politics of the new countries of immigration, Spain,[32] and Italy, who, together with Greece, have played the role of sentinels for the Mediterranean in the "fortress Europe" codified by the Schengen agreement.[33]

---

[30] See AFELSE (Association pour la Fraternité, l'Egalité e la Liberté sans Exclusion). *La ballade des sans papiers*. Paris: n.p., 1996, and Fassin, D, A. Morice, C. Quiminal, Eds. *Les lois de l'inhospitalité: Les politiques de l'immigrationà l'èpreuve des sans-papiers*. Paris: La Decouverte, 1997.

[31] For an overview of the police measures currently in force in Europe against migrants, see Conference Reports from *L'Europe barbelée*. Paris: L'Harmattan, 1998.

[32] Yoldi, L.S. *La immigración extranjera en España: balance y actitudes*. Valencia: Department of Sociology and Anthropology, 1997. Unpublished text, used with author's permission. See also Goytisolo, J. "La frontiera di cristallo." *Internazionale* 247 (1998).

[33] The Schengen Accords of 1985 enforced the abolition of regulations for European Union citizens crossing borders of other EU countries, and also regulated the external borders of EU states. The accords were promoted by France and Germany and is overseen by group of Ministers of the Interior from the contracting states, and the European police. As established by a 1990 convention, a commision of the European Community participates as an observer. Thus, the controls that regulate the movements of migrants and refugees are the product of a "working" accord between the forces of public safety in some European countries, and not the result of a communal deliberation. The Schengen Accords, due to their experimental and yet binding nature,

In the spring of 1996, the government of Spain suffered great embarrassment when the press revealed that illegal Moroccan and Tunisian immigrants were being drugged before being deported. For Southern European countries, closing their borders to migrants is undoubtedly a prerequisite for being accepted into the European club politically and financially dominated by France and Germany.[34] In addition, the Italian incapacity for confronting the migration phenomena in any positive way is of ancient date. During the 1980s, the influx of several hundred thousand migrants did not spur the formation of any strategy for their social integration, but only sparked sporadic and hurried legislative initiatives. No effective provision was adopted to facilitate the social integration of foreigners in the areas of the labor market, housing, health care, education, or culture.

indicate whose authority will control the internal and external public order for "Fortress Europe" in the future. See Christie, N., *Crime Control as Industry: Towards Gulags Western Style*, New York: Routledge (3rd Edition), 2000. Later in this text, I will show how the militarization of the borders in the Mediterranean is not a reaction to the non-existent "invasion" by migrants, but a consequence of construction of Europe as a competitive economic space in regards to the United States, Japan, and emerging economies in southeast Asia, and represents a dominant in regards to poorer countries. See Bigo, D. *L'Europe des polices,* Paris: Complexe, 1992, and "La ragnatela delle polizie d'Europa." *Le Monde Diplomatique-il manifesto* 10, October 1996. See also Busch, H. *Grenzenlose Polizei? Neue Grenzen und polizeiliche Zusammenarbeit in Europa.* Münster: Westfälisches Dampfboot, 1995, and Taylor, I. "The New Virtuality: Cyber-resolutions to the European Union Border Control." Speech at international convention: *Migrazioni, interazioni e conflitti nella construzione di una democrazia europea.* Bologna, 16-19 December 1997. This paper discusses the tendency to increase the harshness of border controls as a consequence of the new European economic order.

[34] In the summer of 1997, Italy officially accepted the Schengen Accords, but German representatives claimed Italy was incapable of protecting its southern borders. See Italian newspapers from 25 January 1997. Then in January of 1998 when a few thousand Kurdish refugees arrived in Italy, the German Minister of the Interior questioned Italy's ability to maintain the Schengen Accords. The Italian Prime Minister affirmed, "When I participate in international meetings, I am held responsible not only for Italian emigration, but for German emigration as well." Prodi, R. "Intervento conclusivo." *Presentazione del rapporto annuale, 1997, sui problemi della sicurezza in Emilia-Romagna.* Bologna, 1 December 1997. 17. This shows how the sovereignty of individual states in Europe is continually diminished. For a discussion of this phenomenon, see Sassen, S. *Losing Control? Sovereignty in an Age of Globalization.* New York: Columbia University Press, 1996.

At the beginning of the 1990s, the substantial indifference of Italian institutions and society opened the way for an ever-increasing hostility, both symbolic and actual. This reaction was reinforced by shocking provisions for public order which legitimated a culture of emergency and exclusion toward foreigners: in the summer of 1991, several hundred Albanians were deported who had been promised work and a *permesso di soggiorno*; in 1995 a military division was dispatched to the coast of Puglia to keep out illegal immigrants; in March, 1997, there was a decision to halt refugees with a naval block of the Italian coastline and several thousand troops were sent to garrison Albania. The blockade was adopted at the height of a campaign of collective hysteria against the Albanian threat, a campaign that was promoted by right-wing political parties, especially the Northern League, supported by the national press, and legitimated by the center-left government, regardless of the fact that the arrival of just over 15,000 Albanians did not in reality provoke any real problem for public order. The Italian position toward foreigners and refugees was sealed when an Albanian raft crowded with women and children collided with a ship in the Italian navy and sank on the night of March 28, 1997.[35]

From the beginning of the 1990s, according to public opinion, migrants have become the cause of the social crises and collective fears that marked the end of the so-called First Republic. If since the mid-1980s, surveys indicated a general indifference or ignorance about migration issues, since the beginning of the 1990s, surveys indicate widespread attitudes of repulsion, if not outright xenophobia.[36] One survey of the members of the major political parties in Northern Italy demonstrated the "political" perception of immigration in that area of our country where the neo-nationalism of the Northern League is growing:

[35] The United Nations High Commission denounced Italy's naval blockade as illegal. See Italian newspapers from 23 March 1997.
[36] For an analysis of these changes, see Dal Lago, A., *The Impact of Migrations on Receiving Societies: The Italian Case*. Research presentation at the DGXII della Comunità europea, November 1998. A review of the evolution in attitudes towards foreigners in Italy is available in Piemonte, Ires. The current research does not indicate that it would at this point be justified to define the current climate as a "xenophobia of the masses;" however, the campaign against foreigners in the press and political culture can be amply documented.

Opinions about Immigrants and Voting (Percentage)

	Northern Lega
Too Many Immigrants Create Problems	66.0
Immigrants Increase Crime	70.7
Immigrants Should Go Home	60.5

Source: Abacus Surveys 1996

Comparative analyses of European attitudes toward migrants show that the rejection in Italy differs from other European nations. In 1988 only 34% of those interviewed felt that there were "too many migrants;" five years later, that percentage jumped to 64%, the highest in Europe. Contemporaneously, the index of ethnocentrism, which was the lowest in Europe in 1988 (1.5 on a scale from 0-5), jumped to 2.75 in 1992, moving Italy into the lead.[37]

The growing hostility on the part of the Italian public opinion toward immigrants is in part created and heightened by the right-wing parties and political movements which are highly adept at taking advantage of urban anxieties and more recent demands for public security so prevalent now in the north of our country. Meanwhile, the left and centrist political forces have not combated the hostility toward foreigners, migrants, nomads, and refugees. Quite the reverse: they have accepted this hostility as an illuminating and incontestable fact of the current trends in public opinion and electoral fluctuations. This progressive yielding to panic in the face of immigration (which grew more acute with the right-wing victory in the March 1994 elections) has seen two distinctive moments: the Dini decree of November, 1995 and the Turco-Napolitano law of 1998. Independent of its practical consequences, the Dini decree had the effect of symbolically stigmatizing migrants as a "social problem" and most of all, as enemies, whether real or virtual, from whom Italian society had to protect itself. The Dini decree was

[37] See Munz, R. "Europa und die großen Wanderungen des 20. Jahrhunderts." *Furcht und Faszination. Facetten der Fremdheit.* Eds. H. Münkler and B. Ladwig. Berlin: Akademie Verlag, 1997. 296-297, which cites the statistics for "Euro-barometer" in January 1988 and January 1992.

supported by the right and also by the center-left largely as "the lesser evil" as compared to the proposals of the Northern League, which were explicitly xenophobic. In reality, this was a measure with limited practical consequences (unless we include the silencing of migrant street vendors, which assigned tens of thousands of migrants to a state of illegality). Before the deadline of March 31, 1996 set by the decree, approximately 250,000 applications for legal status were made.[38] Meanwhile, the deportations were not enforced due mainly to financial concerns and due to the lack of any legislation that required airlines and shipping lines to take responsibility for the repatriations.

However, the Dini decree accomplished political objectives far more important than those outline in the articles of the decree itself: first, it confirmed the principle of closing the borders and expelling foreigners as answers to "the emergency," and second, it functioned as a test case for an understanding between the right and the center-left in the area of immigration, all in the name of national interests. After their electoral success in April of 1996, the center-left government promised a comprehensive re-examination of the problem and comprehensive legislation. Indeed, after a few reiterations of the Dini decree, and long and highly secretive deliberation, new legislation was proposed in February of 1997 by two ministers in the Prodi government, Livia Turco and Giorgio Napolitano. The proposition was clearly more carefully considered than the Dini decree, but in spirit, it resembles the latter. It does provide for a series of innovative measures[39] for the integration and formal equality between legalized foreigners and Italian citizens including active and passive electoral participation in local administrations, the opportunity to take advantage of medical facilities, access to public housing, and obligatory school

---

[38] Caritas, Rome. *Immigrazione. Dossier statistico '96*. Rome: Anterem, 1996. 112.

[39] When this law was proposed in February of 1997, some supporters of the majority declared that they were satisfied because the new law recognizes the "rights" of immigrants. This was perhaps the first time that Italian politicians admitted that, even though immigration has been a constant phenomenon during the past 15 years, the rights of migrants have not been recognized in our country. For the text of the proposal, which is more favorable toward immigrants than the successive law, see Napolitano, G. and L. Turco, *Disciplina dell'immigrazione e norme sulla condizione dello straniero*. Outline of proposed laws, Rome: 13 February 1997.

attendance for minors. These measures, however, also impose entrance restrictions – quotas, seasonal work, and work permits that require a guarantee from the Italian employer – and a path toward legality so torturous it sits at the edge of sadism. "Poor" tourists are limited to a 3-month visa, seasonal workers are limited to 6-month visa (which may be extended to 9 months in certain cases), students are granted 1 year, migrants with a guaranteed job are granted two years legal residence, and for those who can prove their legal status, residency is granted after 6 years of good conduct. The Turco-Napolitano law reconfirms and rationalizes the mentality of closed borders; it introduces a provision for expelling those suspected of criminal action or individuals considered to be socially dangerous, and provides for the establishment of detainment centers for those awaiting deportation.[40]

In the months following its adoption, the Turco-Napolitano law seemed to languish along with other unresolved issues in the Prodi government. Suddenly, in August of 1997, two or three criminal episodes (episodes that were statistically insignificant within the context of the typical crime rates that fill the news every summer) involving foreigners became the occasion for a campaign for alarm and panic that was without precedent in Italian history. Two cases were rapes committed by "*clandestini*" on the Riviera of Romagna, one was a homicide by a Macedonian shepherd, who confessed to the crime. These cases ignited the xenophobic press, the right-wing press, even the independent press did not refrain from making similar headlines and defamatory generalizations, and then came the initiative sponsored by the Northern League which mobilized patrols to hunt down Senegalese and Albanian street vendors. The moderates on the right and the nationalists joined in the chorus until the entire moderate political system literally invented an immigration crisis that was essentially without any basis. National and Northern parties and political movements proposed solutions for the "crisis"

[40] See Napolitano, G. and L. Turco. *Disciplina dell'immigrazione e norme sulla condizione dello straniero*. Outline of proposed laws, Rome: 13 February 1997. art. 5, 6, 7, 11, 12, 13, 14 & 15. These articles remained unchanged in the successive law that was approved in February of 1998. Notice that the police commissioner is given the power to grant visas and residency permits.

that ranged from the gallows to the death penalty for "foreign murderers" and concentration camps for "*clandestini.*" Certain left-wing mayors of cities on the Romagna Riviera proposed instituting "regional" passports in addition to detainment centers and other legal amenities. And it was in this surreal atmosphere in August of 1997 that the government decided to accelerate the approval of the Turco-Napolitano Immigration law.

Between February and March of 1998, the law was approved by both houses of Parliament. During its legislative progression, the law lost some of its aspects that were timidly beneficial to immigrants. The article granting suffrage was eliminated due to opposition from the right. The sections regarding the battle against illegal immigration, deportations, and detainment centers constitutes nearly one-half of the text, thus revealing the orientation of the government to be in line with the dominant European tendency toward closing the borders. As with the Dini decree, this new law seemed to have limited practical consequences in the months following its approval. Without much disturbance, detainment centers were organized in Puglia, Sicily, Trieste and other "critical" locations. The true significance of these centers was revealed between July and August, 1998 when a few dozen "*clandestine*" held in centers at Agrigento and Caltanissetta rebelled against the inhumane conditions under which they were forced to live. Though guilty of no crime, they were kept on bread and water in dilapidated buildings for several weeks, and guarded by police who intervened violently at the smallest sign of protest. Even the press, which initially referred to these as "reception centers," began calling them what they are, concentration camps or Lagers. Overall, this politics of negating human rights did not draw significant protests from any direction, not even from the political left. All in all, the opposition forces were weak in the face of the more repressive aspects of these provisions, as if the associations and political movements on the side of immigrants were unwilling to oppose a "friendly" administration.

2 The "Immigrant Emergency" and Its Victims

While the Italian political system devised essentially repressive legislative measures in the wake of the political and media crises, the hostility toward foreigners and the substantial indifference of the media manifested itself in capillary forms of racism. Periodically in the so-called "at risk" areas of certain Northern cities (Turin, Milan, Genoa, and others), the citizens mobilized against gypsies[41] and "criminal immigrants," and tried to create patrols with the purpose of pushing out not only drug dealers and thieves, but also "disturbers of the peace," that is, foreigners who annoy the citizens with their appearance, with their behavior that does not conform to the habits of the residents, or whose mere presence is an irritation.[42]

Most importantly, in recent years the news has reported a high number of violent crimes against foreigners. An accurate list of killings, assaults, and beatings of individuals in Muslim associations, street vendors, window washers, or gypsies would be several pages long. To give an idea of the dimensions of the hostilities, in 1995 alone there were 301 confirmed cases of violence against foreigners.[43] Statistics for 1996 are even more revealing. According to a study completed by the University of Rome, in 1996 there were 374 violent crimes

---

[41] Frequently the violence against gypsies involves the local underworld. The following news story is an example, "During the protests against gypsies in Quarto, this pair of protestors were on the front line. Yesterday the local police reported them for fencing stolen goods: their house was full of property stolen from apartments in the area." *Il Lavoro*, Genoan supplement to *La Repubblica*, 14 December 1996: vi. Events of this type are not isolated. The native underworld promotes the anti-gypsy or anti-immigrant demonstrations because they draw the attention of the local authorities in those neighborhoods.

[42] One of the most revealing cases of this tendency is the "revolt" of the citizens in a neighborhood in Milan that culminated in attacking a bar with many "Moroccan" clients. See *Corriere della Sera*, 4, 5, and 6 June 1998. The news story relates that the protest focused not just on drugs, but people who "disturb the peace," "get drunk," hang around on the street corners "waiting for who know what," etc.

[43] Caritas di Roma. *Immigrazione. Dossier statistico '96*. Rome: Anterem, 1996. 185. Fifty percent of attacks occurred in public places. See also Buso, A. "Rapporto di ricerca sulle manifestazioni del pregiudizio, dell'intolleranza e della violenza razzista in Italia." *Istituto Piemontese "A. Gramsci."*, Consiglio Regionale del Piemonte, Turin 1996.

against foreigners reported in the press, 68 of which were fatal. During the course of the study, the Minister of the Interior Napolitano admitted that 111 foreigners had been killed in violent crimes,[44] and it was likely that other unreported cases existed. Frequently, homicides and violence against foreigners are minimized or ignored by the press, which makes it difficult to accurately analyze these racist episodes. It is almost as if when an immigrant is killed, a kind of preventative and automatic censorship occurs which causes these homicides to be classified as "fatalities" or news stories that are more or less neutral and devoid of importance. Below are three newspaper stories reporting immigrant deaths, two of which were "accidental," and the third is only slightly different because it was a homicide:

"Tunisian Dies After Attack"

A Tunisian, Habib Hammouda, 37 years old, died of cardiac arrest at the Garibaldi Hospital in Catania where he had been admitted and treated for wounds sustained after being attacked last Sunday in Punta Braccetto outside of Ragusa. In the attack he sustained a trauma to the head and a cerebral hemorrhage. Hammouda, a farm laborer, was attacked and beaten by unidentified assailants around 6 p.m. near the bar where he had gone to work as a parking lot attendant. At the emergency room in Punta Braccetto, the workers thought that the Tunisian was drunk, and did not begin treatment, though he was bleeding from the mouth. Hammouda was then transferred to the public hospital in Ragusa and from there to the Garibaldi hospital where he died.[45]

"Three Suspects Arrested and Freed After Death of Immigrant"

Turin. "We didn't want to hurt him; we only tied him up to restrain him. He had already wounded me with a screwdriver, but I felt sorry for him. You could see

---

[44] See Italian newspapers from 12 June 1997. On the previous day, 5,000 residents in Turin demonstrated against the criminality of immigrants, shouting the slogan, "Who doesn't attack Moroccans is one!" At the demonstration, which was organized by neighborhood citizens committees and right-wing parties, the PDS of Turin also participated.

[45] *Il Manifesto*. 5 July 1995.

that he was desperate," said Stefano Ghedini upon being released from Le Vallette prison in Turin where he and Antonio Lopes, 55, had been held on manslaughter charges. Maria Mattione, 42, wife of Ghedini, had been held in the Nuove prison on the same charges and was also released. All three suspects have been released, but the mystery remains as to the death of N'Hammed Chmina, 54, immigrant from Morocco.

Chmina was found Wednesday stretched out in the yard at a farmhouse. He was bound at the wrists and ankles, and later died. Was it a racist lynching? Hearing the testimonies of witnesses, it became clear that this was actually a tragic story of desperation. Today's autopsy should clear up the mystery.[46]

"Friar Kills Lover. 'I Was Being Blackmailed'"

Bergamo. The death of Aminata Harding, 25, emigrated from Sierra Leon and resident of Alzano Lombardo, would have only merited a short paragraph in the news, except that it was a friar who strangled her to death.[47]

It is not difficult to project the degree to which hostility toward foreigners is reflected in the daily practices of the legal and police institutions, despite the lack of research in this area. The data that does exist indicate a substantial degree of discrimination against foreigners who have been investigated, stopped by police, or involved in court proceedings (consider, for example, police controls of documents, or the reports for misdemeanors or attempted crimes which now involve almost exclusively the foreign population).[48] Numerous episodes of police brutality against foreigners have occurred in recent years. This violence is rarely condemned publicly and is even indirectly justified by some branches of the media with factious and ambiguous news stories. Below are two summaries of illegal police procedures:

[46] *La Repubblica.* 2 June 1995. From this news report, it seems that binding an immigrant and leaving him to die is "normal." Episodes of this type show how in Italy it is nearly impossible to establish the number of victims of racism.

[47] *La Repubblica.* 11 September 1997. 18.

[48] The role of police in identifying migrants as a targeted category represents what Skolnick defined as "justice without due process." See also Skolnick, J. *Justice Without Trial. Law Enforcement in a Democratic Society.* New York: J. Wiley and Sons, 1975.

One year ago I met a young Albanian man who survived by washing the windows of cars as they stopped at the traffic light near my house. We spoke occasionally. One day [...] a patrol car drove up and the police told him to get in. The young man didn't have to be told twice. "I was afraid to disobey," he told me later. The officers took him to the central police station where they sat him on a chair in the middle of a room and they began to beat him, again and again, without even allowing him the question, "What is going on?" Then they let him go.[49]

Chafik Azilag, 18, migrant and homeless, was arrested April 22 in the downtown area of Genoa for attempted purse snatching. The police apprehended him in front of a group of fifth-graders from the Daneo elementary school [...]. The children were shocked and upset by the methods used by the police, and sent a public letter to the newspapers and the police chief Antonio Pagnozzi to relate what they had seen: "First the Moroccan man was punched and kicked by a plains clothes policeman then he was handcuffed to a grate and hit by officers in uniform. One of the officers even went into a bakery to buy some focaccia, and then came out and hit the suspect again." The Moroccan man, it later came out, had to be treated at the emergency room where the doctors diagnosed trauma to the head and knee, a state of stupor (*perhaps he was on drugs*), and recommended 8 days of hospitalization. *Someone described the scene as an example of police methods worthy of the officers in Brazil or Los Angeles.*[50]

Migrants are heavily over-represented in the prison population (an average of 27%, with peaks of 50% in some district penitentiaries), in part because there are no other alternative means of detention for those who are without a *permesso di soggiorno*. Some studies indicate that foreigners accused of crimes are five times

[49] This testimony was recorded in Chistolini, S. "Dal razzismo di strada all'educazione intercultruale nell'università italiana." *Immigrazione e multiculturale nell'Italia di oggi. il territorio, i problemi, la didattica.* Ed. C. Brusa. Milan: Franco Angeli, 1997. It is disturbing that the testimony in question is defined as an example of "racism on the streets" (analogous to insults and other manifestations of hostility) and not institutional racism.
[50] *Il Corriere Mercantile* 2 May 1997: 15. (My italics). The author of the article seeks to convince the readers that the young man who was stopped after a mugging, beaten by a group of customs officers, and treated in an emergency room was lethargic because "he was on drugs."

more likely than Italians to be incarcerated.[51] Furthermore, they are given heavier sentences than Italians for the same crimes.[52] The tendency legal routinization, evidenced in shortened trials and plea bargaining, has even more serious consequences for foreigners, who already face the discrimination implicit in being economically disadvantaged, having difficulty communicating, and being obligated to employ the public defender. The following testimonies of several judges reveals a "normal" discrimination that has less to do with the judges' subjective choices (such as his or her discretion in terms of restricting the suspect's liberty), and more to do with subjecting foreigners to a legal machine that is both inadequate and rigid:

> We don't worry about the defense attorney too much, especially in cases involving foreigners, cases that are handled in ways that are professionally questionable. The quality of the defense is directly proportionally to the how much the client is able to pay. The foreign client has linguistic difficulties, and interpreters are appointed when the client and attorneys simply can't understand each other. The defense attorney is not motivated to make things easier [...]. Years ago a kind of informational handbook on prisoners' rights was circulated in various languages but I don't know if it's still being distributed in S. Vittore. It was published by an initiative of the magistrate's court in Milan. Obviously, telling people to look it up in the library if they want to is far less useful than putting the information directly into their hands with the most relevant parts highlighted. Among the reasons for applying precautionary measures is the

[51] Caputo, A. and C. Putignano. "Immigrazione e aspetti giudiziari." *Immigrazione. Dossier statistico 1995*. Caritas of Rome. Rome: Anterem, 1995. 205.

[52] Lagazzi, M., D. Malfatti, E. Pallestrini, N. Rossoni. "Immigrazione, comportament criminale e sanzione penale. Reflessioni sulla figura dell'"immigrato-spacciatore" nella città di Genova. *Rassegna italiana di criminologia* 1 (1996): 145-164. These authors claim that a discrimination occurs among the foreigners who come into contact with our penal code. Due to this, the data about the number of foreigners convicted of crimes does not indicate a "propensity to commit crimes," as much as a negative selectivity toward them in our legal system. For the methodological and political problems implicated by the results of this type of research, see Bowling, B. "Conceptual and Methodological Problems in Measuring 'Race' Differences in Delinquency." *British Journal of Criminology* 4 (1990): 483-491, and Agozino, B. "Changes in the Social Construct of Criminality among Immigrants in the United Kingdom." *Délit d'immigration. La construction sociale de la deviance et de la criminalité parmi les immigrés.* Ed. S. Palidda. Brussels: CostA2/Migrations, 1996.

danger of the suspect escaping. We have to weigh all the possible precautionary measures and determine which is the most appropriate, and in the case of foreigners who have no stable residence, no documents, and no connections, the appropriate precaution is prison. Foreigners face discrimination not because of race, but because the foreigner's situation allows the law on precautionary measures prosecution to the full extent. If the foreigner has a steady job and fixed place of residence then obviously things change.[53]

The most dramatic issue which affects mainly foreigners, but also Italians as well, is the complexity of precautionary measures other than custody, not because custody is the only appropriate penalty, but because alternative penalties are impossible on the practical level; there are many crimes for which we could sentence house arrest instead of prison, but it's impossible because the suspect has no known residence. Therefore, in these cases, even if all the conditions are right I still can't use any other measures because there is simply no concrete way to employ those other appropriate measures, and often there is a certain culture, which I don't agree with, that believes the only legal measures that a foreigner with an uncertain identity is entitled to would be prison. It's as if all we really needed is a day-hospital, but I still have to put him in containment, do you understand?[54]

I had to go to hearing about a foreigner who was accused of giving counterfeit documents at the government office when he went to pick up his *permesso di soggiorno*, and I happened to ask for a sentence that was disregarded by the judge. He gave a much heavier sentence than the one I had asked for, and he justified it by saying this kind of thing creates a certain social alarm, and there are specific factors that, under a judge's discretion, must be taken into consideration.[55]

In testimonies of judges, lawyers, and prison workers (staff and guards, as well as volunteers and educators) a certain acknowledgement appears that, since the beginning of the 1990s, many migrants, *because they are migrants*, have found prison to be the inevitable endpoint of their migratory movements, independent of whether or not they have committed a crime or if they are

---

[53] Interview with a deputy prosecutor in Milan.
[54] Interview with a judge in Milan.
[55] Interview with a deputy prosecutor in Milan.

effectively a danger to society. To illustrate, I include selections from two interviews, one is with an attorney who specializes in defending foreigners and the other from a prison employee in northern Italy. Though these two individuals could have opposing viewpoints regarding foreigners in prison, their observations agree regarding the penalization of foreigners.

> At a certain point, the foreigner became objectively a criminal; the interests of the various organs of social control became centered on him; every level of police force (city policemen, the federal *carabinieri*, customs officers, local sheriffs) went into action, sometimes in competition with each other but more often carving out specific sectors of specialization in running down every possible illegal or suspected action. The criminalization of street vendors particularly by customs officials and local sheriffs is significant, and the systematic control by *carabinieri* and city police of the places where foreigners meet is likewise significant. This change came about very rapidly. It seemed that overnight nearly all legal firms were assaulted by foreigners grappling with an infinite number of legal problems. The vast majority of them literally did not understand what was going on because a series of activities such as street peddling, selling cigarettes, prostitution, or simply sleeping on a park bench or drinking a beer on the sidewalk were things that nobody considered criminal acts up until the day before and suddenly they became criminalized […]. What I mean to say is at a certain point being an immigrant, a foreigner, an *extracommunitario*, became associated with an image of latent criminality, that being a "foreigner" and being a "deviant" somehow coincided and this connection needed to be uncovered and normed.[56]
>
> *Interviewer*: What kind of evolution did you see in the prisons at the beginning of the 1990s?
>
> *Prison Employee*: At a certain point, everything began to change completely. A prison such as [name withheld] ended up having more foreign inmates than Italian inmates, but even in the non-exceptional cases, the foreigners make up at least 50% of the inmate population. Obviously this brought about a series of radical changes in both the relationship between Italians and foreigners as well as between prison staff and foreign inmates.
>
> The first thing I'd have to say is that the type of foreigner who lands in prison is usually not a criminal, and this can be a real problem even though that seems

[56] Interview with a lawyer in Genoa.

like a paradox. It's a problem because the criminal understands the system and therefore speaks a certain kind of language in which prison plays a very defined role, but detaining non-criminals creates a constant state of misunderstanding that ends up being frustrating and the source of constant conflict. What I mean is that since the beginning of the 1990s, people were sent and have remained in prison who cannot really be compared to what one usually imagines an inmate to be, namely a person who in some way deliberately lives outside of the law. The ones we get are basically screwed, in many cases they don't even realize where they came from, why they're here, what will happen to them, or what kind of system they're in, so the situation inside the prison is always on the brink of exploding.[57]

In other words, the statistics that show an increase in the number of immigrants who are arrested, sentenced, and imprisoned do not reveal a higher propensity for criminality but an actual "penalization" of foreigners.[58] Numerous indicators show that suicides and accidental deaths of foreigners in prison are attributable to capillary discriminatory practices, enhanced by the chronic emergency situation and neglect of the Italian prison system.[59] Not just active and deliberate discriminatory practices, but the effect of an inadequate system of legal assistance, of superficiality, lack of interest and indifference on the part of state functionaries, judges, lawyers, and doctors. Prison acts as a kind of black hole, a dumping ground where foreigners naturally occupy the lowest rung of the ladder, the weakest among the weak. As the testimonies of those in the legal system attest, the hostility aimed at foreigners is not the fruit of some ideological racism. Instead, it is part of that logic that says the weakest pay

[57] Interview with a prison employee.
[58] For an analysis of the problems born of the use of the penal statistics relative to immigration, see Tournier, P. and P. Robert. *Etrangers et delinquances. Les chiffres du débat.* Paris: L'Harmattan, 1991.
[59] Consiglio d'Europa. *Rapporto degli ispettori europei sullo stato delle carceri in Italia.* Palermo: Sellerio, 1995; Passarella, D. and A. Spinelli, eds. *Gli stranieri in carcere.* Rome: Ed. Sinnos, 1994; Ruggiero, V. "Flexibility and Intermittent Emergency in the Italian Penal System." *Western Penal Systems: A Critical Anatomy.* Eds. V. Ruggiero, M. Ryan, J. Sim, London: Sage, 1995; Caritas Rome-Fondazione Zancan, *I bisogni dimenticati. Rapporto 1996 su emarginazione ed esclusione sociale.* Milan: Feltrinelli, 1997. 157.

more, which is the logic of the normal functioning of the prison mechanism. Following are a newspaper article that gives an idea of the conditions and fate of foreigners in prison, and an excerpt from an interview with a prison worker.

"Fasting in Cell and Dies. Scandal Behind Bars. He Always Claimed, 'I Am Innocent.'"

Padua. Melad Meftah, 43, Algerian, or also Mohamed Oussane, 31, Palestinian [...]. In prison awaiting sentencing for possession of drugs, he swore he was innocent. He was without documents, without money to pay for a lawyer who truly cared about his case, without friends or relatives. He went on a hunger strike hoping to be heard. Weeks of fasting, reduced to a skeleton [...] but the truth is that he was killed. Not by the pneumonia he contracted in the hospital where he was transferred but by the merciless justice system and the indifference of all.
He had been stopped by the *carabinieri* on February 7 [...]. There were 7 of them in the farmhouse, all Maghrebi, assembling packages of heroine. When the police burst in, the heroine was thrown out of the window, 20 grams. Melad ended up in handcuffs. "I had nothing to do with it. The drugs weren't mine," he swears, but no one believed him. On the advice of another inmate, Melad contacted Cesare Vanzetti, an attorney in Padua [...]. Who knows if the Algerian will be able to pay the lawyer's fees, but you never turn down a job. Vanzetti barely remembers Melad. "It was routine," he says. The fact remains that there was never even a request made to consider house arrest. "Where would we put him?" the attorney explains, "He had no permanent residence and he didn't know anybody." So Melad went back to his cell. And he made the only form of protest available to him: a hunger strike. "It always happens with Maghrebi, they self-inflict injuries or similar things. Then they calm down," his lawyer added. Melad, though, held on [...]. What he wanted, no one knows, because no one would listen. The prison warden sent a report to the public prosecutor's office but nothing happened, not until Melad actually became very ill and they decided to transfer him to the hospital. [...] At the beginning of May it became obvious that the poor man was at death's door. And what did the hospital do? They assigned a psychologist to visit him. His diagnosis: Melad is capable of understanding his surroundings, of expressing his will and he has no intentions of suicide. [...] They gave the patient a sedative and then kept him alive with intravenous feedings. But by then, his body was so completely debilitated that he easily fell prey to other illnesses. A few days later they

diagnosed him with severe pneumonia which was unresponsive to antibiotics. They intubated him, thus keeping him alive with a machine for his circulation. But it was pointless. He was struck down by a heart attack. Amen. One less irritation for everyone. But where was his lawyer, the judges, or anyone who could have convinced him to stop his fast before it was too late?[60]

"Interview"

In prison, have you seen specific forms of racism aimed at foreigners?
No, I think that the racist actions and hatred toward foreigners are the fruit of a profound moral decay that actually has little to do with what you could call the immigration emergency. Prison is fertile ground for any kind of expression of this type; you must understand that when people [prison guards] amuse themselves by setting fire to cats or by mocking those infected with AIDS asking them, "So when are you dying?" When there are people who act this way, I think it is difficult to attribute such actions to a conscious racism. If tomorrow there were no more blacks, no more cats, and everyone with AIDS was healed, there would still be subjects acted upon by these same mechanisms. The older officials and deputies still talk nostalgically about the restraining beds used more than 20 years ago, and back then there were no foreigners in the prisons. It was the most desperate or the most rebellious who ended up tied to their beds, nowadays it would be the foreigners, and clearly among the foreigners the ones who would end up like that I'm sure would be the Moroccans, that is, the weakest.

Xenophobia and institutional discrimination against foreigners, whether that discrimination is ideological or occurs in actual practices, have become characteristics of Italy, at least since the end of the 1980s. Nevertheless, neither the social organs of communication and information nor the research in sociology or political logic (except for a few exceptions) have decried or analyzed this reality and its implications for our society. While the Italian press has given ample attention to the attacks on immigrants that occurred in Germany after reunification, from 1990 to the present, and has reported individual cases of racism and discrimination that have occurred abroad, the

[60] *La Repubblica.* 1 June 1997: 21.

press has never undertaken any serious investigation of the xenophobia in Italy. This xenophobia is invisible in that it is not the object of a legitimate public discourse; in other words, it has been subjected to an implicit censorship.[61] If the events in Rostock or Lubeck aroused strong reactions in Europe and fierce political reactions in the German Federal Republic, the aggressions against foreigners in Italy have slipped widely unnoticed among the daily criminal news stories. When immigrants are attacked, the juridical and public safety authorities raise doubts as to the xenophobic nature of those acts of aggression. The press, for its part, tends to present even the most extreme forms of violence against migrants, as the effects of a situation that is "objectively" serious, i.e. ultimately a situation caused by immigration and not as actions that are deliberately xenophobic. Following is a news article that is on some levels representative of a raid by a band of Naziskins in Turin on April 17, 1997.

> There were about 50 of them, some witnesses say even as many as 80. Shaved heads, black jackets loaded with spikes, military boots. Armed with baseball bats, iron bars, boxing gloves filled with sand, faces covered with scarves and ski masks, they "marched" on Murazzi, the district along the Po River near the center of Turin. Every night, hundreds of young people patronize the businesses and clubs open until late in the evening, and drug dealers and their clients also gather. Thursday night, just after midnight it happened [...]. A disc jockey of French origin, originally from Guinea, had just left his business to get a coffee, and he was savagely beaten and severely injured while the other victims of this "punitive expedition" declined medical assistance, since they do not have *permessi di soggiorno*. That the situation at Murazzi is extremely serious is evident in the arrest that occurred one hour after the raid: Rachid Samir, 21 years old, Moroccan, a previous offender and once deported, had a Beretta 6.35

[61] Every social phenomenon, in order to be visible, must be the object of an autonomous social discourse which is often produced by legitimate and specific initiatives. Unlike the "immigration emergency," xenophobia in Italy is not yet the subject of legitimate social debate. For a theoretical discussion of this problem see *American Journal of Sociology* 5 (1996), and Jacobs, R.N. "Civil Society and Crisis: Culture, Discourse, and the Rodney King Beating." *American Journal of Sociology* 5 (March 1996). See also Van Dijk, T.E. *Racism and the Press*. London: Routledge, 1991.

pistol in his pocket which he attempted to throw away when police agents apprehended him.

"We want to clean up Murazzi," shouted the executioners during the racist raid. *Investigators tend to indicate a different number of thugs ("There were at the most 30," claim the police). Some police authorities such as Filippo Dispenza of the Volanti and Antonio De Santis of the Digos have advanced the suspicion that underneath this outbreak of racist violence are battles between drug dealers.*[62]

As will be demonstrated in detail later, the minimization of the xenophobia by redirecting attention (the "extremely serious" situation), the citing of facts that have no relation to the violence in question except for the "criminal immigration" (the armed Moroccan, "previous offender and once deported,") and the minimization of the events on the part of the police officers interviewed, are all constant characteristics in the information circulated relative to the problems of immigration. It is a direct effect of this treatment in the news that the xenophobia of Italians, the emergency for migrants, has become literally invisible and unmentionable.[63] In July of 1997, again in Turin where the attack by Naziskins occurred, a young Moroccan man was killed under atrocious circumstances. During an argument with a group of young Italian men, Abdellah Doumi was hit and fell into the Po. From the banks the young Italian men threw beer bottles and other objects at him (including a vacuum cleaner) to prevent him from climbing out. The young man drowned. Of course in the press, even this death had nothing to do with racism:

"They Made Him Drown While They Laughed"

A Moroccan died in the Po: they kept him from reaching the shore
Turin. They say that Abdellah Douomi floundered for a long time before he went under the turbid water of the Po. Though he didn't know how to swim, he tried desperately to reach the shore, but he fell back beneath the hail of bottles,

[62] *La Repubblica* 19 April 1997: 21. (My italics).
[63] While many sociologists and criminologists have expressed interest recently in the "propensity of immigrants to commit crime," there is very little research regarding the violence *against* immigrants.

cans, and pieces of wood that the group of young Italian men threw at him, laughing […]. *"Of course this is not an episode that can be ascribed to racism,"* underlines Claudio Cracovia, leader of the homicide division of the Turin police force, "no less serious, it was the tragic conclusion of a conflict between drunken individuals."*[64]*

3 Democratic Exclusion

Another type of discrimination exists, not of direct hostility against foreigners, that does not enter into the current definitions of "racism" and "xenophobia" in the tally of violent acts and victims. While at first glance, it appears less lethal than violence, it probably has greater negative effects upon the overall existence of migrants. I refer to a strategic hostility hidden in the neutral technical definitions used in the laws and decrees periodically adopted in order to "regularize" the legal condition of foreigners. These definitions have no relation to the racism of the Naziskins or ideological intolerance, and are in fact, adopted in order to combat the racism, to establish law, and to put in order. Their foundation is nothing more than the common, democratic, public opinion, "what the people think" of immigration: namely, that migrants constitute a problem or a threat against which our society must defend itself, though within a context of "tolerance," and "respect for other cultures," and "multiculturalism."

The Turco-Napolitano Law is interesting from this perspective because it expresses a view point not from the political right, even less from the xenophobes, but rather from progressive political culture. This law efficiently summarizes exactly what civil democratic society and its political representatives think about immigration and what practical measures they intend to adopt in order to regulate it. Under this provision, declarations of inalienable principles and attempts at recognizing fundamental universal rights coexist with pure and

[64] *La Repubblica.* 20 July 1997: 6. (My italics.) A few days later in Milano, three more Moroccans were seriously wounded by young Italian men throwing malatov cocktails. Once again, the investigators had no explanation for the event, but tended to exclude the "racist matrix." All these episodes without explanations are either considered to be mysteries, drunken outbursts, effects of the summer heat, or the more generally "due to the gravity of the situation."

simple police measures. This duality depends exclusively on the division of migrants into legal *regolari* and illegal *clandestini*. In the first place, there is a timid attempt at recognizing a fundamental right to existence, while in the second there are exclusively norms for public order. In the text of the law, the distinction appears subtle, but it carries decisive consequences:

> *The foreigner present in the Italian territory has fundamental human rights* provided under the internal national laws, international conventions now in force, and principles of international law generally recognized (article 2, paragraph 1).

> *The foreigner legally residing in Italy* is entitled to all civil rights attributed to Italian citizens, unless otherwise indicated in international conventions in force for Italy or under current Italian law (article 2, paragraph 2).

Distinguishing between "fundamental human rights" and "civil rights" means drawing a line between who can be subject to any provision of public order (being stopped by police, expelled, held in a detainment center), presumably without suffering any mistreatment that would violate the individual's human rights, and those who are *regolari* and thus equipped with the same civil capital as Italian citizens. It has been widely noted that international conventions do very little to unite individual nations in regards to the "rights of the individual."[65] Only rarely are the most serious violations reported and spark controversy. The fact that foreigners residing in Italy who are not *regolari* are without civil rights means in practical terms that they will be subject to legal orders and entrusted to the discretion of the police to learn about their individual freedoms. The section of the law that regulates expulsions and detainment camps for "*permanenza temporanea*" gives a detailed outline showing what foreigners can expect:

---

[65] I disagree with the opinion of S. Sassen, who sees the "international regime of human rights" as a limitation of the sovereignty of individual states. See Sassen, S. *Losing Control? Sovreignity in an Age of Globalization*. New York: Columbia University Press, 1996. For the issue of international acts and declarations of human rights, see Fauré, C. *Ce que déclarer des droits veut dire: histoires*. Paris: Presses Universitaires de France, 1997.

It is not always possible to immediately expel a foreigner by escorting the individual to the border or by deportation when certain procedures are necessary, such as medical assistance, supplementary verifications regarding nationality or identity, obtaining required travel documents, or when appropriate transportation is not available. *In these cases the police commissioner arranges for the foreigner to be held for the minimum time necessary in the nearest* "centro di permanenza temporanea e assistenza," *among those designated and established, preferably one near to the border, by decree of the Minister of the Interior together with the Minister of Internal Affairs and the Minister of Finance* (article 12, paragraph 1). (Author's italics).

Under law, the foreigner is held in the Center to insure the necessary assistance and full respect for his/ her dignity. In addition to the provisions outlined in article 2, paragraph 5, the foreigner is guaranteed free access to correspondence outside of the center, including telephone contact (paragraph 2). [...]

The police commissioner, along with law enforcement, adopts effective measures of surveillance so that the foreigner does not leave the Center unduly, and will undertake the immediate correction of a situation in which these regulations are violated (paragraph 7).

The legislators' intent, as indicated by the officious prose, is undoubtedly to intern foreigners awaiting deportation in camps which have been organized near the borders and are under police control;[66] camps that resemble prisons, although their visitors are not subject to legal proceedings. As previously mentioned, these tactics have already been adopted by other European countries (Germany, England). But in Italy, these proceedings have had both officious and extreme expressions (the internment of Albanian refugees in the Bari stadium in August, 1991, and the camps created after the arrival of boat people in March, 1997) and which now have assumed normative value. Those candidates most likely to become guests in these camps are, first of all, the "*clandestini,*" those migrants without a legal "*permesso di soggiorno,*" the undesirable, because they are socially dangerous and therefore suspect.

[66] On 1 June, 1997, Minister of the Interior Napolitano reaffirmed that immigration is a police matter, from legalization to imprisonment in detainment centers. *Il Manifesto.* 2 June 1997.

According to the Turco-Napolitano proposal (which recasts article 7 of the Dini decree),[67] these individuals can be expelled under article 1 of law 1423/1956 ("Preventative Measures for Those Endangering Public Security or Morality") which defines who can be considered "socially threatening."

1. Those whom evidence suggests are habitually given to criminal acts,
2. Those whom evidence suggests and whose conduct and tenor of life indicate that they maintain themselves, even in part, by criminal acts,
3. Those whom evidence suggests and whose conduct shows that they are given to crimes that offend and endanger the moral and physical safety of minors, or the health, safety, or peace of the community.

Here it is important to note that these and other norms (such as article 203 and those following in the Penal Code) authorize restrictive measures (and in the case of foreigners, even authorize preventive detention in camps while awaiting expulsion) against the personal liberty of individuals who have not been reported to the police, much less found guilty of any crime. They are condemned on the basis of a belief in their dangerousness, when "evidence suggests" relative to their "conduct and tenor of life" that they are "given to criminal acts" that "offend and endanger the moral and physical safety of minors" or "peace of the community." If these norms are applied to foreigners, they allow authorities under the pretext of public safety to expel a traveling salesman selling trinkets on a beach, a migrant who gets drunk, or an Albanian who demonstrates by his "tenor of life" hints of criminality. These norms, which are not applied to Italian nationals, turn foreigners into dangerous subjects on the basis of arbitrary evaluations. These evaluations arise easily from public opinion, and above all, from media representations as shown by the following new article about the expulsion in September, 1997 of some Albanians considered to be socially dangerous.

[67] For the text of the Dini decree, see *Il Sole 24 Ore*. 2 December 1995: 20.

"Albanians with Money and Cell Phones Expelled"

Bari [...] Another Albanian just outside the train station wriggled away, pulling off his t-shirt to show journalists the scratches forming an X on his back: "I don't want to leave, I don't want to leave," he cried, flailing wildly, "first I have to go and get the car I left in Turin." *Many* "clandestini" *have cell phones and don't even try to hide it. Some even use them to communicate with who knows...*[68]

The following chapter will examine how "facts" that are actually non-existent become indications in our society of potential social danger in the case of foreigners. In the text reported above, it is the suspect's cell phone that is seen as the visible indicator of arrogant ("he didn't even attempt to conceal it") and illicit trafficking and untold criminal strategies, even though cell phones in Italy ring constantly in every public place and are proudly gripped by drivers, adolescents, managers, and every other citizen (including even journalists, probably), and are even found in situations of deprivation and poverty. These are the "behaviors" that will most likely destine the "dangerous" foreigner for detention and expulsion. At any rate, given the obvious similarity between detention centers and prisons, and detainees and inmates, there are few guarantees that the "*permanenza*" of the detainees with be "*temporanea*" or that their dignity is insured, as promised by article 2, paragraph 5 of the Turco-Napolitano Law.

Because they have the same rights as Italian citizens, legally documented foreigners should be able to avoid the condition of radical exclusion, but even foreigners who are *regolari* cannot escape special legislation, evidenced in article 6 of the law:

The foreigner who cannot exhibit a passport or other identification document, or a *permesso di soggiorno*, when requested by the officers and agents of public safety, will be punished by arrest of up to six months and a fine of up to 800,000 lire (paragraph 3).
In addition to providing the required identification, public safety officials may also require information from foreigners verifying the availability of funds

[68] *La Repubblica.* 11 September 1997: 18. (My italics).

either from employment or another legitimate source that are sufficient to maintain the individual and all other family members residing with them in the Italian territory (paragraph 4).

Paragraph 4 of article 6 is clearly discriminatory because it abrogates to the authorities of public safety the capacity to investigate the income and economic status of those who, theoretically, are entitled to all the same civil rights as Italian citizens. Those rights include the right to privacy, explicitly protected by the Rodotà law. However, another threat to the rights of foreigners, implicit but no less serious, is contained in paragraph 3. That point is quite obvious for a political culture that for years has been obsessed with legality. It is in keeping with legislation that assigns decisive importance to paper documentation of citizens' identity and assigns to public safety officials the power to demand identification from anyone at any time. We should recall that in other countries identification cards DO NOT exist, and requirements of this type are considered harassment if not outright violations of civil rights.

The problem here is: how does an officer accurately determine an individual's identity if that person is a foreigner? In addition to this law's clearly oppressive nature (6 months under arrest, fines of 800,000 lire), behind it lies the thinly disguised, wide spread, and banal reality of random identity checks. Under the authority of such checks, everyone, if their appearance or skin pigmentation causes concern, can be stopped and eventually arrested if for any reason they cannot justify their lack of an adequate identification document. In reality, this article does nothing but validate what happens in cities and urban centers considered "at risk" for years due to social alarm, nourished largely by the media and political opportunists: San Salvario in Turin, the historic downtown of Genoa, some areas of Milan such as Porta Venezia. Many migrants have informed me that in these areas (downtown Genoa, for example) an immigrant can be stopped by police as many as 20 times in a week. If such a thing happened to us Italian and European citizens, we would consider ourselves to be living in a police state. How do we describe such a law, if not as discriminatory, though with a degree of self-satisfaction, its own proponents have termed it "favorable to immigrants."

The law in question makes evident the ambivalence of democratic political culture in confronting the problems of migration and foreigners in general. On the one hand, we dogmatically accept and even advance the presupposition of the "immigration emergency." We follow the political right toward mobilization against an invasion; we contemplate discriminatory legislative measures, we treat immigration as a disease or a problem.[69] On the other hand, we promote demonstrations against racism, we organize debates about multiculturalism, and we endlessly discuss "diversity," all without coming to the obvious contradiction between the principle of equality that everyone proclaims but no one acts on, and principles of diversity which everyone sustains and subscribes to. Touting diversity is appealing not just because it so conveniently satisfies contemporary cultural modes, but because diversity legitimizes the significant desire to separate foreigners from Italian citizens and immigrants that are *"regolari"* from those who are *"clandestini."*

4 A Sense of Hostility

When confronted with the issues of migration, our country not only reacted initially with a negative and excluding form of indifference, but also turned its own incapacity in dealing with migration phenomena against the migrants themselves. The racist violence demonstrated by the ideological minorities, the indifference veined with hostility of the silent majority, the discrimination inherent in the legal system, and the social exclusion are all different forms in which society that is essentially unified in its fear of migrants (despite its ideological and political differences) manages to erect a unassailable barrier between "us" and "them," even while some of "them" are allowed to temporarily reside among us. "They" are all those who would presume to live among us for whatever reason, and yet are not like us. This "diversity" has

---

[69] For a critism of this cliché, see Rushdie, S. *Imaginary Homelands*, New York: Penguin, 1992.

nothing to do with race or culture, at least not in principle, but rather has to do exclusively with their foreignness to our legitimate space, albeit national or extranational.[70] What Moroccan, Algerian, Senegalese, Romanian, gypsies, Albanian refugees, Bosnian, and Kurdish migrants all have in common is exactly this fact that they do not have the right to live in our national space because they are not Italian, not Western European, not "first world," and not rich. It is beyond evident that what we are saying about foreigners and the social, political, and legislative discrimination they face does not hold true for Japanese, North Americans, Swiss or other foreigners who would technically also fall into the category of "*extracommunitari.*"

Everywhere that the terms "foreigner" or "*extracommunitari*" appear – in legal decrees, in the press, in "scientific" debates – those terms actually apply to those migrants in search of a job, a refuge, a new existence. The barrier that our society erects against them is not constituted only by the empirical forms of violence and discrimination examined earlier, but is foremost, *political.* As such, the discrimination is not manifest only the usual forms of defending our borders (repressive military and civil apparatus), but of a symbology that transforms purely empirical distinctions between "us" and "them" into an oppositional ontological stance between worlds that are radically opposed.[71] Before being discriminated against in actions, migrants and refugees are discriminated against in the language that our society invents to represent them. This language, despite its constant modification, nevertheless remains unaltered in its characterization of these human beings as aliens: "immigrant," "*extracommunitari,*" "*clandestini,*" "*irregolari,*" "third-worlders," and so forth. These labels appear in every type of discourse: common usage, legalistic language, political discourse, bureaucratic terminology. Not only do they falsify the social and existential reality of the

---

[70] For this definition, see Sayad, A. *L'immigration ou le paradoxe de l'alterité.* Brussels: De Boeck-Wesmael, 1990.

[71] The necessity of borders as a political condition of ethnic differentiation has been analyzed by Frederik Barth. For Barth, the ethnicization of cultures is a process that involves the interaction of changing groups. See Barth, F. "Introduction." *Process and Form in Social Life. Selected Essays.* London: Routledge and Kegan Paul, 1981.

migrant, but they act as a catalyst for every sort of negative meaning. The migrant, thanks to this sort of language of exclusion, is naturally impoverished, threatening, and has criminal tendencies.[72]

This hostility becomes even more apparent when national borders come into play as the silhouettes of national society. While it is objectively complicated to turn a group into a national enemy that resides within the interior of the state, nothing is easier than transforming foreigners into enemies when they try to cross our borders. In this case as well, identifying the foreigner as an enemy is the result of implicit procedures, often represented as the descriptions of real situations. Consider the following report from Lampedusa, which every summer becomes the border area where Italy wages war against immigrants:

"Border Lands, Lampedusa, Europe's Weak Point"

The Tunisians keep arriving, the inhabitants of the area revolt, the *carabinieri* surrender in the face of laws that are too permissive [...]. Judging from the numbers, the situation in Lampedusa is serious and paradoxical. According to the *carabinieri*, from January to October, 1,874 *extracomunitari* have "conquered" the islands' beaches. Now all of them have left Sicily to swell the ranks of the army of "*clandestini*" that roam our country.

The situation is dire because nothing can stop the waves of these desperate people. And this upsets the islanders, their intolerance becomes violent, and there is a ripple of terror that the negative publicity caused by this "Tunisians in Lampedusa" phenomenon will provoke a crisis in the tourism industry, the economic base in this slice of land, the southernmost part of Europe.

And here is the most paradoxical and grotesque element of the entire episode: Commander of the *carabinieri* of Agrigento, Col. Renato Gatti spreads his arms and says, "There is a law, the so-called Martelli law, and a decree from last September[73] that allows for the explusion of illegal immigrants. But in order to expel an individual, I must first determine the subject's exact nationality. Because none of them ever have any documents, we must send our requests to

[72] On the heterogeneity of the justifications for qualifying another as "enemy," see Simmel, G. "Der Munsch als Fiend. Zwei Fragmente aus einer Soziologie." *Aufsätze und Abhandlungen 1901-1908*. Vol. II. Frankfurt: Suhrkamp, 1992. 335-343.
[73] The Dini decree was actually dated November 1995.

the Tunisian Consulate. While we are waiting for the information from Tunis, the *extracomunitario* who snuck into Italy can do whatever he wants." [...] Why don't you prevent them from landing? "How would we do that? As soon as we get close to them, they throw themselves into the water. Naval code obligates us to save them from drowning. So we have to haul them out and take them to Lampedusa." Then they go to Agrigento, and on to freedom...
It was no accident that last October 7 a group of young men attacked some Tunisians who had hidden in a refrigerated storage compartment for fish. A gray Fiat Uno drove up, [one of the passengers] opened the storage unit and threw in a Molotov that fortunately did not function properly. Only one Tunisian was wounded and everyone was frightened.[74]

Equating the migrants with the enemy might seem misleading in so far as it is associated with a political definition of foreigners. It goes without saying that no war has ever been declared against migrants; and they don't display, obviously, their relative status as enemies. But migrants are in fact treated as enemies because they have the temerity to invade our national space. It is in fact typical of wartime legislation to intern, expel, or deprive "enemies of the state" of their civil rights. These same practices are explicitly provided for in the laws regarding migrants. In our own peaceful era, wars are fought but not recognized as such by those who fight them. Wars are no longer declared[75] and are officially considered "international police operations" (the Gulf War) or "peace missions" (Bosnia, Somalia, etc.). This normalizes and neutralizes the violence of the troops that officially do not fight but how are assigned to re-establish order in the name of peace. "We killed a few hundred Somalis," an Italian general confirmed when the scandal broke over the parachuters who had tortured civilians.[76] It is worth noting that similar news stories are reported only marginally as mere side notices

[74] Piervincenzi, E. " Pericolo Lampedusa. Viaggio sull'isola presa d'assalto dagli immigrati nordafricani." *Il Venerdì di Repubblica*. 1 November 1996: 28. For another point of view, see Ouazani, C. "Avec les sans-papiers de Lampedusa." *Jeune Afrique*. 10 December 1996.
[75] Hobsbawm, E.J. *Ages of Extremes: The Short Twentieth Century 1914-1991*, New York: Pantheon Books, 1994. The author argues convincingly that the era of war declarations has effectively ended.
[76] Declaration made by General Carmine Fiore, the commander of the Italian contingent in Somalia in 1993. *La Stampa*. 8 June 1997: 9.

in reports about torture; even more troubling is the fact that these stories do not arouse any particular reaction in public opinion. In other words, it seems absolutely normal and obvious that a "peace" force would kill hundreds or even thousands of a country's inhabitants that it was supposed to pacify, declaring that (according to military reports) these individuals were "bandits" who tried to steal food from the peace-keepers compound.

As the following chapter shows, this "normalcy" presupposes a racist attitude that is simultaneously implicit, undeclared, and hyperbolic on the part of the soldiers (and the public opinion of the countries that send them) toward human beings who are not treated as part of an inferior race but as a kind of lower-order animal.[77] From a political and military point of view there is no consistent solution between peace keeping in a foreign country and the military defense of our own borders from "illegal" foreigners. The troops deployed are essentially the same and the rhetoric of national interest is analogous. The main difference consists in the impossibility of using the "normal" violence within the Italian state as is enacted against foreigners. But as we see in the case of thousands of migrants who drowned attempting to reach our country, "peace keeping" was left to the elements and to death.

Though the migrant is reinvented daily as an enemy and a threat to our stable demography, jobs for our children, security for our cities, our cultural homogeneity, our values or any other element that characterizes our identity in reality or in our imagination, the migrant is preliminarily assumed to be and therefore constitutes an enemy. In this sense, A. Sayad[78] maintains that the exclusion of migrants is a result of the "mindset of the state." The migrant is considered ontologically, i.e. in his essence to be an enemy because he is seen as a threat to the very foundation of the state's order, the nation itself. As the image (political, symbolic, historic, cultural, and ideal) that the members of a society call "nation" advances the pretext of existing, of being real, even more

---

[77] This article that revealed the tortures Italians inflicted upon Somalis further revealed how the Italians also tortured animals; they treated the animals and Somalis in the same way. See Porzio, G. "Somalia. Gli italiani tortuavano i prigionieri: ecco le prove." *Panorama* 23, 12 June 1997: 20.

[78] Sayad, A. "La doppia pena del migrante. Riflessioni sul 'pensiero di stato'." *aut aut* 275 (1996): 10.

will it require "enemies" that can symbolically define borders. This is why a movement such as the Northern League that defends – or believes it defends – the mundane material interests of its electorate, practices an extreme, irrational xenophobia against "*extracomunitari*" (see Figure 1).

Figure 1

Poster for the Northern League, August, 1998. "Stop Them! They are arriving by the millions!"

The transformation of the foreigner into an enemy is a way to symbolically legitimize the pretext to dominate a territory. In fact, precisely because it is representative of a neonationalistic movement, the political culture of the Northern League, based on xenophobia, demonstrates how the invention of an enemy is intrinsic to nationalism. When nationalism is no longer in its formative phase, but is already consolidated, the hyperbolic forms of racism will be substituted by the procedural, democratic, legal and scientific forms of racism. These forms don't need to declare hatred against another, but limit themselves to actually treating the other as an enemy.

In short, migrants are enemies of the national society because they allow it to be defined and recognized as such. In discriminating against migrants –

foreigners in search of a job or refuge – national society seeks an essential justification for its own existence. Paradoxically, our societies need the migrants that they exclude, they need to exclude them as enemies. And this can explain the double game that the old and new societies of immigration play regarding migrants, even more than their economic usefulness: the rigidity of the norms against the *"clandestini"* and acceptance of a certain flow of migrants, the coexistence of exclusion and multicultural ideology, of denying civil rights and exalting cultural diversity, the obsession with police controls of foreigners, and the tolerance for illegal labor, and so on.

Naturally, the existence of an ontological enemy not only satisfies the need for a national identity, but also has practical repercussions that are of no small importance. Once they have been admitted by our host society, both legal and illegal immigrants (even if temporarily deprived of their enemy status) are little more than unwelcome guests, modern *metoikos* that the national society can treat according to its pleasure, excluding them from normal civil rights or perhaps conferring them with a few rights that can either be maintained or removed, excluding them from the norms that regulate the rights of legitimate workers with their jobs, treating them as illegitimate members or society, or second-class citizens. As guests that are tolerated only to a certain degree, migrants offer clear advantages to the host society: as underpaid workers, and if working illegally, they can hardly demand their rights. There are also social advantages in that the migrant will do anything to avoid social disturbance and expulsion, and thus avoid falling into the category of public enemy. In ancient Athens, a *metoiko* was hardly more than a slave. In our free society, which abolished slavery centuries ago, an immigrant-guest is a subject that can easily fall into the category of neo-slavery.

The symbolic and economic functions of the migrant as enemy are evident in the terminology that our legal, political, and conversational culture have invented to represent them as a category. I refer to the arbitrary and meaningless distinction – though still obsessively employed by politicians and the mass media – between legal immigrants (legitimate guests or suspected enemies) and the *"clandestini"* (illegitimate guests and enemies that have infiltrated national space). The media talks continually about the invasion of "*clandestini*" laws and propositions to repress "*clandestini*" immigration, demographers and research institutes try to quantify the illegal "*clandestini.*" Actually, the definition of illegal immigrant should be applied only to those few thousands of foreigners who tried to enter the country without passing the official borders. This would be easily determined, especially in this era of satellite surveillance of land and sea. The preoccupation with the invasion by "*clandestini*" has no other foundation than the distorted representation of immigration among different social groups and institutions. This is why a volunteer can speak of 300,000 *clandestini*, while Confcommercio (an organization that represents shop owners concerned about unlicensed street traders) speaks of 1,500,000 "*clandestini*" and the Northern League speaks of "millions."[79]

But if the "*clandestini*" number in the tens of thousands, then an enormous number of migrants has been "clandestinized" in the image that our society has constructed of them. In fact, the term "*clandestini*" normally defines the migrants who are outside of the condition of legality, for example, those who enter the country legally as tourists but can't manage to acquire a *permesso di soggiorno* or those immigrants who are legal but become illegal if they can't satisfy the legal and bureaucratic conditions imposed by the legislation currently in force. It bears mentioning that the term "*immigrato clandestino*" ultimately connotes not a formal condition but an anthropological one. "Thousands of *clandestini* from Albania are ready to flood into Italy," warns a radio broadcast from February of 1997. Being "*clandestini*" thus becomes the natural characteristic of those who are feared by our society, a ubiquitous threat. Following are two telling examples, the first from a letter that a reader sent to the newspaper editor and second are reflections of a well-known political scientist:

One reader writes, "In a letter from a few days ago, there was the affirmation that the '*clandestino* is not synonymous with criminal.' I'm sorry but this is simply not the case. A *clandestino* is already in the category of outlaw, and

[79] Eurispes. *Rapporto Italia '96*. Rome: Koiné Edizioni, 1996. 70.

because of this simple circumstance, he's already a criminal. Also, *clandestini* are already potentially dangerous and so they should be subject to every kind of governmental control.

"It's like giving a basket of edible mushrooms jumbled together with poisonous mushrooms to a person who is unable to tell them apart. Even though the person would check them out, he would need to get rid of them, the bad together with the good."[80]

Who is the immigrant and who is the "*clandestino*"? He is a person who enters a country secretly but also is caught and stopped at the border, and manages to disappear [...] if citizens are required to follow State laws, in the same way, *the State must protect citizens from those who evade the law and who do not legally exist.*[81]

I wish to highlight not only the metaphors employed in these texts (in the first, migrants are compared to poisonous mushrooms that must be gotten rid of as a group; in the second text, they are entities that don't "legally exist), but notice also the implacable logic: the "*clandestino*" is outside of the law, and is therefore an outlaw and a criminal; he is dangerous besides being non-existent. The consequences of this logic are reminiscent of the Joseph Heller novel, *Catch 22*: whoever wants to excused from active military service must apply under article 22, but whoever applies under article 22 cannot be excused from active service. The "catch 22" of the migrants situation is essentially the same: "We only accept immigrants that are not criminals. A foreigner that tries to immigrate is '*clandestino*' and therefore a 'criminal who does not legally exist,' but he doesn't exist, so he can't immigrate."

In the obsession over who is not "in line with the law" or who is illegal, clearly other factors typical of the current social organization come into play: on the one hand, an increase in police controls, the desire to know virtually every aspect of the individual's condition, and on the other hand, the fear of the unknown, or indifference of those who, for whatever reason avoid conforming

[80] *La Stampa.* 26 August 1997: 31.
[81] Sartori, G. *L'Espresso.* 11 September 1997: 68. (My italics.)

to social codes. And thus, the individual who "does not have his documents in order," even if he has committed no crime and has nothing to hide, slips into the social condition of being a danger to society.[82]

5 The Logic of Public Opinion

The preceding pages describe how Italian society has adapted to the immigration phenomenon. From the outset, the institutional disinterest and social indifference have made the migrants (regardless of their insignificant numbers) create a reality that is completely marginal to Italian society. From the early 1990s on, the "immigrants" have become not just aliens but the target of an ever-increasing symbolic and actual hostility. The traditional sociological tools are inadequate to explain this hostility, which could be defined as the social construction of the migrant as enemy. First of all, the sociology of migration tends to neglect the symbolic elements and political determinants (with a few notable exceptions)[83] in constructing this public enemy. Secondly, immigration is not just a "problem" or specific sociological argument but a formidable catalyst for real and symbolic conflicts of local and national discourses and rhetorical campaigns. The processes through which migrants tend to become public enemies exceed the traditional interests of sociological studies of migration because they have to do with society as a whole; therefore, traditional sociological studies end up becoming a mirror that deforms the reality they examine.[84]

The quantitative dimension of immigration *in and of itself* cannot explain the social hostility. Migrants represent just over 1.5 million foreigners, approximately 2% of the Italian population. Before becoming popular, a reaction characterizes a society's political and intellectual orientation, the

---

[82] One of the best literary illustrations of the transformation from "*clandestino*" into "non-person" is the novel by B. Traven, *The Death Ship*, New York: Lawrence Hill Books (2nd Edition), 1991.
[83] For the themes discussed in this study, the concept of "people without a state" has been fundamental, as expanded by Hannah Arendt, *The Origins of Totalitarianism*. Cleveland: Meridian Books, 1958.
[84] Sayad, A. *L'immigration ou le paradoxe de l'alterité*. Brussels: De Boeck-Wesmael, 1990.

systems of the mass media. To explain the aversion toward foreigners as a reaction to the presence of a few window washers at the traffic intersections, the supposed criminal propensity of foreigners, and a competition for jobs that no one has ever been able to prove, is something that could be satisfying to popular opinion or the new social swing to the right, but is inconsistent with social theory. When social science examines such explanations closely, one quickly discovers the presence of clichés. For example, the classic argument made by neighborhood watch groups that unlicensed foreign traveling salesmen compete with the small local shops has no empirical foundation. The same is true for the wide spread anxiety about the criminality of foreigners or simply their presence.[85]

However, while these public opinions are scientifically false, socially they are "true" because they are capable of crystallizing into social dogmas. According to sociological theory, public opinion is constituted by "what everyone thinks" and acquires a tautological value of truth simply because it is "what everyone thinks." When sociology began to concern itself with the cognitive structure of public opinion, it became evident that the social actors were involved in constructing reassuring and tautological models for their daily reality.[86] Further elaborations of these theories shows that the social actors were able to construct an infinite number of ad hoc justifications of their model of the world as soon as that model was assumed to be true, just, and normal.[87] So the public opinion which should be able to describe the world actually constructs the world according to its performative and productive character.[88]

[85] See "I problemi della sicurezza in Emilia-Romagna. Secondo rapporto annuale 1996." *Quaderni di città sicure*. Region of Emilia Romagna, 1996. See also Duprez, D. and M. Hedli. *Les mal des banlieues? Sentiment d'insécurité et crise identitaire*. Paris: L'Harmattan, 1992. Research conducted in other countries arrive at similar conclusions. Lagrange, H. *La civilité à l'èpreuve. Crime et sentiment d'insecurité*. Paris: Puf, 1995.

[86] Schutz, A. *Collected Papers, Vol. 2: Studies in Social Theory*, Heidelberg: Springer, 2007.

[87] Garfinkel, H. *Studies in Ethnomethodology*. Englewood Cliffs, N.J.: Prentice Hall, 1967.

[88] For the concept of "performativity," see Austin, J. *How to Do Things with Words*, Oxford: Oxford University Press (2nd Edition), 1976. For the performative character of public opinion, see De Certeau, M. *The Practice of Everyday Life*, Berkeley, CA: University of California Press, 2002.

This seems even more true in our day, when the media hold enormous power to orient viewers or readers about the world's complexity. The following chapter will include an in-depth analysis of the role of the media in the construction of immigrants as public enemies. At this point, above all I wish to unravel the mechanisms that power the construction of public opinion when those mechanisms apply to delicate "problems" such as racism or the relationships between natives (Italians) and foreigners. One model for an explanation emerges from the comments in a newspaper's letter to the editor in which an Italian citizen reports being the victim of a racist incident:

"My Incredible Story of Racism"

At the train station in Parma, Favour Iyamu tries to stamp his ticket, but the machine is out of order. He goes to a worker who reassures him, validates his ticket by hand, and tells him to board the train because his round-trip ticket had already been validated on the first leg of the trip. When the conductor comes to check tickets, he responds to Iyamu's explanation by warning, "Oh, it's always the same story with you blacks! Pay the fine or get off!"
Fayour Iyamu refuses to do either and then ignores the conductor's protests. At the station in Bologna, the shouts of, "Where is the black guy?" echo through the train car as four police officers leap onto the train, reach Favour Iyamu, and ignoring his explanations, grab him and force him to the ground, shattering the bones in his hand.
At the central train office in Polfer, a great discovery is made: on his identification documents, it reads, "Favour Iyamu, Italian citizen. Employed by the city of Florence, Environmental Office." Now, even more disturbing is the fact that how he is now treated immediately changes and Favour Iyamu re-acquires his civil rights. After hearing all of the excuses, he is given a new ticket for free and invited to take the next Intercity train. Iyamu underwent an operation on his left hand at the Rizzoli hospital in Bologna. He needs to wear a cast for 29 days and will miss work for an even longer period.

Favour Iyamu, Florence

"Barbara Palombelli Responds"

When I read stories like Favour Iyamu's, I must confess that I feel tremendously uncomfortable. I have always personally been pained over racism. For the last four years I have suffered even more intimately for the racism aimed against the black skin of my beloved son (though he calls it "brownish.") I hope that Favour Iyamu's shattered hand doesn't leave you feeling indifferent, but that it jogs the sleepy conscience of those who would like to break the hands of those foreigners who wash car windows at the intersections *(and speaking of that, if there was greater regulation at the traffic lights and better enforcement of laws against "clandestini" and criminal immigrants, we would all be more tolerant.... helping our brothers and sisters doesn't mean supporting illegal actions, which we wouldn't allow our fellow citizens).*[89]

Here we have a textbook example of the discourse of public opinion as applied to foreigners. Using the third person, the reader denounces a case of *double racism* (double racism because it occurs against a person whose appearance is different as well as against a presumed foreigner). This illustrates what we have termed emergency *for* the immigrants. A citizen who is mistaken for a migrant is harassed by an employee of the train lines, he is mistreated and wounded by four officers of the law. These actions are completely unjustifiable and in any other country would have created a scandal. The journalist Barabara Palombelli simply informs us that "intolerance" (fracturing someone's hand is "intolerance") is caused by a lack of "regulation at the traffic lights," and thus intolerance is caused by the presence of the window washers, those people who commit "illegal actions which we wouldn't allow our fellow citizens."

Developing the presuppositions inherent in the discourse of public opinion in this response, we arrive at unforeseen conclusions. Someone is victim of an act of racism because he appears to be a foreigner, but he's actually Italian. Whose responsibility is that? Evidently, it is not the responsibility of those who acted (the train employees, the police officers). Palombelli's letter doesn't say a word about them. Nor is it anyone else's responsibility, but the event is the

[89] *La Repubblica.* 8 June 1997: 12.

fault of an "intolerance" provoked by the "illegal" status of the foreign window washers. *We must therefore conclude that if a foreigner is the victim of racism, then that is the foreigner's fault. Ultimately, the responsibility belongs to that class of people that the victim belongs to, at least in appearance.* Obviously, the journalist didn't write any such thing and would disdainfully reject such an interpretation of her statements. But this obsession for attributing the causes of any "immigration problems" to the "illegal status" doesn't just prompt absurd statements (why should washing windows at intersections be an criminal act?), but it also produces non sequiturs that actually become true for millions of people (such as, "If you're the victim of racism, then that must be *your* fault.") In the following chapter, we will see how the above example is quite revealing of the journalistic representation of migration issues.

The discourse of public opinion is one way to explain social events and problems, however it really explains nothing. Opinions merely become popular, "*common*," because they reproduce incessantly what the public thinks and therefore, what the public wants to confirm. Fed on illogic, tautologies, myths of various types, "public opinion" still demonstrates certain regularities and conforms to a kind of logic. As shown earlier, the discrimination against foreigners materializes via multiple practices and multiple actors all with various points of view. However, these practices come together into a central, explicit expository mechanism that establishes itself as indisputable. This central mechanism could be summed up as the transformation of the victims into the guilty. The "sense" produced by this mechanism can violate with impunity logic, truth, or any other value vaunted by the implicit actors, as long as the procedure employed is consensual and therefore incontrovertible. An excellent example of this mechanism of inescapable guiltification is offered by that great scholar of the perversion of logic, Lewis Carroll:

> The King turned pale, and shut his notebook hastily. "Consider your verdict," he said to the jury, in a low trembling voice.
> "There's more evidence to come yet, please your Majesty," said the White Rabbit, jumping up in a great hurry: "this paper has just been picked up."
> "What's in it?" said the Queen.

"I haven't opened it yet," said the White Rabbit; "but it seems to be a letter, written by the prisoner to – to somebody."

"It must have been that," said the King, "unless it was written to nobody, which isn't usual, you know."

"Who is it directed to?" said one of the jurymen.

"It isn't directed at all," said the White rabbit: "in fact, there's nothing written on the *outside*." He unfolded the paper as he spoke, and added "It isn't a letter, after all: it's a set of verses."

"Are they in the prisoner's handwriting?" asked another of the jurymen.

"No they're not," said the White Rabbit, "and that's the queerest thing about it." (The jury all looked puzzled.)

"He must have imitated somebody else's hand," said the King. (The jury all brightened up again.)

"Please your Majesty," said the Knave, "I didn't write it, and they can't prove that I did: there's no name signed at the end."

"If you didn't sign it," said the King, "that only makes matters worse. You *must* have meant some mischief, or else you'd have signed your name like an honest man."

There was a general clapping of hands at this: it was the first really clever thing the King had said that day.

"That *proves* his guilt, of course," said the Queen...[90]

---

[90] Carroll, Lewis. *Alice's Adventures in Wonderland.* 1865. Ann Arbor: University Microfilms, Inc., 1966. 180-182.

III The Fear Machine

The distortion of reality in reportage is what is truthful in the reportage of reality.[91]

The sociologist cannot ignore to the ideology of race simply because it is idiotic from a scientific point of view: many social situations are efficiently controlled by the definitions of idiots.[92]

1 Someone to Hate

Traditionally, every discrimination or persecution of internal or external foreigners occurs through recourse to mechanisms of the victimization of the aggressor and assigning guilt to the victims.[93] The aggressors are usually the "victims" of wrongs that must be righted or the weaker citizens abandoned by the institutions, and who band together to enact their own justice. Those who are attacked or discriminated against are the foreign bodies, invaders, corrupters or enemies of a defenseless society. Often, the role of defenders of an offended society is assumed by what I will refer to as the "*imprenditori morali*,"[94] the avant-garde who takes on the role of shaking up a passive or unaware public opinion. At times, individual institutions or influential centers of power mobilize society against individuals or groups.[95] Transforming the

---

[91] K. Kraus, *Dicta and Contradicta*, Champaign, IL: University of Illinois Press, 2001.

[92] Peter L. Berger, *Invitation to Sociology: A Humanistic Perspective*, Jacksonville, FL: Anchor, 1963.

[93] In the analysis that follows, I was aware of the work of Mary Douglas: *Risk and Blame: Essays in Cultural Theory*, New York. Routledge, 1994, *Purity and Danger: An Analysis of the Concepts of Pollution and Taboo*, New York. Routledge, 2002.

[94] Becker, H.S. *Outsiders: Studies In The Sociology Of Deviance*, New York: Free Press, 1997.

[95] For a theory of the formal sociological properties of "the police report," see Garfinkel, H. *Seeing Sociologically: The Routine Grounds of Social Action*, Boulder, CO: Paradigm Publishers, 2005. On the cultural significance of these practices, see also Gellner, E. *Plough, Sword, and Book: The Structure of Human History*, Chicago: University Of Chicago Press, 1992.

victims into the guilty naturally assumes different forms, and displays various intensity according to the political organization of society, and the existence and force of public opinion independent of political power.

The persecution of internal foreigners (heretics, witches, deviants of every type) or external foreigners (Jews, gypsies) is a recurrent phenomenon in European history.[96] The first Crusades, especially the popular ones, were accompanied by a "resolute" ejection of the Jews, as historical records attest.[97] The panic caused by the Black Plague that decimated the European population in the middle of the fourteenth century resulted in the persecution and the first mass extermination of the Jews and laid bare the indifference of the political authorities of the time who should have protected them.[98] After an initial tolerant phase, until the fifteenth century, gypsies suffered widespread persecution from local governments and from religious and political authorities. Even in periods of relative peace and tolerance, foreigners were already identified as the potential source of danger to and corruption of society, and were therefore to be feared. Diffused and uncontrolled rumors circulated (analogous to our own urban legends)[99] that accused Jews and

[96] Ginzberg, C. *Storia noturna. Una decifrazione del sabba.* Turin: Einaudi, 1989. 36. See also Wippermann, W. *Wie die Zigeuner: Antisemitismus und Antiziganismus im Verleich.* Berlin: Elephanten Press, 1997.

[97] Runciman, S. *A History of the Crusades Vol. I: The First Crusade and the Foundations of the Kingdom of Jerusalem,* Cambridge: Cambridge University Press, 1987.

[98] Bergdolt, K. *La peste nera e la fine del Medioevo.* Casale Monferrato: Edizione Piemme, 1997:184. Indifference can have economic advantages, when the Jew's belongings were appropriated. I will demonstrate how the mechanism of economic exploitation of collective fears is not new in our society when migrants are involved.

[99] By urban legend, I mean news of an event that is without any foundation, often unusual or parodic, but that becomes "true" because it circulates widely by word of mouth and is even taken up by the press or by other branches of the mass media. See Brunvand, J. *Leggende metropolitane.* Genoa: Costa & Nolan, 1993. As will be shown, the image of the foreigner as criminal depends on the exaggeration of their illegal activities and by the construction of a perverse circle of rumors and information provided by the mass media. On this point, see Bastenier, A. "L'immigrazione nel quotidiano. La funzione sociale della diceria." *Rassegna sindacale.* XXII (1991): 79-80. On the concept of "rumor," see Kapferer, E. *Voci che corrono.* Milan: Longanesi, 1987.

gypsies of sacrilegious practices and terrifying crimes such as stealing children.[100] In the modern period, the culture of fear was secularized and extended to internal enemies, first including the working classes as "dangerous classes" and then including all types of deviants and criminals who are periodically the object of collective fears. Between the nineteenth and twentieth centuries in the long process of including the urban working classes into Western society, the role of internal enemies becomes progressively reserved for hooligans, thugs and delinquents, in addition to the other minorities historically discriminated against.[101]

The anti-Semitism at the end of the nineteenth century is one of the most extreme manifestations of the persistence of the social mechanisms of the persecution of minorities in Modern Europe. But the event that institutionalized the mass fear of the enemy in European culture is certainly the First World War, with its network of national hatreds and sequels of civil wars and revolutions. It was precisely among the millions of soldiers packed into the trenches that the widespread rumors began about betrayal and the secret troops that aided the enemy from the inside.[102] After World War I, it is the totalitarian regimes that take advantage of the availability of group hatred to impose the institutional persecution of the Jews, as in the case of Nazism.[103] A common element in the stigmatization of internal and external foreigners (independent of its specific historical forms or political mechanisms) is the fear of contamination, of mixing of races, of sexual promiscuity, of spreading foreign diseases.

---

[100] These legends survive in our day. Foreigners, inasmuch as they are "strange" for our culture and "demand" to live among us, are seen as typically guilty of horrifying crimes. So Albanians are accused of using children as "human shields," the racket of Slaves and Albanians makes martyrs of the "child prostitutes," and nomads are believed to force their children to steal, Moroccans make their children steal and beg, etc.

[101] Cohen, S. *Folk Devils and Moral Panics*. London: MacGibbon and Kee, 1972; Pearson, F. *Hooligans: A History of Respectable Fears*. London: Macmillan, 1983. For a general discussion, see Escobar, R. *Metamorfosi della paura*. Bologna: Il Mulino, 1997.

[102] Fussell, P. *The Great War and Modern Memory*, Oxford: Oxford University Press, 2000.

[103] Beck, U. "Wie aus Nachbarn Juden Werden. Zur politischen Konstruktion des Fremden in der reflexiven Moderne." *Modernität und Barbarei. Soziologische Zietdiagnose am Ende des 20. Jahrhunderts*. Ed. M. Miller and H.-J. Soeffner. Frankfurt: Suhrkamp, 1996. 318-343.

If this kind of collective fear fed the extreme forms of racism in the past, now this fear is reborn in the anxiety manifest by the requirement of medical exams for foreigners and the "pathologization" of foreigners.[104] An example of this process of stigmatization is evident in the following interview of an activist in a committee of Genovese citizens who essentially equates the "nationality" of an *extracommunitario* with "disease."

> There was a convention for doctors in Naples and one of the doctors is a friend of mine. He sent me a summary of all the diseases that they've seen… it shows how diseases have increased and everything… I have the evidence from this convention in Naples […] about the *extracommuntario* diseases and all that […] But they also told me this, they said, "Keep this information to yourself […]." But I say, if a foreigner doesn't want to tell me his nationality, that's not a problem. I'll just take an X-ray of him, and from that, I'll know what his nationality is. The convention in Naples brought this up to educate us about these things. So when they back me into a corner, we can ask and find out the nationality. We'll just add this requirement: for every citizen of unknown nationality, just take an X-ray according to the procedure outlined by this doctor… that way we'll find out their nationality.

Unlike the traditional internal and external enemies, nowadays migrants come into contact with society that is officially secularized and removed from collective myths. Now, however, the *imprenditori morali* are infinitely more effective than in the past, because they are capable not only of instantly communicating the fear of an enormous number of people, but also feeding and even in some cases creating the fear. Hearsay, urban legends, prejudices, and fears circulating in local society via the mass media become first a symbolic resource and then social, objective truth resurrecting stereotypes that have lain dormant for centuries in the collective consciousness – the foreigner as

---

[104] The racist obsession with contamination transcends migration issues and has to do with any contact between "our" world and another. The following author, in his text on the Ebola virus, advances the hypothesis the spread of this lethal virus is due to the ease of international communication and contact. See Preston, J. *Area di contagio. Una storia vera.* Milan: Rizzoli, 1994.

"plague-spreader," uncontrollable vagabond, monster, kidnapper, and rapist. These images enter into circulation thanks to the media and find confirmation in the reports on the crime pages, whether those stories are true or false, real or invented, but are nevertheless ideal for feeding deep-seated fears. Consider the following news article that reports rumors about the criminal and occult practices among gypsies:

"Stealing Is Easy Here"

The secret code of the gypsies returns. It's really a cruel joke, and it seems to work effectively, catching dozens of victims. Over the last few weeks, strange "symbols" written in pencil or scratched with some sharp instrument have appeared in the neighborhoods of Genoa: crosses, circles, triangles, letters are all signs used by gypsy thieves. The police and *carabinieri* have long understood the code. [...] This summer the occurrence even came to the attention of Parliament and last month, a flyer with these symbols came across the desk of the chief of police, who distributed it to all police sectors. The joke works like this: someone is upset with his unpleasant neighbor, so he draws a sign next to his doorbell, and when the neighbor discovers it, he's terrified [...] "But there have not been any gypsy thieves. Someone was just joking..." say the *carabinieri*.[105]

This is almost a textbook example of contemporary urban legend, legitimized and reproduced first by institutions and then by the channels of mass communication. There is no actual proof of any contemporaneous use of this "gypsy code." Furthermore, if the flyer in question is closely examined [Figure 3] we see that these symbols have nothing criminal about them. These are merely a worked-over version of the symbols used in the past by hobos on the "begging" maps [Figure 2]. They fell out of use and disappeared in Italy at the beginning of the 1960s. It is more probably then, that during the campaign against the nomads in Genoa in the Autumn of 1995, some one came across these symbols

---

[105] *Il Lavoro*, Genoan supplement to *la Repubblica*, 27 May 1997: vi.

Figure 2

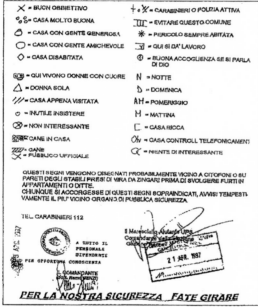

Figure 3

and attributing them to gypsies, sent them to the chief of the Genoa police who distributed them by reproducing the flyer in Figure 3. But the real issue is different: while claiming to explain a "joke," the article confirms the pre-supposition that citizens are "terrified" by these mysterious, sinister activities of the nomads. The fact that there are not any thieves is not mentioned in order to show how ridiculous the legend is, but only to condemn the "jokers." In reality, what are the nomads accused of, thanks to these legends which have been taken as truth, "interpreted" and legitimized by the local police and diffused by the media? Nothing more than marks scratched on the doors indicating that "Stealing is easy here," just as Manzoni's "plague-spreaders" were accused of "greasing" the doors of people's homes in order to contaminate them during the time of the Black Plague.

That foreigners are in fact responsible for events recounted in the crime pages thus becomes seen as empirical proof for the generalizations reported as truth by the mass media. If a foreigner commits an act of violence against a woman, that is because all foreigners are potential rapists. But if two foreigners save an Italian citizen from an attack, that fact cannot be generalized because it is implicitly considered to be an exception to the rule. Fear of the foreigner thus becomes a standing resource that can be used for all ends: for the media it is an endless source of sensational stories, for politicians or *imprenditori morali* this fear creates the opportunity for creating consensus. Only rarely is this utilization of the dangerous foreigner blatant enough for us to discern the perverse web of collective fear, media sensationalism and public instrumentalization. Below is a news report that could be relegated to the realm of local Boccaccian legend, if not for the serious implications it contains for the true victims: foreigners.

"Woman Fakes Rape To Cover Up Lover"

Woman Confesses: I Made up the Story about Albanian Rapists
Brescia. Oh, God, what will my husband say? It must have been a little domestic drama, the kind that keeps the neighbors gossiping for weeks in the town of Capriolo. But Ms. Maria Angela and her friendly, dim-witted lover had a stroke of genius. And that's how they started a story that for days sowed terror across the wide-open, hard-working area that extends beyond the south of Brescia. The supposed band of Albanians, or maybe it was Slavic rapists or thieves, was a carbon-copy of the famous criminal Ljiubisa Urbanovic, nick-named Manolo, who wrecked havoc in this same area seven years ago. But now the climate had changed and together with the *carabinieri* and the police, this

news story even unleashed the Northern League: the MP Caldiroli announced that green-shirted squads of Northern League supports will begin to patrol, and Mayor Rigamonti, also a Northern League supporter, called for a special city council to catalogue all immigrants.[106]

This is the report of a grotesque story that apparently ends "happily." On the same page as this report, Natalia Aspesi can easily be about this local "Padana" story ("in the area there is real resentment toward *extracommunitari* due to actual problems, crimes, and fear.").[107] Even Northern League supporters dauntlessly insist on utilizing the episode ("Now they will say: 'Poor foreigners, they've been falsely accused.' Poor foreigners, my eye!").[108] For once it seemed that a racist tale had been publicly ridiculed to the relief of democratic public opinion. And yet, this story of infidelity and slander has a sinister undercurrent which becomes readily apparent by examining the news stories published before the "happy ending." Following are reports of two alleged assaults published in two well-known national papers:

"Squads Mobilize"

Brescia. After Attack on a Storeowner, the Slavic or Albanian Bandits Tried to Rape His Wife.
Brescia. [...] The crime occurred between Thursday and Friday night. Oliviero Signori, 42, owns a small motor import-export business. Around 2 a.m. he heard noises from the next room where his wife, who had been sick with the flu, was sleeping. In the doorway he found a man with a stocking pulled over his face. The intruder hit him over the head [...] Then while one intruder held a pistol to Olivero's throat and threatened his son, Massimiliano, the other tried to rape his wife. [...] The local *carabinieri* have few doubts. It was either Slavs or Albanians. They spoke Italian but they were clearly foreigners. Olivero Signori and his wife were able to give the following descriptions to the police: one intruder was 1.75 meters tall with long, curly black hair and dark eyes. His

[106] *La Repubblica.* 21 April 1997.
[107] Aspesi, N. "Non era l'immigrato ma l'amante." *La Repubblica.* 21 April 1997.
[108] "'Ma le ronde servono le stesso.' Intervista al senatore Francesco Tabladini." *La Repubblica.* 21 April 1997.

accomplice was shorter, about 1.60 meters tall, dark bowl-cut hair and a round face. [109]

"Woman Raped in Front of Her Husband. Man Hunt for Two Immigrants in the Area Terrorized by 'The Slav'"

After the Night of Violence Minister Napolitano Promises to Send a Task Force. Brescia. It couldn't have been Manolo, the Slav who has terrified the isolated houses around Brescia [...] That icy-eyed killer is still in prison in Serbia. But he threw out a final threat after his extradition and sentencing (15 years, punishable up to 5 years), "I'll come back to Italy." But last night's attack in the small village of Capriolo in which two men assaulted Oliverio Signori, 42, and his wife Maria Angiola, 32, has a very similar "signature."

News of the recent Brescia case has reached Rome. Senator Tabladini, after a meeting with the mayor of Capriolo, Fabrizio Rigamonti (who had just announced plans to make an official count of *extracommunitari*) had called Minister Napolitano who promised to send a task force of superinvestigators from Milan. Police have compiled two descriptions reconstructed by the victims, who were still in shock. "They were foreigners, they spoke in broken Italian, but they were white." Probably Slavs, like Manolo or perhaps Albanians.

Maybe they are some of the people camped in the woods who scrape a living with odd jobs and send their children out to beg [...] The new police commissioner Gennaro Arena urges all citizens to collaborate with the police. Does the current investigation suspect *extracommunitari*? Arena says, "Here in this province there are 2,400 legal immigrants. But there are thousands of *clandestini*. They move around constantly. It's impossible to check up on them.

Maurizio Marinelli, from the Department of Public Safety in Brescia, is the Director of the National Center for Studies and Research of Police Issues. He has just published a study on the sudden increase in crime in the province after the increased number of *clandestini*. "We need weapons. The provisions for expulsion only exist on paper and too many officials just act as 'gatekeepers.'" [...]

In Pontevico, Guido Viscardi, who survived when his family was murdered, counts the days until Manolo is released. "He wants to come back to Italy to kill me," says Viscardi. "When he gets out, just give me a gun."[110]

---

[109] *La Repubblica.* 20 April 1997.
[110] *Corriere della Sera.* 20 April 1997.

This is the version of the "facts" that the readers of this major paper were able to gather from the media before everything imploded. The authors of these articles have forgotten the most fundamental requirements for any professional journalist: to qualify and use caution when reporting facts without evidence ("It is said," "It appears," "We suppose," etc.) Thanks to the affirmations in the news media, the opinions of the investigators ("the local *carabinieri* have few doubts,") automatically become the official version of reality. Especially in the article from *La Repubblica*, these versions even include "testimonies" about nonexistent physical details with obvious racial symbolism ("dark curly hair," "dark eyes.") My point is not to uncover inexperience or condemn the superficiality of journalists, but to reveal how the news media is naturally situated within an interpretive frame.[111] That frame holds that "foreigners and criminal immigrants are our enemies," and is validated by the "obvious" connection between the current story and an earlier one: the crimes of Manolo, which have nothing more in common with the alleged assault in Brescia than the "foreign" nationality of the infamous "icy-eyed killer." The imaginary connection is legitimized with the authority of the experts' opinions – various police officers and the police commissioner – who offer details such as, "There are thousands of *clandestini*," or "we need weapons.") The quotation from the relative of victims of a different crime who asks for a gun to defend himself from Manolo adds a touch of Hollywood Western to the entire episode.

Attributing to foreigners (whether "*extracommunitari*," "Serbs," "Slavs," or "nomads,") a non-existent crime is not exclusively the construction of facts by journalists. I emphasize construct and not mere invention[112] because journalists only refer to a frame, a symbolic resource, obviously available as the immediate political stances show (Northern League supporters, Minister Napolitano's promise to send a task force). Ultimately, journalists just confine

---

[111] By "frame" I intend the symbolic outline that gives meaning to a social fact. Goffman, E. *Frame Analysis, The Social Organization of Experience*. Harmondsworth: Penguin, 1975.
[112] This case is not one of false information or "invention," nor is it mere gullibility, but rather an example of the news as a demonstration of "what we already know."

themselves to pouring "facts" into an ever-ready and willing media outlet.[113] Thus the curious fact remains that journalists "naturally" and "in good faith," and "without malice," do nothing more than help render credible a stereotype that they themselves have helped to create. The episode in question clearly shows once and for all not just the close connection between local gossip and national news (a circularity that can be defined as "the tautology of fear,") but also shows the ease with which abstract, generic, or innocent individuals can be accused of non-existent crimes.[114]

2 The Tautology of Fear

Examples of "facts" like those in Brescia suggest a circuit connecting local public opinion ("they were Albanians") with political initiatives (such as patrolling squads) and generalizations made in the media ("The Manolo Nightmare Returns"). Thanks to these, the foreigner is incessantly constructed and reconstructed as the enemy. Independently of their local context, these facts acquire meaning, visibility, and reality thanks to the attention granted by the press, the decisive actor in this circuit. If the information relative to migration showed great variability during the 1980s, since the beginning of the 1990s, the daily news has dedicated a constant, growing attention to immigration. In large part, this attention has been negative, creating the image of immigration as a "serious social problem." For example, out of the 824 news articles published about immigrants in the seven national papers during 1992-1993, 47% of the articles were reports of crimes committed by migrants or else

---

[113] For a discussion of the social mechanism of the construction and reconstruction of moral stereotypes, see Berger, P. and T. Luckmann, *The Social Construction of Reality: A Treatise in the Sociology of Knowledge*, Port Moody, BC: Anchor, 1967, and Douglas, J.D., ed. *Deviance and Respectability: The Social Construction of Moral Meanings*. New York: Basic Books, 1970.
[114] The fact a category or class of subjects is being accused is even more serious individuals, because *any* foreigner who in that class or category can be accused of any misdeed. The process of labeling constitutes the cognitive foundation of racism. For a discussion of these mechanisms, see the works of Van Dijk, T.A. *Communicating Racism: Ethnic Prejudice in Thought and Talk*. Newbury Park: Sage Publications, 1987.

public order enforcements relative to migrants; only 8% of the articles reported cases of racism or xenophobia. Even more than the quantitative prevalence of negative information, the image of migration as "social problem," "plague," or "threat" is constructed and transmitted by the media through the constant use of headlines written for shock value, and stylistic choices that seem calculated to provoke revulsion in readers. Following is a brief list of such headlines:

"Forced to Drink Dog's Water" (*Corriere della sera*, January 15, 1995)
"Hell on the Third Floor. Police Sweep in Piazza Arbarello Reveals Story of Exploitation among Connationals. 28 North Africans Living in 4 Rooms" (*La Stampa*, September 2, 1994).
"North African Minor Raped. A Street Vendor by Day, Prostitute by Night" (*La Stampa*, September 8, 1994)
"[…] Immigrants for Sale. In Foggia, Tunisian Prostitution and Illegal Labor Ring. For Field Workers, Low Wages, No Food, and Sex at Bargain in Prices" (*Il Piccolo*, September 1, 1994).
"Albanian Women, Enslaved Street Walkers" (*La Gazzetta del Mezzogiorno*, September 19, 1994).
"'Officer, Please, Arrest Me,' 14-Year Old Moroccan Boy Begs. 'That Way I'll Eat Every Day.' 'Pony' Boys: Stories of Misery in the Battle between Africans Who Use Minors to Push Drugs" (*La Stampa*, September 20, 1994).
"Eight Months Out in the Cold with My Mother the Beggar. Nomad Girl Hospitalized for Malnutrition" (*La Stampa,* September 24, 1994.)[115]

These headlines are all from the time period in which the "immigration emergency" was on the rise, and are actually tame compared to what the media circulated in the following years about the connection between immigration and criminality. It is necessary to point out that Italy is still far from the self-

---

[115] Istituto Piemontese "A. Gramsci" – Consiglio Regionale del Piemonte. *Rapporto di ricerca dulle manifestazione del pregiudizio, dell'intolrenza e della violenza razzista in Italia.* Turin, 1994. p. 74, footnote 78.

regulation the American press imposes by not publishing the race of alleged suspects when reporting crimes. Nearly 30 years ago, an American criminologist noted how the ethnicization of crime on the part of the media – and which he viewed as parallel to the stigmatization of minorities in court proceedings – was decreasing due to pressure from civil rights groups.[116]

In Italy no one would write about "Venetians Stopped for Nighttime Disturbances," or the "Tendency toward Violence among People of Tortona." However, the ethnic, national, or racial affiliation is an absolute constant in the media definition of migrants stopped by police or arrested for any minor crime or infraction. Recently, a local paper in Genoa published the front page headline, "Albanian Pirate Overpowers Woman."

The quantitative and stylistic variation in the presentation of information on immigration reflects a decisive thematic shift. Beginning in the 1990s, immigration is almost exclusively defined in terms of illegality and urban decline, while the privileged news source is constructed by a new social actor: the citizen who protests urban decline, which is equated with immigration. As one sociologist noted who has extensively studied the "social construction of immigrants," the reports in the press about immigrants are not filtered through the voices of the direct actors, but are dependent on their relative contexts, constructed by the implicit equation of immigration with public disorder. These two elements together compose the typical narrative plot that invariably includes the "siege of citizens by criminal immigration," the "neighborhood protest," the "arrival of our people [the police]" and even "the temporary relief of honest citizens."[117]

From a textual point of view, the existence of recurring narrative plot reveals a stable mechanism of media production of fear. I call this mechanism "tautological," because simply sounding the alarm (i.e. "the invasion of criminal immigrants") demonstrates the reality of that which is being decried.

---

[116] Schur, E.M. *Our Criminal Society: The Social and Legal Sources of Crime.* Englewood Cliffs, NJ: Prentice Hall, 1969.
[117] Maneri, M. *Stampa quotidiana e senso comune nella costruzione sociale dell'immigrato.* Sociology Doctoral Thesis, Università di Trento, 1995. 115-116.

These "autopoeitic"[118] mechanisms are well known in sociology and are based in W. I. Thomas' concept of the "definition of the situation," in which he explains that "if individuals define a situation as real, then they are real in their consequences."[119] In other words, a social situation is one that the actors define as such. This will seem less obvious considering that a social agreement between different social actors frequently has the ability to impose the official definition of a current situation, even if the social definition in question is false, bizarre, or improbable, as P. Berger alludes to in the epigraph at the beginning of this chapter. In the autopoeitic construction of meaning, subjective definitions of a situation become real, that is, objective, and this is even more true in tense social situations such as "fear of the enemy." Erving Goffman refers to this kind of intersection of subjective perceptions and objective definitions in his study on "producing reality: "

> ... the term [alarm] is an example of that troublesome class of words that refers in common usage both to that which produces a state in the perceiver and the state itself.[120]

---

[118] "Autopoeisis" in biology is the capacity of living systems to riproduce themselves and their subsystems and relationships but maintain their homeostatic balance. Maturana, H.R. and F.J. Varela. *Autopoiesis and Cognition: The Realization of the Living*, Heidelberg: Springer, 1991. I use the concept of "autopoeisis" as a limited analogy for communicative systems, because I disagree with those (including the authors of the text cited) who would used biology to explain complex social mechanisms. In sociology, a concept similar to "autopoeisis" would be "self-referentiality." See Luhmann, N. *Social Systems*, Palo Alto, CA: Stanford University Press, 1996, and Callon, M. and B. Latour. "Unscrewing the Big Leviathan: How Actors Macrostructure the Reality and How Sociologists Help Them to Do So." *Advances in Social Theory and Methodology: Toward an Integration of Micro- and Macro-Sociologies*. Eds. K. Knorr-Cetina and A.V. Cicourel. London: Routledge & Kegan Paul, 1981.

[119] Thomas, W.I. *The Child in America*. New York: Knopf, 1928. 584. Cited in McHugh, P. *Defining the Situation: The Organization of Meaning in Social Interaction*. Indianapolis: Bobbs-Merrill, 1968, remains one of the best studies in this field.

[120] Goffman, E. *Relations in Public*, New York: Basic Books, 1971, p. 247. From a rhetorical point of view, alarmism resembles "Catonism," that rhetorical style that admonishes the reader in terms of "the end of civilization," imminent "civil war," and an "invasion of the new barbarians." This style was at one time considered "critical," but now plays upon the social anxieties. See some selected works by Enzesberger, H.M. *Prospettive sulla guerre civile*. Turin: Einaudi, 1994, and *La grande migrazione*. Turin: Einaudi, 1995.

The capacity that an alarmist definition has to become objective, and thus determinative, depends on several strategic factors: first, the understanding between the social actors bearing any kind of title to generate definitions, and second, their legitimacy or their right. It seems self-evident that in a crime with victims, it is the victims themselves who have the right to say what happened and not the supposed guilty party, even if guilt has not been established. When "guilt" is in play – social alarm is always concerned with individuating "guilt" and "responsibility" – the accuser assumes the right to make the primary definition of the situation, which allows him or her to condition the subsequent definitions of the situation. This is obvious in the progress of criminal trials, the ritual of accusation par excellence in our complex society, but holds equally true for the production of fear and alarm when those definitions are created by the press.[121]

This constitutes the third strategic factor of transformation: the ability of the press to impose the "definition of the situation" depends upon its fundamental function of *agenda-setting*, i.e. the construction of the topics that are relevant to public discourse, the current modes and implicit methods of news manufacturing, such as the selection of which stories will be printed and the choice of language that will be employed. The more these modalities seem current, reliable, automatic, and self-evident, the more they confer objectivity to the alarmist definitions of reality, thus transforming them into a habitual cognitive background.[122] The media's definition of "dangers" is thus legitimized and

[121] Graber, D.A. *Crime News and the Public.* New York: Praeger, 1980.
[122] The press is the principle source of "what everyone knows," or public opinion. The press serves to maintain the "background" of public opinion. Notice the different roles played by television and the press. The former is connected with the portrayal of "events," "theater," "ceremonies," i.e. occurrences that at designed to maintain the public's attention for short periods. See Dayan, D. and E. Katz. *Media Events: The Live Broadcasting of History*, Cambridge, MA: Harvard University Press, 2006. The press, on the other hand, demands a constant and continued attention. Even though the reading public is far smaller than the viewing public (tens or hundreds of thousands of readers versus millions or tens of millions of viewers) the specific influence of the press has a far greater ability to define situations. In addition, the press is far closer to "local" opinion, more sensitive to alarm, and prejudice against foreigners. See Champagne, P. *Faire l'opinion. Le nouveau jeu politique.* Paris: Ed. De Minuit, 1990.

confirms the existence of acts that vindicate the representation of the local society. In fact, local society is the most threatened by the danger (e.g. the criminality of foreigners). When the voices of citizens are interpreted or represented by a legitimate political actor as in the Brescia case (this role tends to be assumed in Italy by the Northern League), the problem of the alarm becomes a political issue of national relevance that public authority cannot ignore. The full process of the tautological construction of social alarm can be represented thusly:

Through surveys and investigations, the press can determine what the current perception is of social "problems" such as immigration and crime. Television wields this power to determine "what is important" by selecting instead the "big" political events. See Gans, H.J. *Deciding What's News: A Study of CBS Evening News, NBC Nightly News, Newsweek, and Time.* New York: Pantheon Books, 1979. For an analysis of the autopoeitic mechanisms used by the media, see Bourdieu, P. *On Television*, New York: New Press, 1999.

Figure 4
Tautology of Fear

Symbolic resource: Foreigners are a threat to citizens because *clandestini* are usually criminals

↓

Subjective definitions of legitimate actors: "We're afraid. Foreigners make us feel threatened." (Witness the urban decline of our cities, individual acts of violence, the "Brescia case.")

↓

Objective definition of the media: "Foreigners are a threat. The [legitimate] social actors--interviews, surveys--proves this, as well as events that are continually occurring."

↓

Transformation of symbolic resource into dominant frame: It has been proven that *clandestini* threaten our society and therefore "the authorities must act."

↓

Subjective confirmation of legitimate social actors; "We can't stand any more. What are our mayors, police, and government doing?"

↓

Intervention by "legitimate social representatives": "If the government won't intervene, we will defend our own citizens."

↓

Legislative political and administrative measures that confirm the dominant frame.

Thanks to the recent appearance of citizens who protest, constructing themselves as the "victims of immigration," the reactions and subject confirmations inevitably translate into a political resource feeding the rhetoric of political groups who "represent the common citizen." Opposition parties must demonstrate that the government is unresponsive to the needs of ordinary citizens

while the government must demonstrate with legislative measures that it is aware of the situation and can act rapidly. Because this political resource can be utilized by different institutional and political actors, it doesn't need to correspond to general public sentiment, but must simply be evoked and confirmed by the active voice of the "protagonists." News reports regarding citizens' protests against urban decline renders those protests an unquestionable, dominant reality, and above, a representation of "what the people think." The critical connection in this short circuit of politicians and *imprenditori morali* (who are legitimated even by the "neutral" observers, as discussed in the following chapter) enables the local political resource to acquire the level of primary, global, universal resource for a political agenda. And this is how the "immigration emergency," nurtured by the very political rhetoric that created it, has shifted from being an abstract entity, a sort of political-media "blob" to becoming an indisputable truth, capable not only of expanding indefinitely, but of promoting heated national political debates, governmental interventions and legal measures. [123]

3 Actual and Virtual Citizenship

In the "tautology of fear" model, the citizen plays a strategic role as *imprenditore morale* or "subjective definer of the situation" because he or she constantly acts as "the voice of the people" in the media and justifies the transformation of symbolic generic resources into a dominant social, moral

---

[123] In the sociology of communication, the cumulative interaction of factors capable of creating a dominant opinion is known as a "spiral of silence." When a rumor is progressively legitimized by the media, it becomes practically impossible for other sources to negate it. See Noelle-Neuman, E. *Die Schweigespirale: Öffentliche Meinung – Unsere soziale Haut*. München: Piper, 1980. This explains why the mobilizations of citizens committees, while statistically insignificant when compared to the numbers of people who participate in anti-racism demonstrations or marches in support of immigrants (which have had as many as 50,000 participants at a time), are universally considered representative expressions of "what the people think" about immigration. The analysis of Noelle-Neuman integrates the classic studies of A. Hirschmann with the cyclic factors in these public protests. See Hirschman, A.O. *Exit, Voice, and Loyalty: Responses to Decline in Firms, Organizations, and States*, Cambridge, MA: Harvard University Press, 2007, and *The Passions and the Interests*, Princeton, NJ: Princeton University Press, 1976.

frame. Before examining exactly how this relatively new character functions, it is necessary to mention specific transformations in Italian society that have permitted this character to rise to the level of legitimate social actor. The most revealing is certainly the so-called "crisis of the First Republic," with its attendant moral and legal redefinition of public life. One of the principal legal effects of the "Tangentopoli" trials was bringing the entire political system under accusation, and the following formation of certain innovative rhetorics, i.e. the corruption and therefore untrustworthiness of politicians and administrators, the citizens placed in opposition to the system, the substitution of a political paradigm for the legal one in defining what occurs in public life, and therefore the predominance of "legality." This alteration in the political code among "the people" is accepted in different ways by the two privileged observers of these phenomena quoted below. The first is employed by the police force, the second is a criminologist.

[...] I've noticed this since my return to Milan. I'd been gone for two years. I left before the explosion of Tangentopoli and I came back when Tangentopoli was full-blown. I noticed a profound disillusionment in everyone, which was as it should be, right? And that disillusionment slowly transformed into dissatisfaction and then a demand for immediate reform.[124]

[...] Judicial power has often functioned as a catalyst and force for order in emergencies and from time to time during those emergencies, various groups have constructed discourses that have shaped not just the juridical environment, but they often managed to shape social perception: I think I can definitely say this about the terrorism emergency, the mafia emergency, the Tangentopoli or "*mani pulite*" emergency, and the immigration emergency. The logic of an emergency seems to be intimately connected to the juridical culture of this country, a kind of permanent need; so the immigration emergency is naturally just inserted into a place where this kind of logic gains continual strength. The logic of the decay of justice or its justicialism doesn't come from immigration. If anything, the immigration issue in the justicialism comes under the area of

[124] Cited in Palidda, S. "Verso il 'Fascismo democratico'? Note su emigrazione, immigrazione e società dominanti." *aut aut* 275 (1996): 143-168.

racism, and maybe it's become much easier to spread emergencies when justicialism and ethnicity are joined. If we consider how all of the "honest" politicians joined together during *"mani pulite"* and that type of executionary, Jacobian mentality created a category: "the honest politicians" (a category that anybody would have trouble verifying), then it's even more understandable how easily the "native population" is grouped against the "foreigners."[125]

The Northern League was able to use this paradigm shift to its advantage in the early stages of its political adventure: its early slogan was "Rome is a thief!" The League confirmed that paradigm shift with the nexus of certain notions that are not only hyper-localist and secessionist, but indirectly and directly xeno-phobic (such as their interpretation of citizens' protests, and their mobilization of citizens' patrol squads). The fundamental ideology that assumes the "social autonomy" of citizens actually translates urban public opinion into a fight to the death against every "threat" whether real or imaginary. This battle is more symbolic than real, more publicized than practiced, but is extremely effective from a rhetorical point of view. This technique has made the Northern League (even though it was not the direct political representative of those "citizens who protest the immigration problem") the political force during the 1990s that was most able to utilize the symbolic resource of the "immigration threat" as well as retranslating that "threat" into a political key, a kind of "upping the ante" that characterizes this very strategy:

> During the 1990s, the Northern League distinguished itself as the most active in its use of mobilizations and propaganda against *extracommunitari*, gypsies, and petty criminals [...] The League's activity in this area frequently took the form of organized patrols to protect the populace of Northern cities besieged by *extracommunitari*, gypsies, and most recently, Albanian refugees. While these initiatives were without concrete results, they raised issues that influenced popular opinions and attitudes and created powerful symbols that characterized the nature and role of the Northern League's political movement.[126]

[125] Interview in Genoa.
[126] Biorcio, R. *La Padania promessa. La storia, le idee, e la logica d'azione della Lega nord.* Milan: Il Saggiatore, 1997. 270-271.

In other words, the Northern League has progressively attained the role of political interpreter for the voice of the people. Originally the role of legitimate "definer of the situation" was assumed by generic, apolitical citizens, particularly in the cities of the industrial triangle: Milan, Turin, and Genoa. The citizens committees that formed at the beginning of the 1990s were rather heterogeneous from the standpoint of political positions. In Genoa, certain political actions were born from self-started initiatives from the inhabitants of the historic downtown area. Often these initiatives came from the political left and took a stance against drugs or "urban decline," a term that has become synonymous with the presence of immigrants. Many initiatives were short-lived or spontaneous, like the anti-gypsy committee formed in Genoa's Levante neighborhood in 1995. In Milan, these initiatives have older roots, organizational traditions that are more solid and reflect different ideological points of view. Turin seems to have raised more dramatic though intermittent initiatives, particularly in the San Salvario area in the Autumn of 1995 and 1996 and the Spring of 1997.

The social composition of these citizens groups also varies widely. Depending on the location and point of development, they include professionals, businessmen and shop owners, and in some cases, craftsmen and manual laborers. Actually, the social composition and the ideological viewpoints are not very relevant compared to the territorial insignia with which the group identifies. In fact, from the very beginning, it is the neighborhood (or sometimes the street or piazza) that determines the group's identity, in terms of action and ideology both practically and symbolically. Here, territoriality has a double meaning: first, it can refer to the "place" where we live and must therefore be protected from all threats; second, it means the environment that extends beyond traditional social and political distinctions and allows for a new kind of "identification." The prevalence of territoriality and abandonment of traditional political matrices in the culture of the "ordinary citizen" is evident from interviews with some of the supporters of these citizens committees:

Seven or eight years ago with the arrival of the first *excommunitari* and the urban blight that began in the historic downtown, the mothers of Sarzano asked

'territorio' una

the prefect for permission to carry guns to defend themselves from criminals and drug dealers. From this initial movement, others arose: the citizens committee of Fossatello, Maddalena, and others.[127]

The left-wing political parties have usually supported grassroots movements, and in some cases even organized them. But with citizens committees, the political parties had difficulty. Even important people like Burlando had difficulty because the committees outstripped him by a long ways. He thought he'd be able to manage them, to work along the same limes, but then he caved in. When it comes to problems of public safety, the right- wing has just fanned the flames, without offering any kind of solution, and that's an issue that the right has always used as a rallying cry... They exploit the malcontents, and go on T.V. [...] but they haven't been able to make any improvements. [128]

The first citizens committees were spontaneous gatherings that started around 1989, mostly in the Sarzano area because the people living there came home and saw drug deals taking place right outside their windows in plain sight in the middle of the day. So they rebelled against a situation that they felt was unjust. Even before immigration, drugs were the main problem.[129]
After July 1993, the attitude of the officials changed radically, I think. The criminal elements got under control and most of all, citizens had more control over the territory [...] crime still exists, but the biggest victory was certainly taking control of the territory and getting the criminal elements under control so that the normal people in Genoa could go on living, go shopping, things like that. [130]

The "territoriality" referred to in these interviews indicated a profound change in general feeling of local society. The skepticism toward the traditional parties on the right and left shows not only the "autonomy of the citizen" from the

[127] Interview cited in Petrillo, Antonello. *Insicurezza, migrazioni, cittadinanza. Le relazioni immigrati-autoctoni nelle rappresentazioni dei "Comitati di cittadini": il caso genovese.* Sarzano, Fossatello, and Maddalena are respectively the names of two piazzas and a street in the historic downtown area of Genoa.
[128] *Ibid.* 209. Burlando was once mayor of Genoa, has been an MP in Prodi's administration, and is the most important figure in Genoa's PDS.
[129] *Ibid.* 213.
[130] *Ibid.* 212. In July of 1993, a group of racists incited serious altercations with immigrants in Genoa's downtown area.

political system (one of the public discourses produced by the crisis of the First Republic) but also a refusal to use political codes for interpreting social occurrences. The "territory" no longer accepts definitions "imposed" from the outside, but stands in immediate and direct opposition to any threat. The "knowledge" of their safety as explained by these citizens takes the form of oversimplified equations ("drug deals in plain sight… immigration," "arrival of *extracommunitari*… guns to protect ourselves from criminals and drug dealers," "*extracommunitari* equals urban blight.") The problems expressed by these oversimplifications are solved by defending fundamental territorial needs ("shopping, living"). This is a uniform, universal "knowledge" that appears in dozens of interviews with members of citizens committees.[131] It's knowledge that, since the 1990s, became legitimized as the prevalent criteria for morality and legality:

> President Barbino, who coordinates the citizens committees in Milan, works as a consultant. In an article published in *La Voce* entitled "Security and Legality: Prerequisites for Solidarity," Barbino quotes Vattimo and Veca [to support his positions]. And after quoting them, Barbino follows the philosophers' lead by saying, "Ultimately, the committees have their finger on the people's pulse, they testify to a profound change in the way people feel. For a long time, most people were convinced that the, "It's-prohibited-to prohibit" approach that dominated the culture of the 1970s has lost its effectiveness […]. And what about solidarity? According to the committees, solidarity needs to be "demanding and severe. Understood in this way, it's not in opposition to the forces of public order and safety." [132]

It's easy to think that such generic formulas are inevitable when new political *imprenditori morali* are doing the talking (what does "demanding and severe solidarity" mean anyway?) Furthermore, these clichés have progressively acquired the role of official definition of reality: they are employed by nearly all the political parties in their obvious attempts to claim they represent the voice of

[131] *Ibid.*
[132] Fantini, L. *Milano 1994. Percorsi nel presente metropolitano.* Milan: Feltrinellli, 1994. 65-66.

the people, as well as the public opinion of the educated as voiced when needed by generic intellectuals and even by objective observers. The cliché about the need to increase public safety returns in a similar form in the words of two other citizens, a local political leader from the moderate left and a sociologist who has become the spokesperson for his neighborhood.

"Isn't it a legitimate right for a citizen to protest when he finds his mailbox full of used condoms because every night the streets around his house are full of drug dealers or he is subjected to seeing scenes of love-for-sale right on the street? Or because his son's mountain bike gets stolen and his wife is afraid she'll be attacked? [...]" says Sergio Chiamparino, 46, regional secretary for the PDS, father of a 16-year old son (who fears his mountain bike will be stolen). He lives in Murazzi, on of Turin's hot spots between Vittorio Veneto and Corso Vittorio Emmanuele, where the residents have organized protests against the Senegalese and Moroccans.[133]

There is another terrible criminal practice in several forms common among various groups of immigrants: the exploitation of minors. Rom children forced into begging, stealing and prostitution with threats, abuse, and even torture; Moroccans used as windshield washers at traffic lights to win the drivers' pity, Chinese employed illegally of course to work for next to nothing in restaurants or the fur and clothing industry. And it's difficult if not impossible to win attention from the authorities responsible for overseeing the enforcement against such crimes [sic!]. From personal experience, I know this very well, having written repeatedly and unsuccessfully to ask for police intervention, even when I've asked in the official capacity of Head of the Commission for Social Problems in Zone 3.[134]

Company consultants who invoke a new morality on the heels of well-known philosophers, and mobilize their neighbors in protests against *immigrati clandestini,* local political leaders offended scenes of love-for-sale, intellectuals who embrace secular mythologies about monstrous nomads and unsuccessfully

---

[133] *Corriere della sera.* 18 October 1995: 7.
[134] Melotti, U. "Criminalità e conflittualità: il disagio metropolitano." *Milano plurale. L'immigrazione tra passato, presente e futuro.* Ed. S. Allievi. Milan: IREF, 1993. 163.

call for the attention of public officials against crimes such as washing windshields at traffic lights. This rhetoric irresistibly brings to mind the Italian trash cinema of the 1970s (*Crime on the offensive, the police do nothing, the citizens rebel*). One could perhaps smile in response to this if it didn't confer a political-intellectual coating to that social process I defined earlier as the "tautology of fear."

With the legitimization of the common feeling among "citizens" by those who manipulate symbols (old and new political forces, intellectuals, the media) the pioneering function of citizens committees has virtually ended. It is true that periodically them make themselves heard to point out new emergencies, to sound the alarm or rouse the authorities, but the rights of primogeniture in the "definition of the situation" passes to politics, with its procedures and rhetoric. The neighborhood *imprenditori morali* can go back to their regular jobs or their micropolitical adventures. Fear is no longer the business of company consultants or disappointed political activists, but a primary resource in the political theater of the media, a frame with its emergencies, unexpected events, or the difficulties of public life can be retranslated and managed to the general satisfaction.

4 **What Every Citizen Knows**

Before discussing the functions and general political rhetoric of public opinion, it will be useful to focus on some characteristic aspects of the negative representation of migrants, other than its uniformity.[135] Any in-depth interview, public declaration by citizens or their self-appointed moral, intellectual or political leaders, any slogan or citizens committee flyer or similar fixed set of complaints shares the same idea: "We can't live with (immigrant) criminals, thieves, drug dealers, window washers, prostitutes (in our territory) anymore."

---

[135] The uniformity of public opinion transcends national and European boundaries. A novel published in the United States relates the same embarrassment, discomfort, and defensiveness toward Latin immigrants in the United States. See Coraghessan Boyle, T. *The Tortilla Curtain*, New York: Viking Penguin, 1995, which portrays the legal, cultural, and physical barriers that separate Latinos from "Americans."

This uniformity of thought is nothing more than the urban version of the dominant frame, "Immigrants as enemy." This hides the less evident operations of those discourses responsible for generating public opinion. First is the elasticity of the category of "criminality" and its extension to behaviors that are not criminal or that fall into the category of administrative infractions, or in sociological terms, "crimes without a victim" (prostitution, purchasing drugs).[136] Theft and drug pushing are crimes from a penal perspective, while being a prostitute is not an offense (unless it involves solicitation, at least in Italy), and it is even doubtful if this is a crime. However, washing windows at traffic lights can be an administrative infraction at the most. On the other hand, "illegal labor" in a restaurant or clothing factory, which are big business in our economy, are framed as crimes for the employer but not for the worker. In other words, "criminality" usually means general social deviance, an extremely wide category that includes everything from disturbing the peace to selling drugs. Clearly, since the citizens' protests refer to such a wide spectrum of activities, they have the effect of lowering the level of tolerance as to what public opinion feels is a threat to daily life.

Secondly, the extension of criminal categories is selective because it is not generally applied to all members of society but only to foreigners. This conflates criminality with deviance, penal action with informal social practice, those crimes with victims and those crimes without victims, petty infractions and behaviors that are at most only debatable in those cases in which immigrants are involved. And while this extension is activated automatically only for immigrants, it's not difficult to deduce that the uniformity of their negative categorization has one meaning: as a category, immigrants are criminals (while the behaviors ascribed to them have the function of empirically demonstrating

---

[136] By "crimes without victims" I intend behaviors that are punished by the law but that do not inflict damage on a third party. More than any other behaviors, crimes without victims are the product of prevalent definitions of morality incorporated in "rights" and are therefore an example of deviance. See Schur, E.M. *Crimes without Victims.* Englewood Cliffs, NJ: Prentice Hall, 1965. See also Matza, D. *Becoming Deviant*, Upper Saddle River, NJ: Prentice Hall, 1969, and Becker, H.S. *Outsiders: Studies In The Sociology Of Deviance*, New York: Free Press, 1997.

"what we already know.") This aspect is evident in the interview of a committee supporter who responds with commendable sincerity to a question about racism among citizens:

> Question: Do you think there are any cases of racist actions among [members of the citizens committees]?
> Answer: Yes.
> Q: So, do think there is an underground culture of racism in the city?
> A: Yes, deep down, there is. It's difficult to disconnect that from the brain. Even friends, people from the political left [...] are somewhat racist, fundamentally. Because we don't have the cultural background [...] [Our city] has always been hospitable to these people but then a lot of other strange people arrived [...] and that's when the racism started. [...] Even if we don't like to admit it, so we say we're not racist, but fundamentally, deep down, I see my friends who say, "Gypsies can't stay here!" Personally, I think how things are now is no good: you can't say, "Give us a place to stay with water and electricity, etc," but deep down I think, "Ok, let's try to give them a house like everybody else." But then people think that it's not all right to have them in the piazza, it's not ok to give them a house, because giving it to them seems like taking it away from us [...].
> So, maybe we do have a little intolerance [...] but that doesn't mean [...], well, it's not true that then we're racists. At the end of the day, if I talk to a person of color, I'm always thinking he's [...] different. I mean, when I consider the drug problem, it goes without saying that my fellow Italians are in on it, but I still say that it's because of the *extracommunitari*.[137]

The idea that immigration and criminality are nearly synonymous in common belief and public opinion emerges in two revealing articles. The first is a news article about an alleged racist episode in which a well-known political commentator replies to the question, "Is Genoa a racist city?" The second is a "neutral" article about inconveniences in the city during the summer.

---

[137] Interview made in Genoa (my italics).

"Are We a Cold, Racist City?"

Is Genoa cynical and racist? "No, Genoa and its residents have always been very patient and tolerant. *They have tolerated the problems of the* extracommunitari, *the nomads, and the failure to find any solutions for the immigration problem.*[138]

"Illegal Gypsy Camps at Marassi and Lagaccio"

Genova. Alarm over the Gyspies in Marassi.
Residents of the two areas are under siege by groups of nomads who set up camp quite some time ago in front of the Luigi Ferraris stadium and around the sports fields in Lagaccio. In this city that is usually empty at the end of August, even the streets downtown are now crowded with camps of hobos, punks, and drifters that have sprung up along side the nomads. It's easy to run into groups of young people sitting on the ground playing little flutes and begging for change (with little success). They all resemble one another, from their dirty, ragged clothes to the numerous dogs that accompany them, their faithful travel companions.[139]

Immigration, nomads, and *extracommunitari*, grouped together with gypsies, drifters, punks, and dogs, are something that citizens put up with, thus demonstrating their tolerance. Immigration therefore becomes a metaphor for social deviance, which the authorities recognize either implicitly or explicitly, as evidenced in the following comments by two police functionaries:

In my opinion, there's been a definite change and public opinion is much more interested in cases of petty crimes. Yes, minor crimes have become a real priority. There aren't many of those dramatic cases from earlier, kidnappings and terrorism. Clearly, the problem of lesser crimes increased, and includes a wider spectrum. But it's also probable that people have become less tolerant, people act less tolerant [...] The problem of minor crimes stays the same, but people are intolerant and demand more security. I don't think the demand for

[138] Statement made by Baget Bozzo, G. a *Il secolo XIX*, 15. The article comments on the case of a young Nigerian man who was stopped on a bus because he had no ticket and was subsequently arrested and imprisoned for four days.
[139] *La Stampa*. 24 August 1997: 35. Marassi and Lagaccio are neighborhoods in Genoa.

security has changed in nature, just in degree. It has increased and it has to do with these kinds of phenomena: prostitution, *extracommunitari irregolari,* drug dealing, drug use, and obviously purse snatching and theft in general.[140]

People in general are afraid. "I don't know you. You scare me." People are suspicious, and especially frightened by the presence of people who are physically distinguishable. You know, maybe a white criminal, if you don't know he's a criminal, frightens you less. Someone dark-skinned, you can already distinguish and he can become the black boogey man out of fairy tales. People, when they're superficial, are especially frightened. I look at my mother, who comes from a certain social context [...] she'll often follow a line of thinking that scares me.[141]

Over all, those are the kinds of offenses committed by *extracommunitari*: sometimes even inflict bodily harm, but they're not moving towards other kinds of offenses: kidnappings don't come up because the people who keep committing muggings or kidnappings (crimes against people) are Italians. *Extracommunitari* sell some drugs, pimp prostitutes. I think these are the most prevalent offenses [...]. When I've been outside of Liguria, I don't see *extracommunitari*, but ten or twelve Albanians together. People told me that they'll go and sit in the same bar all day long. They just go and sit there, they don't work or do anything. A few might work, watering gardens, but the others just sit at the bar, drinking and arguing, sitting there all day. But the crimes we've seen with Albanians have been more serious. You see, Albanians are more violent, more dangerous. There are a lot of attempted homicides, they use weapons immediately, just like the few Slavs we have, it's connected to problems over women, it's tied to their culture, and their use of alcohol.[142]

In that area, especially in the historic downtown, people are exasperated. They can't take it any more. And sometimes when we arrive on the scene, people vent their anger, say there's been a fight, maybe a group of these *extracommunitari* got drunk and broke bottles and raise a ruckus at night, and in an outburst of anger you might here some citizens say, "Could you just club them all over the head and drag them off?" But since we're there to enforce public order, we

---

[140] Interview with police officer in Milan (my italics).
[141] Functionary of the PS in Genoa.
[142] *Carabinieri* official in Genoa

aren't vigilantes, we can't go in there and beat people over the head just because they are creating disturbances and breaking bottles.[143]

In these interviews with police agents and *carabinieri* officials, what unanimously alarms citizens regardless of their cultural or political orientation is this double equation of criminality with immigration. On the one hand, these experts highlight specific crimes attributed to immigrants (minor drug dealing, fights, prostitution and pimping, drunk and disorderly conduct). At the same time, they are aware that the public alarm, "what people fear," extends to immigration as a metaphor for social deviance: increased intolerance, identification of "the other" as criminal ("the black boogey man" from the second interview), irritation with the unemployed. Among those interviewed, some functionaries admit that many calls made to police emergency services are reactions to the caller's pure and simple panic when there's a foreigner in the neighborhood or on the street, while others note that a fear of the foreigner is typical of elderly people living alone in the city. Others underscore the increasing role of certain types of immigrants in the drug trade (young Algerians and Tunisians) and still recognize that the drug problem transcends the immigration problem: "A lot of drugs circulate among immigrants, [...] but [the drugs] come from Italians [the suppliers]."[144]

I saw this verified on a specific occasion: in Genoa, after the Dini decree was approved in November 1995, for several weeks, immigrants who were not in the country legally as well as those involved in minor drug trafficking were afraid of a police crackdown and being deported so many immigrants wouldn't leave their houses. They often had an older immigrant with a *permesso di soggiorno* go out and buy food for everyone.[145] Consequently, the "pony boys" (the foreigners who are small-time drug dealers) disappeared from their typical corners and streets, and were quickly replaced by young Italian men. One police agent said,

---

[143] Officer on patrol in Genoa's historic downtown area.
[144] PS Agent in Genoa.
[145] Testimony of T., a Senegalese immigrant in Genoa.

Sure, they all work together [the drug dealers], and they do the work of the "pony boy" as it's called, the lowest rung on the ladder, so to speak. They do the real work, I mean, going around with the packets in their pockets, and deliver them to the users. Who gives them the packets, I don't know, but of course there are territories, apartments, places where they keep the stuff, and the distribution is organized. Of course there is a real organization to it, but I can't say how it all works. [...] There are other offices that deal with that.[146]

If we compare the testimonies of the police officers and *carabinieri* with the typical affirmations used commonly about the "criminality of immigrants" a "moral microscope" emerges. Public opinion, both educated or uneducated, political or non-political, enlarges any infraction whether real or virtual that interferes with its interpretive lens, but typically refuses to admit the existence of far more serious forms of crimes when they are organized, hidden, established, and consolidated. Drug dealing is visible, but the organizations that perpetuate it are not; the protests against the "*viados*," the foreign prostitutes, are visible, but not their clients, the landlords who rent the rooms, or the complicitous hotel owners. People become hostile towards street vendors or windshield washers, but with few exceptions, they don't see the illegal labor of migrants, or if they see it, they don't see the Italians who profit from illegal labor. But even when public opinion "sees" all this, it transfers its perception of major crimes onto the most convenient symptoms, for example, as when "immigration" becomes synonymous with "mafia:"

I'll tell you, immigration, especially in Genoa, is controlled by the criminal underworld. Immigration has made drug dealing – which used to be organized in a certain way – more widespread. I mean, once you couldn't find a piazza, a brick, a car anywhere without a drug dealer on it. Since immigration, let's just say [...] you can't even ask to see someone's ID anymore: you don't know who was selling drugs anymore, who was and who wasn't [...] so immigration was, and still is controlled by [...] organized crime, by the mafia, essentially.[147]

---

[146] Interview in Genoa.
[147] Representative of a citizens committee in Genoa.

In short, the knowledge of "citizens" is symptomatic and therefore different from that of the police, at least when this knowledge functions strategically and doesn't complete mere superficial operations for appearances sake or to reassure people (such as patrolling or checking IDs in areas considered high-risk). Thus, the typical citizens' protest against police indifference is born, as well as a certain attitude of distance or irritation on the part of some police agents towards citizens:

> In my opinion, an Italian who hires an *extracommunitari* is two-faced. On the one hand, he could say, "I feel sorry for these poor people. Rather than see them out selling roses on street corners, I'll give them something for taking care of my yard." On the other hand, if you give someone a job illegally, then you, as an "employer" don't pay any taxes, you don't help pay for their health care, you don't help pay for any assistance this worker would need if some work accident or anything like that happened.[148]

The social phenomenon most representative of what "every citizen knows," of the creation of public opinion in its most extreme or most hidden aspects (intolerance for visible offences, immigration as metaphor for social deviance, the myopic and microscopic hypervaluation of the symptoms of criminality) is the prostitution of both male and female foreigners. Unlike other forms of deviance, whether real or imagined, prostitution is not a phenomenon with which citizens have direct contact unless it's in the role of client. If specific forms of microsocial tension caused by the activities on the street (such as fights and late-night disturbances), then prostitution is, or should be, outside of the citizens' area of concern. In the forty years since Italy abolished brothels, certain neighborhoods and streets have become "open zones" for prostitution (the Maddelena area of Genoa, the park and streets around the central train station in Milan, etc.).[149] Independent of the widespread demand for this service (one

---

[148] *Ibid.*

[149] As in many port cities, in Genoa both male and female prostitution has long been accepted socially. In a large section of the downtown area, a regular prostitution business exists, including foreign prostitutes, which the citizens have never protested.

scholar estimates that in large cities, 20% of the male population are either occasional or regular clients),[150] prostitution didn't created any particular social alarm until the appearance of foreign men and women on the streets. While traditional prostitution found outlets that were more lucrative and discrete ("masseuse" or "fortune tellers"), the prostitution of foreigners – *viados*, Albanian and Nigerian women – became highly visible, and this is what sparks the clamorous protests by citizens. In Milan during the 1980s the residents in the area of Melchiorre Gioia mobilized against the *viados* while the protests against foreign prostitutes was increasing in general. Below is a representative text from a citizens' protest:

In the last few years, the number of foreigners in street prostitution has multiplied. The Brazilian *viados* (as well as the Italians who imitate them, and pass themselves off as South Americans) work mainly in Viale Abruzzi at night. From early evening, the Slavic and South American women are out on Corso Buenos Aires and the surrounding streets, along with all the drug addicts; the Moroccan women who have mainly Maghrebi and their own countrymen as clients operate around via Benedetto Marcello, along with the older Italian prostitutes and the ones that are less appetizing. The male Tunisian prostitutes wait in the evening for the homosexuals around Porta Venezia; the African women, together with the Slavs and South Americans work later in the morning hours around Piazza Aspromonte which one member of a citizens committee describes as "an open-air amusement park for sex," due to all of the hotels and rental rooms involved, some with and some without business licenses, and which are tolerated by the police (who knows why) [...]. Few residents of the neighborhood have dared to protest against this disgusting activity though it depresses the entire area and brings fights and bloody conflicts among the people involved in these illegal activities. [...] This situation has prompted a consistent percentage of the population to demand greater involvement from the forces of law and order, but with few results. The public safety officials tend to

---

[150] Cutrufelli, M.R. *Il denaro in corpo. Uomini e donne: la domanda di sesso commerciale.* Milan: Marco Tropea Editore, 1996. I consider these estimates too conservative. Individuals who operate in the Lila street area of Genoa have placed the percentage around 60%.

underestimate the destructive effects of criminality, and openly admit that they have other priorities (even if they won't say what those priorities are).[151]

What is representative in this text is not just the typical alarmist tone, nor the ritual polemic raised about the indifference of the police, nor even the titillating allusion to the attractiveness of aging prostitutes, but the absence of Italian clients (aside from the mention of homosexuals, the only clients mentioned are "Maghrebi," as if to suggest that the demand for prostitution only involved foreigners). The general public opinion of the citizens committees doesn't see that its own citizens are buying what the *"viados,"* African, and Slavic women are selling. To explain this dismissal, rather than appealing to Freudian analysis and the ambivalence men feel toward prostitution,[152] it is necessary to refer to someone with empirical knowledge of the phenomenon:

> Realistically, about 60% of the Italian male population tends to consistently use the new [foreign] prostitutes. I've discussed the principal mechanisms: domination and creating inferiority. In the personal stories I've gathered, the prevailing desire is to enact violence that is not negotiated. We're not dealing with lovers who practice sado-masochism, this is not about technique. This is about seeking the feeling of being the complete master of another body, a body that can be used and tortured because of its "submissive" nature.
> What I'm trying to say is that the practice of physical violence – punches, slaps, binding, unannounced use of knives and whips – is extremely frequent, as is forced oral sex without a condom. Another common practice is gang rape. This practice is very well-established. Generally a group will hire a young Albanian girl, promise her extra money (which is almost never paid), drag her to some isolated part of the city or private house and use her for as long as they feel is opportune. There are no limits to what "use" means: for example, burning her breasts with cigarettes is a well-established practice. What emerges from the

---

[151] Melotti, U. "Criminalità e conflittualità: il disagio metropolitano." *Milano plurale. L'immigrazione tra passato, presente e futuro.* Ed. S. Allievi. Milan: IREF, 1993. 166.
[152] Freud, S. "Notes upon a Case of Obsessional Neurosis" ("Rat Man"), J. Strachey (Ed.), *The Complete Psychological Works of Sigmund Freud*, Vol. 10, pp. 153-249, London: Hogarth Press, 1959. Freud's observations regarding the "pathology of eros" are useful but must be integrated with contemporary ethnography regarding the demand for prostitution. Foreign prostitutes are at a greater risk of becoming the victims of violence than their Italian counterparts.

accounts of these young Albanian or black women is the overwhelming sense of ∽ entitlement that empowers the Italian male. Nothing seems to be more appealing than finding a body whose "natural" destiny is to be submissive. In the accounts in these women, what continually resurfaces is the women's non-existence, whether their clients are individuals or in groups. Most prevalent among the clients is a sense of competition either with themselves or with others, and the prostitutes body is utilized simply as a technical "instrument."[153]

These observations are confirmed by young foreign women who granted interviews as well as by the testimonies of volunteers and police officials.[154] In addition to the typical kinds of non-violent crimes against prostitutes (purse-snatching is considered a professional risk), the violence of the sexual relations is common and is enacted against women that are young, defenseless, and marginalized. The "normalcy" of this violence appears in an episode that I observed personally:

In Genoa, the Foce neighborhood [the area where foreign prostitutes, especially Nigerian and Albanian women congregate], one Saturday in September, about midnight. I was at a bar, sitting at a table outside. A four-wheel drive roughly accosted a black woman on the sidewalk. Two middle-aged men jumped out of the car and grabbed the woman, shouting, "Come with us." Two more were waiting in the car. The woman struggled free. A man seated near me, about ten yards from the scene observed, "They must be police officers." (They looked as if they had just come from a party). The two who had jumped out of the car shouted, "Give him a f**k!" and forced the woman's head into the car. A few minutes later the woman was thrown from the car, fell to the ground, and the four-wheel drive roared off with its tires squealing.

---

[153] Interview with F. Pivetta. In a study from the 1930 on the psychology of tyrannical attitudes, Manès Sperber showed how extreme aggression can be the effect of a sense of powerlessness. ∽ See Sperber, M. *Zur Analyse der Tyrannis: Das Unglück, begaht zu sein. Zwei sozialpsychologiche Essays.* Wien: Europa Verlag, 1975.

[154] Tartarini, L. *Migrazioni femminili e devianza: una ricerca sulla prostituzione nigeriana nella città di Genova.* Masters Thesis in Criminal Anthropology, Department of Law, University of Genoa, 1995/1996, which documents the frequency and "normalcy" of violence against prostitutes. See also Rahola, F. *La prostitution immigrèe en Italie. Les cas des femmes albanaises et nigerianes à Gênes.* Mémoire de Dea, Université Paris 7 Diderot, Paris 1998..

The condition of foreign prostitutes is absolutely atrocious. In addition to the violence intrinsic to the relations with clients, there is the violence inflicted by pimps and boyfriends. The papers report the violence against these young women who have no *permesso di soggiorno* and are doubly vulnerable to exploitation. The perception of violence is exclusively one-way, and not just because the violence is a phenomenon confined to the shadowy corners of everyday life and because it occurs in the marginalized area of immigration. The existence of these women is noticed only when it provokes irritation among the citizens. Analogously, prostitution is inevitably associated with the activities of criminal gangs who battle over territory. Except for theatrical initiatives to "clean up the city," the reality presented by the problem of the prostitution of foreign women is regularly ignored by the media, the *imprenditori morali*, and by the majority of those who study social phenomena.

The dismissal of the violence that foreign women are subjected to manifests the micro-morality of everyday citizens and conceals something more sinister. Hannah Arendt noted, following Péguy, that it is in fact the "family man," the ordinary citizen obsessed with safety who is most likely to "sacrifice his own beliefs, honor, and human dignity" to blindly follow political flag wavers along the path of demagogery.[155] Today's citizens don't even require this sinister greatness. They tend instead to focus their hostility at those on the margins of society, those whose obvious presence represents what public opinion abhors but to which it is irresistibly attracted: explicit eroticism, offers of facile sex, promiscuity, exoticism. As Susan Bordo has noted,[156] the female body is always the object of a double-bind: while public opinion demands that a woman who has been raped can prove her innocence, that she in no way provoked her attacker either directly or indirectly, that same public opinion reads the body of the prostitute as an object that attracts but is simultaneously available for abuse. Following are two testimonies that both reflect this

---

[155] Arendt, Hannah. *The Jewish Writings*, New York: Schocken, 2008.
[156] Bordo, S. *Unbearable Weight: Feminism, Western Culture, and the Body*, Berkeley, CA: University of California Press, 1995.

contradiction, though the witnesses represent opposing positions. The first is from a Brazilian woman, the second from a police functionary.

> There were a thousand, maybe two thousand people. I'd seen a storm like it before. It gathered from far away, with a lot of threatening flashes and bangs. The invasion started in via Melchiorre Gioia, in San Siro, and Monumentale. The residents were all upset. They said, "The police don't provide protection, so we'll handle this ourselves! Condoms and needles in the parking lots where kids play! Lines of cars, fights, car horns honking until 5 a.m.! We've had it! We're cleaning this up!" There were a lot of headlines in the papers and protests shown on TV. But it was the first time I'd seen a storm with bats and umbrella handles in Milan. I was afraid, but I didn't feel lost. Here in Europe they won't kill you right on the street [...] Then the police showed up with their sirens and their lights flashing, exchanged some tense words with the protesters, fights, and screaming dulled the anger and for all of us who were running away, the only risk was being give an expulsion order.
>
> At the Clara Hotel that night, a lot of women were really pissed off. They said they saw their clients out there with the protesters.[157]

The citizens of [city withheld] who use these immigrants and exploit them have exactly the same profile as the clients of transvestites, and are the same people who then dispute them. It's the people who rent the rooms to blacks that come in and report that some blacks are camped out illegally. These are the people who will rent some rotten room to an immigrant, then when they find out that ten are staying in it, they come and report them all, saying that the immigrants were living there illegally and the Moroccan is telling you he's been paying for the room and paying a lot. The Moroccan has no reason to lie, what would make him say that he pays 400,000 lire a month to stay in a basement. He's reported to the police anyhow. It's the people who have a screw in their cars with a transvestite, the Brianzoli businessmen in their 50s with a wife and kids and a nice car, they're in that category that always says we have to throw out all the blacks, transvestites, and fags. Among the clients of transvestites, I've never found a single blue-collar worker or an anarchist

---

[157] Farias de Albuquerque, F. and M. Jannelli. *Princesa* Rome: Sensibili alle foglie, 1994.

political agitator, no way, never. It's always a well-dressed man in his 50s in a fancy car who undoubtedly votes for the Northern League, that's always the group he belongs to.[158]

5 Material Evidence and Criminal Bodies

In addition to the annual heinous crime that goes unpunished, the massacre on the highways from car accidents among vacationers, every summer has a new "immigration emergency." In 1993 the campaign to "oust the immigrants" from the center of Genoa showed everyone that immigrants exist and "they are a problem." In 1995 the crusade against gypsies set off a campaign that resulted in the Dini decree. In 1998, the arrival of *clandestini* in Sicily created the opportunity to experiment with detention centers for foreigners. But the events of August, 1997 eclipsed all precedents and challenged any observer of social behavior to maintain theories of rational social behavior. "Events" is an inadequate term for describing the escalation of xenophobic fury in the media and in politics that was based in a few isolated criminal offenses. The three principal acts in that summer's drama were:

Act One: Waves of sexual crimes were committed by clandestini. Between August 11 and 12, 1997, two or three Moroccans were arrested in Rimini, the vacation capital of the Adriatic, for the rape and attempted rape of foreign tourists. The police and carabinieri patrolled the beaches. Stories in the press about a brawl between "young Italian men and *clandestini*" are picked up by the TV news. The images show an Italian man kicking a foreigner, *carabinieri* who blandly attempts to calm a young, foreign-looking woman who is screaming, "Why are they beating up my boyfriend?" The reports talk about the problems of urban decline in this Italian Disneyland: worried hotel owners,

---

[158] Police functionary from a Northern Italian city. Independent of their position in regards to migrants, nearly all 50 of the police officers, prison employees, and judges whose interviews I transcribed concur with these conclusions.

desperate immigrants, terrified women, the imposing diligence of the forces of law and order, "who do what they can, but it's not enough." One of the more colorful stories published in the news draws an analogy between individual human "decline" and a parallel decline in the urban area. Following are two excerpts from news stories:

> There's the stench of wine and urine from the closed beach umbrellas and deck chairs stacked up on the beaches of Miramare [...] Walking along the beach, I'm afraid. Where are the patrols and the police who should be here? [...] I have the feeling I'm being followed, I've become someone's prey. A young man appears from under a pile of rags, wavering on his feet. He has to be Maghrebi, he's drunk, and he's coming closer. "H-h-hey, b-beautiful," he wheezes in Italian, "C-c-come 'ere." He starts to follow me. He's fast. He could drag me under the deck chairs. I try to walk in a sliver light. I know I can't make a mistake, I can't hesitate, I know others could appear along the beach front as if it were high noon. I smell the stench from the alcohol. He's too close. I jump over a wall and escape from his hunting field. [...]
> Fear mounts as the hour gets later and the night gets darker. It grows just like the milky scum that appears just beyond where people swim [...]. If the heat keeps up the terrible blanket of slime will keep growing. Over there, where the *extracommunitari* have made beds on the sand [...] only a few have gone to sleep. There they are, strangely friendly to one another, Albanians, blacks, dirty, drunk and tomorrow they will try to erase every trace of their stay here. [159]

The "pursuit" mentioned here isn't aimed at immigrants (the Northern League declared that immigrants should be "ousted" after the "waves of sexual crimes" in August), and it's not a reference to the Senegalese vendors on the Rimini beaches a few days earlier who were forced to take refuge in the water for "a few hours" to the presumed amusement the defenders of the law. (Both Italian and foreign beachgoers protested this police action, thus showing a shred of human decency). Nor does it refer to the "pursuit" of Albanians, which became all but a national sport in the Padana region in 1997. This refers to a pursuit by Maghrebi, drunk and filthy (smell of alcohol, stench of urine) for the

[159] De Luca, M.N. "Scene di caccia in Riveria." *La Repubblica.* 14 August 1997. 7.

white woman, an intrepid journalist who acts wisely when she realizes she has become the "prey" ("I know I can't make a mistake, I know I can't hesitate"). Furthermore, the individuals are "strangely friendly" although they are Albanians and Maghrebi (i.e. "whites" and "blacks"). More than anything else, it is the nocturnal fear that transforms this vacation spot into a filthy place with a "milky scum" and "blanket of slime" extended across the dirty sea where immigrants come from.

A few days previously, a fight among immigrants in Padova made front-page headlines. Right-wing political parties demanded the expulsion of *clandestini* while the Northern League proposed, "*Clandestini* should be sent to work camps."[160] The "green shirt" Northern League supporters jumped into action against street vendors, but were careful to relocate their efforts to the Ligurian coast near Alassio[161] after their efforts to patrol the beaches in Rimini ended in an embarrassing retreat (the sailors at the port authority had to protect them from angry swimmers).[162] A few days later near Sulmona, a Macedonian shepherd (immediately described in the press as "the wolf-man") killed two female tourists from Venice and wounded a third. The papers unanimously cried, "He should have been deported, but he was still here!" On August 23, 1997, the headlines on the front page of *la Repubblica* read, "Macedonian Shepherd Interrogated. Minister Napolitano Says He Shouldn't Have Been in Italy. The Killer Confesses. Debate Explodes over *Clandestini*. The Great Invasion." (End title by A. Cavallari).

Act Two: The government decides to intervene. Faced with "an invasion," the government moves quickly. August 14, two days after the events on the Riviera, then Prime Minister, Romano Prodi, cuts his vacation short to meet

[160] See Italian newspapers from 14 August 1997.
[161] "Alassio, un deterrente per gli ambulanti. E le camicie verdi entrano in azione." *La Stampa.* 15 August 1997: 40.
[162] "Scontri in spiaggia contro le camicie verdi. Turisti contro ronde anti-immigrati." *La Repubblica.* 4 August 1997.

with Minister of the Interior Napolitano in Rome.[163] They decide to speed up the Parliamentary procedure proposed by the Turco-Napolitano law, and to proceed with the expulsion of Albanian *clandestini* who had left the detainment camps, even though no Albanians had been involved in the events in Rimini and Sulmona. The Undersecretary of the Exterior Fassino declared that funds were insufficient to expel all the Albanians. Minister of the Exterior Dini, an economist aware of finances, proposes instead *instituting refugee camps in Albania for the Albanians*.[164]

Act Three: "We will defend our cities." Mayors from the Riviera revolt.[165] A mayor from the political left proposes "regional passports" for immigrants. The government is cautiously skeptical. MP Livia Turco defends the humanity of her proposed law and therefore of the detainment camps in general, but is against regional passports. MP Borghezio, from the Northern League suggests putting the *clandestini* in Lagers. One official from the National Alliance proposes the death penalty for "*extracommunitari* murderers." The Alassio League awards the militant patrols who are most active in identifying *clandestini*. The majority leader from the Northern League in Acqui Terme votes in favor granting rewards of one million lire for Albanians in hiding, while the minority left-wing representatives abstain from voting and the mayor explains, "It was just a way of starting a discussion." The left-wing mayors along the Adriatic Riviera unite with the right-wing mayor of Milan in a "Promise for Action for Urban Safety." In September, police sweeps of Albanians and other *clandestini* begin in Milan and Turin. At the end of September, the Mayor of Mondovi, a Northern League supporter, calls for citizens to report *clandestini*.[166]

---

[163] "Allarme immigrati, vertice Prodi-Napolitano." *Corriere della sera.* 15 August 1997: 13.
[164] See the Italian newspapers from 27 August 1997. I believe that no other similar proposition has been made anywhere in the world. The Albanian government declined the offer and no further discussion followed. See "Profughi, un altro no da Tirana. Respinta la proposta di creare campi in Albania. In Puglia nuovi sbarchi." *Corriere della sera.* 28 August 1997.
[165] "Riveria. Sindaci in rivolta. 'Cacciate i delinquenti'." *La Repubblica.* 13 August 1997.
[166] See Italian newspapers from 24 September 1997.

Inserting these events into the paradigm of the "tautology of fear" gives an idea of their surreal quality and reveals the capacity of urban legend to shape or become social, political, and normative reality.

Figure 5
Tautology of fear at work, or how legend becomes reality

Fundamental symbolic resource: "Foreigners represent a threat to citizens."
↓
Subjective definitions of legitimate actors (mayors, politicians): "They rape and kill our women. We're afraid. Throw them all out."
↓
Objective media definition: "Foreigners are a threat, murders and rapists roaming free, mentally imbalanced and dangerous, yet tolerated by an inefficient government system."
↓
Transformation of symbolic resource into dominant frame: "It has been shown that *clandestini* are a danger to our society and so the authorities must act immediately."
↓
Legislative, political and administrative measures that apply the dominant frame. The government declares, "It's time to draw the line. We will enforce the law and throw out *clandestini*."
↓
Supplementary intervention or variations on a theme by "legitimate political representatives" (right-wing parties, the Northern League, right- and left-wing mayors): "If the government doesn't act soon, we'll take care of defending our own citizens."
↓
Confirmation of the dominant frame which can then be reinvoked for any new emergency.

The model outlined in Figure 5 differs from the one outlined in Figure 4 in that the ordinary citizen has now become extraneous. The legitimate political actors have now been substituted by the local representatives of the right and left wing parties. The overall tautological mechanism remains the same. In the summer of 1997, this mechanism functioned very rapidly, synthesizing the entire process of the social construction of the foreigner as enemy. The "fear machine," powered by heterogeneous factors, became autonomous, and it is therefore probable that it can now function automatically on the level of institutional and normative practices. Before examining this aspect, it will be useful to discuss the cultural consequences of the entire process, particularly the new symbolic dimension opened by the institutionalization of the "enemy" interpretive frame.

6 A New Kind of Racism

The most important form of neo-racism is certainly the implicit and explicit redefinition of immigrants. First of all, common iconography represents immigrants not only as delinquents but as ethnicities, thus suggesting that delinquency and ethnicity go hand in hand. Consider the political cartoons about the "immigration emergency" printed in August 1997 in the three highest-circulating newspapers in Italy.

Figure 6/8: The Black Man – The "Mafioso" - The Black "Mammy"

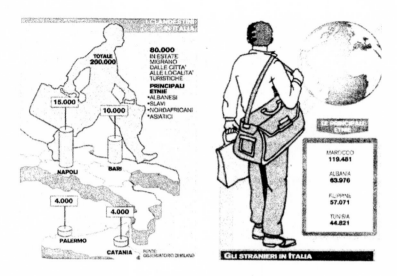

Figure 9/10: *Clandestini*" in Italy - Foreigners in Italy

In Figures 9 and 10 from *la Repubblica*, *clandestini* are represented as "men who come and go," divided by ethnicity (Asians, North Africans, etc.) In Figure 6 from *Corriere della Sera*, a foreigner with his head bowed seems to be admitting some kind of guilt (the *clandestino*, the evil black man), while Figure 8 from *La Stampa* shows the smiling black woman wearing a kerchief, the "mammy," the good black woman, i.e. servant. In Figure 7, the Albanians are depicted as the typical mafia characters from 40 years ago (moustache, sideburns, bowler hat). The distinction between good and bad foreigners proposes the classic division between "useable" women and "enemy" men characteristic of the fascist iconography of Africans ("Views from Abyssia," Figure 11). What is significant in these images is not only the prejudices of the artists who designed them, but their ubiquitous obviousness, their semiotic ubiquitousness, the fact that these were circulated by three papers that together are capable of reaching 2 million readers every day.

Figure 11: Slaves and Enemies
(From *La menzogna della razza*, Bologna: Grafis Edizioni, 1994.)

But there is something even more deeply disturbing in the ethnicization of immigrants. If two or 3 sexual crimes and one homicide set the fear machine in motion to its greatest extremes, that is because "facts" taken out of context and exaggerated to the point of paroxysm by the press and political representatives carry enormous symbolic significance, unlike those rapes committed by Italians as well as the murders of immigrants that took place during this same period but that were completely ignored by the press and the politicians, and therefore *did not exist* because they were not included in the tautological fear machine.[167] The significance of these events was so troublesome as to annul

[167] Between August and September the press reported several incidents: an Italian in Biella killed his lover, a Nigerian prostitute; a priest in Bergamo killed lover, a black woman who was blackmailing him; an Albanian was killed in Sardinia; due Moroccans were killed in Bologna by a drug addict. The events in Rimini and Sulmona were only the pretext for a campaign of xenophobia demonstrated by two circumstances: 1) rapes by and gang wars between Italians were reported all during the summer without arousing any particular reaction and 2) when a Tunisian man was accused of having raped several elderly women in Puglia there was no significant reaction because

another emergency that occurred the month previous, namely the increase in murders in Naples and Campania that forced the government to send in the military to help the police battle the camorra.[168] The Moroccans, or Macedonians (Tunisian, Albanian, or any other foreigner) constitutes the material evidence for the whole history of August, 1997, or rather their bodies become the materials that are criminalized. Their bodies are seen as murderous bodies, oversexed bodies and phalluses, filthy animalistic bodies ("the wolf-man"), and at the same time, alien and formless bodies ("milky scum," "slime,") and therefore by metaphor, bodies that must be contained, removed, eliminated. Because their danger is symbolically charged, because the "enemy" frame is affectively convincing and highly emotional, the formula "foreigners – criminal bodies" equates immigrants with animals of another race, with the monstrous, as in the racist ideology of every age (for example, the Klu Klux Klan). Figures 12, 13, and 14 show the continuity between the image of the foreigner in the fascist period with the image of the foreigner reported in an Italian paper from the time of the events in Rimini.

the "tautology of fear" had already redefined "immigrant" as equivalent to "criminal." In September, the government announced that it had removed the right to vote from the newly proposed immigration law. See the Italian newspapers from 22 September, 1997.
[168] Headlines from *La Repubblica*, 20 July, 1997 included: "Bloody Saturday in Naples. 17-Year-Old Killed by Mistake. The Kid Was with a Friens on His Motorcycle when the Killer Struck." "Four Victims in a few Hours in Campania. A Grandma Was Killed by Burglars in Front of Her Grandson." "Minister of the Interior Giorgio Napolitano: The Camorra Is More Dangerous than the Mafia."

Who Attacks a White
Woman and Who
Defends Her,
Past and Present.

Figure 12. Rimini: police patrols on the beach, *la Repubblica*, 12 August, 1997.
Figure 13. Montage of fascist propaganda and a cartoon from
Il Giornale, 14 August, 1997.
Montage published on the front page of *Il Manifesto*, 15 August, 1997.
Figure 14. Propaganda, "Difendila!" from a fascist poster, 1944.
(From *La menzogna della razza,* Bologna: Grafis Edizioni, 1994.)

These are limited cases, of course. Perhaps residual symbolic content of these images merely found occasion to re-emerge.[169] But even more than these alarming images, the reduction of the foreign body to animal body is implicit in typical representations of the immigrant. If the female foreigner is the body to abuse (therefore "prostitute" becomes equivalent to foreign woman, for she is visible and therefore "obscene"), the foreign man is the threatening body. Even if he has committed no crime, not raped our women, he is dirty and he dirties everything else ("urban decline," "stench," "slime," "milky scum"). He is out of place, like gypsies and dogs, he is aggressively obscene. In a "humorous" cartoon from the 1930s, the black body is civilized by the Italian with a violent washing (Figure 15). In a photo published in numerous papers and magazines

Figure 15   Figure 16

in August, 1997, the bodies of Moroccans are exposed in their "natural indecency" (Figure 16). This last image requires an explanation. The foreigners in the photo were stripped by police searching for drugs. News reports in

[169] On the perpetuation of symbols in the history of culture, see Warburg, A. *Ausgeqählte Schfriten und Würdigungen.* Berlin: Teubner, 1932.

September (which used images from news programs dated August 13-14) presented the foreigners' nudity as "exhibitionism."

> Hidden among deck chairs two agents from the Rimini narcotics division watch the drug dealers' movements. The first clients arrive, the sale takes place: first the clients pay, then they pick up their hit. There's no direct contact with the merchandise. The buyer is told were the drugs are hidden. The pusher doesn't keep anything on him. The police try to stop some kids who have just bought drugs, they point out the dealers. Then there's a chase along the beach, soon backup forces arrive. The pushers are caught trapped and they fight back. They get mad when they see our videocamera and they don't mind proving to us in their own way that they're "clean." A free exhibition that shocks the dozens of tourists standing by. [This image in no way proves that the figures in the picture are drug dealers. They are undergoing a strip search and for that reason are naked].[170]

The representation of the foreigner-animal is so dominant that it conditions and frames even anti-racism discourses. For example, in a cartoon published on September 20, 1997 in *Boxer*, a "vu' cumpra" is attacked by a gang of Italian racists who are shouting, "Filthy nigger!" The victim reacts by zapping them with his voodoo magic (Figure 17). Thus the equation of "foreigner" with a "criminal body" that is capable of reacting diabolically. It's unnecessary to explore in-depth that tradition in the popular imagination in which the devil is represented as a goat, and which finds its culmination in this cartoon supposedly from the political left. Together with countless other examples, this cartoon shows the secondary cultural fallout from the media campaign of August, 1997, that is, the normalization of racist imagery of foreigners. The general "frame of the enemy" is institutionalized in public opinion reinforcing each time the unbridgeable difference between "us" and "them." Inverting the sense of difference, as in the cartoon from *Boxer* in which racist Italians are

---

[170] Transcriptions of the television programs *Tg2 Dossier*. 19 November 1997 and *Rimini '97*. 19 November 1997.

Figure 17

vanquished by the diabolical black man, does nothing to diminish the framework of "foreigner as enemy" but rather perpetuates it.

Although a significant number of symbols and traditions associated with racism surfaced in the media campaign during the summer of 1997, we will focus now on one problem and interpret it as a "regurgitation" or "reflux." As the images reproduced here demonstrate, an evident parallel does emerge between the racism of previous years and today. However, if racism historically proposed a hyperbolic line between whites and the "inferior races" (see the Roman sword in Figure 18), today's racism assumes plural forms that are not necessarily bound to historical racist mythology.[171] The specter of difference includes race and

[171] In my opinion, this question has remained unanswered by research about racism in Italy. For example, a study by P. Tabet (*La pelle giusta.* Turin: Einaudi, 1997) about the image of the other

bestiality, filth and drunkenness, deviance and criminality, disorder and danger without any definite symbolic hierarchy.[172]

Figure 18

And it is precisely because of this that racism enjoys such an extraordinary freedom of word and image, disconcerting to a culture that would rather not be racist and that is unable to discern racism in its new forms. The noose that appeared on the front page of *La Padania* on August 22, 1997 (Figure 19) has the same function as the Roman sword in Figure 18, with the difference that it would not immediately be connoted as "biologically" racist. Nevertheless,

in the school writings of children in elementary and middle school examines the role of fear, but ignores the context of the media and government's war against immigrants.

[172] In other words, racism may be defined as the symbolic code of absolute inferiority, which can be justified by different types of stigmas. Consider the image of the Irish as "animals" in English writings from the sixteenth and seventeenth centuries.

sociologically, it is racist in a new or at least a different form. But as a symbol of summary vigilante justice, the preferred form of punishment used by the Klu Klux Klan against "rebellious" blacks, this noose does not merely recall the separation of the races, but the subordination of one race to another ("keep in your place, or else …")

Figure 19

Contemporary Italian culture has made no protest, except in very limited cases, against the new racism mainly because the issue of race takes a secondary role. For example, if the Northern League and the right wing wave nooses, form patrols, propose quotas, promote secret accusations, and try to throw out *clandestini* (on a verbal level), our democratic society seems able only to interpret these as political initiatives of questionable legitimacy ("only the state can enact justice") and not as a new form of racism. Thus, the enormous social import of these local initiatives is never highlighted because there is an underlying consensus about the "values" that these initiatives entail, though not in their forms or methods. The campaign to "oust the street vendors and *clandestini*," illegitimate as practiced by the Northern League, is normally conducted in less picturesque forms by the legitimate forces of the law (for example, the police sweeps of the *extracommunitari* in Milan and Turin in September 1997, which were widely covered in the press). Ninety per cent of the political forces gives their blessing to such actions, while at the same time the vast majority of them would proclaim themselves anti-racist and would condemn any extremism, which can only be termed "political double-mindedness." Their sincerity is indisputable. Because the kinds of racism they are thinking of are the racisms of 60 years ago, historically codified as deviance or moral degeneracy in the course of history. Naturally, in a pluralist society every thing can flow back from the past. We see in some of the Northern League's publicity, Jews are associated with the "*extracommunitari*" threat. But what seems most decisive in the entire social construction of fear is not just the refuse of some distant nostalgia but the re-appropriation of every possible xenophobic symbol that creates the "us" vs. "them" opposition. As the following chapter discusses, contrary to every illusion of modern moral thinkers, this reappropriation occurs today under the aegis of legality.

IIII Society Defends Itself

They told me briefly that in order to combat racism in France, we needed to send all the immigrants back to their homes. I kept silent, but it seemed strange to me that you would combat an idea by putting it into practice.[173]

1 Legality Pills

The definitive inclusion of the "immigration emergency" on the political agenda signals the disappearance of real, living citizens from the political scene. Rumors, even if voiced by a minority, are destined to become background noise, a rhetorical resource for whatever political party wishes to cross the line of legality at any cost. This line, after the 1990s, enjoys the comfort of certain international consensus. After the Republican Mayor of New York, Giuliani, launched his campaign of "zero tolerance" for petty crimes (a strategy enthusiastically endorsed by the German Social democratic candidate Gerhard Shröder), then in England, Prime Minister from the Labor Party, Tony Blair rediscovered the pedagogic value of beatings for juvenile delinquents. In Italy, where the center-left government prefers a more charitable approach, such tactics are eschewed. With the exception of the Northern League and a few callous fans of the gallows, the political system holds the line, and prefers a forceful campaign in favor of legality. A government authority explains,

Have the supporters of the left who call for security in S. Salvario become right-wing? What about everyone who listens to Radio popolare? What about Giuliano Amato who wants to defend the embryo's right to life? What about Livia Turco who is against the legalization of marijuana? [...] Tony Blair's

[173] Van Cauwealert, D. *Un aller simple*, Paris: Albin Michel, 1994.

Labor Party supporters have voiced uncomfortable truths (like "Law and Order") and now, twenty years later, they're in a position to govern Great Britain. The democrats who support Bill Clinton have even said extremely harsh things against welfare, and they're in power in America. Mitterrand had to make some very difficult choices for the left, but he changed France.[174]

Before analyzing the salient moments of this campaign and its effect on the "immigration emergency," it will be useful to examine the overall significance of political rhetorical rituals. From Max Weber,[175] we know that in politics (not the ideal of Aristotle, but actual politics, or *petite politique*), the aim of professional politicians is the solidification of their own and their party's prestige and power. Obviously, even a modern political democracy is based on this assumption, so it should shock no one when politicians use any means for achieving their prime political objective. The most common means is the search for consensus, or the approval of the electorate. Political consensus, however, is more mercurial in a representative system that provides periodical verification of what the electorate thinks of its government and representatives. As Winston Churchill learned bitterly after having lead England to its victory over Hitler, there is no heroism or wisdom that protects a leader from an electorate in a bad mood.

The advent of new means of mass communication has offered new resources to professional politicians. They have learned that they can win the approval of the citizens by inducing them to believe that their point of view has been adopted by the politicians. Dictators have communicated their own will to the people and created an instant sense of communality. (Hitler favored the radio, and Stalin used it skillfully, as in his famous speech to the Russian people to mobilize against the oncoming Nazi attack.) In modern democratic society, that kind of communality is unthinkable, because the piazzas in which

---

[174] Veltroni, W. "Non sarà la nostra Ustica," *Corriere della sera.* 3 April 1997. Notice that the pleas for legality and its political advantages were made three days after the Albanian ship sunk in the canal of Otranto.

[175] Weber, M. *The Vocation Lectures: Science As a Vocation, Politics As a Vocation,* Indianapolis, IN: Hackett Publishing Company, 2004.

citizens once listened passively to speeches over loudspeakers under the eye of the military have been substituted by the "virtual piazza"[176] of television in which everyone physically remains at home. And also, representative democracy involves a plurality, albeit limited, of political positions. If the objective of dictators was to connect people in an instantaneous and passive communality, the objective of a politician's communication in a democratic state is to convince the public, the voters, the people, to make his or her viewpoint their own by choosing him or her from a limited list of options.

In a mass mediated, democratic society, a politician or a party operates under a regime of competition, both analogous and financial. Their objective consists in convincing the public to buy their line of politics. As in any kind of market, in the political market, success will smile on those who know how to interpret and provide for the needs, the moods, and the whims of the consumers (marketing), in addition to effectively hawking their own product (advertisement). As in the market for goods, the political market offers different advantages and disadvantages. The principle advantage is that the advertising is free, because the media provides ample, free venues for "political theater." The disadvantage is that the frequent upheavals and emergencies in political life don't allow for planning the marketing campaigns. Opinion polls taken by political parties or by commissioned specialists cannot reasonably foresee what will unsettle the public's mind or what subterranean changes of opinion are occurring. Thus, a keen "sense of smell" remains the fundamental quality of a political leader. Knowing how to sense in which direction the political wind is blowing, and above all, knowing how to anticipate and produce it (thanks to a real "bellows effect") allows the able politician to go beyond the limits of marketing scientifically applied to the political arena. Powerful leaders celebrated for their abilities have found themselves in ruins from one day to the next after having

---

[176] Meyrowitz, J. *No Sense of Place: The Impact of Electronic Media on Social Behavior*, Oxford: Oxford University Press, 1986. The author analyzes the virtual character of new social communication. The fact that community is virtual (everyone is exposed to the media privately, particularly television) renders the influence of the media and who controls it simultaneously very extensive and highly ephemeral.

trusted completely in opinion polls indicating their popularity (as happened to Benito Craxi in 1992). At the same time, other politicians just breaking in to the political market have created tremendous followings for themselves despite their apparent extremism because they knew which way the political wind was blowing, as well as how to whip it up (Le Pen in France and Bossi in Italy are obvious examples of this ability at self-promotion).

As the former chapter discusses, during the 1990s safety and immigration became the dominant social concerns thanks to the "tautology of fear," a mechanism capable of uniting local opinion and media opinion into an unbeatable political duo.[177] These concerns are ideal for the political market for several good reasons. First of all, they are recurring, or cyclic, and can therefore be met without prior planning. Every time an "immigration emergency" explodes, the scripts are all ready. Second, as essentially *symbolic* concerns they can be resolved inexpensively with symbolic responses,[178] unlike tricky issues such as "the reform of the social state" which involves intense conflicts between interest groups and painful, unpopular choices. Third, they are *disturbing* and take over the political and media scene, marginalizing periodically the other difficult and controversial issues. It is unnecessary to resuscitate worn-out rhetorical games such as "Who is this helping?" I only wish to simply point out that thanks to the vigorous citizens' protests and the "problems of public order" that those protests involve, the return to the forefront of the issues of public safety and immigration allows several actors to play a leading role in the market for consensus, or in the political theater: the right will advocate the gallows, the

---

[177] For years, German cities had been considered among the most peaceful and secure. For a discussion of the vicious circle of citizen's fears and media hype that has grown in Germany, as in Italy, see Diederichs, O. "Kriminalität und Kriminalitätsfurcht," *Bürgerrechts und Polizei/Cilip 57* 2 (1997).

[178] On symbolism and the rituality of power, see Kertzer, D.I. *Ritual, Politics, and Power*, New Haven, CT: Yale University Press, 1989, a compelling study that should be integrated with the work of Dayan, D & E. Katz, *Media Events: The Live Broadcasting of History*, Cambridge, MA: Harvard University Press, 2006, and Turner, V. *From Ritual to Theatre: The Human Seriousness of Play*, New York: PAJ Publications, 2001, and *The Anthropology of Experience*, Champaign, IL: University of Illinois Press, 2001.

center will call for time to reflect, the democrats will call for tolerance, and the government will attempt to show its competence and concern for the needs of "the people."

Thus legality has become the dominant question in Italian politics in recent years. Legality "pays" symbolically, even if the concrete effects of the relative campaigns are nil or even negative. Just as the use of the death penalty never solved the problem of crime, but actually, paradoxically made it worse. The American justice system increased the number of executions in order to demonstrate its own punitive power, which rendered the rise in crime more evident and that in its turn produced an increase in executions with a cumulative effect that could be seen as grotesque if it were not so tragic. The campaign for legality in Italy will have no other effect than to amplify the illegality and thus produce a strange consequence, i.e. the more citizens demand public safety, the more they will be convinced that the environment in which they are living is unsafe. This is not merely an example of "the perverse effect of social action,"[179] which depends on the intrinsic illogic of human action when compared against ideals,[180] but is more due to the fact that maintaining fear among citizens can become an excellent, "logical" political objective, like so many others.

The somewhat artificial obsession with legality is a prime example of political rhetoric. I use this term to highlight not its evident vacuity so much as its *autonomous* functioning in the political theater. Once a certain level of legitimacy has been acquired, this rhetoric fears no contradiction – it's impossible to confute a piece of theater[1] – and it can easily coexist with the very practical knowledge that would contradict it, if it could do so legitimately. We have seen how the specialists of issues such as "legality" and "public safety" (police officers, magistrates) tend to interpret in a different light, and even minimize "emergencies" such as "the criminality of immigrants." Specialists are not attempting to enter the political theater or the market of public opinion,

---

[179] Boudon, R. *Gli effete perversi dell'azione sociale*. Milan: Feltrinelli, 1981.
[180] Boudon, R. *La logica del sociale*. Milan: Mondadori: 1979.

(1) unless it's done aesthetically, ie the ugliness of non-solidarity)

but tend to underscore the continuity and normalcy in their work, in part because the anxiety over the "crime waves" coming from citizens' groups or politicians sounds like an implicit criticism of their own performance. In addition, the specialists know how to distinguish between symptoms and causes, appearances and structures of criminality, and above all, between different types of criminality. While they, too, are subject to the pressures of public opinion and are obviously influenced by public opinion, it is highly unlikely that they would confuse drug use with drug dealing or the organized drug rings, or confuse prostituting with hiring a prostitute, or confuse a fight between drunks with gang warfare. These very confusions form the basis of the public's obsession with public safety. Naturally, the specialists are subject to the issues that politics and public opinion assigns to the state machine, thus the "emergencies" will not cool down and will re-enter the chorus when the exigencies of political rhetoric on stage require it.

Ever since Tangentopoli and the "crisis of the First Republic," the dominant interpretive political frame[181] has been decisively oriented toward "legality." Currently in Italy this term has assumed a different connotation than in the rest of Western Europe. In addition to the political corruption in our country, the networks of organized crime are widely diffused and deeply rooted in several regions although their offshoots, especially financial, have acquired national and international dimensions. Periodically, the military is sent in to control the territory in those regions, such as "Operation Sicilian Vespers," against the Sicilian mafia, or to deal with kidnappings and highway robbery in Sardegna, or against the camorra in Campania. The official objective of these operations is to aid the public safety officials in maintaining order in the territory and the implicit political objective is to reassure public opinion that "the government is in control." However, in general, these operations demonstrate the inability of the government to use the forces of order to conquer organized crime, for it still

[181] See Luhmann, N. *Political Theory in the Welfare State*, Berlin: Walter De Gruyter Inc., 1990. The political code can be defined as an elementary binary system that defines political options. I use the concept of "code" broadly, and include the underlying discourses and rhetorics that are capable of creating consensus.

remains an efficient power and in some cases is the alternative power to that of the state. (Remember that during the terrorism of the 1970s, the military was not employed to aid police in maintaining public safety). Nevertheless, the mafia, camorra, and 'ndrangheta do not constitute fertile terrain for cultivating the political rhetoric of legality. On one hand, their very existence demonstrates the inefficiency of the Italian State. On the other, their existence doesn't create a consistent alarm among "the people," or rather, the electorate. With the exception of some regions in the south, public opinion doesn't "see" the effects of organized crime, just as it doesn't see the international traffic of drugs and weapons, another industry for which our country acts as a crossroads. With the exception of elaborate media ceremonies, such as the funerals of Judge Falcone or Borsellino (which were read by the media as evidence of the "crisis of the First Republic" and symbolically interwoven with the anguish of Tangentopoli), organized crime simply doesn't create a constant reaction.

Microcriminality, however, predominantly functions independently of organized crime: burglaries, muggings, prostitution and "crimes without victims" have no connection to the mafia but rather with small, local, organizations. Drug dealing, however, is to organized crime what retail trade is to the fluctuations in international business. Microcriminality is therefore the perfect area for the rhetoric of legality, because its effects, whether real or imagined, can rouse "the people" to a cause. Furthermore, in order to maintain a relative level of alarm – once fear has passed from the neighborhood to the political dimension – a few translation exercises are necessary. The first consists in rendering organized crime and petty crime rhetorically homogeneous, thus transforming a symptom or epiphenomenon into a "cause" or "structural fact." The second requires equating crimes with deviance, and the third is finding a representative character for the rising illegality, a figure that we recognize easily, the foreigner (or immigrant), who finally finds himself, thanks to the sort of rhetoric being analyzed here, consecrated as the *public enemy.* To illustrate these three exercises in translation, below are statements from politicians and high-level state functionaries, as well as citations from public documents, all of which are representative of the process by which the "tautology of fear" transforms itself into political resource and rhetoric.

Microcriminality and organized crime are the same thing, two sides of the same coin. In reference to organized crime, Luciano Violante, former judge, firm supporter of the PDS and currently president of the Chamber of Deputies, points out that the data regarding microcriminality is encouraging, overall, given the steady decrease in robberies, thefts, and Italy's position in the international classifications of crime rates. He also acknowledges the anxieties of average citizens:

> While Italy's position in the international classifications of crime rates is good and there has been an overall reduction in crime, this does not reassure the average citizen who is uninterested in the situation of New Zealanders and doesn't see evidence of our 3 % reduction in robberies nationwide. The average citizen continues to fear he is at risk and worries that those who commit crimes will go unpunished. To feel vulnerable and defenseless increases one's sense of individual insecurity and mistrust for institutions.[182]

Even the vice-chief of police, Gianni de Gennaro, who knows the data, doesn't seem to question the reality of this new threat: a flood of microcriminality. The same concern for the citizens' security is voiced by De Gennaro in the same magazine, one year after Violante's article appeared. Significantly, De Gennaro's article was entitled, "Democratic Repression."

> Just as serious [as the problem of organized crime] and with analogous intensity we warn people about *the danger of wide-spread, frequent, petty crime usually termed reductively, "microcriminality."* Muggings, robberies, auto theft, purse snatching, drug dealing: a multitude of microtraumas that the social body is forced to absorb every day and which most often afflict the weakest strata of society.
> The collective result of these traumas, if ignored, risks becoming a *true emergency in the future.* An eventual and inauspicious resignation among people and *an increased climate of illegality and impunity* which discourages people from

[182] Violante, L. "Apologia dell'ordine pubblico," *Micromega* 4 (1995): 124.

turning to the justice system because they anticipate that the system will be dismissive to their personal drama; a progressive extension of such forms of criminality, erroneously considered "minor," can actually result in more serious crimes due to an unjustified increase in the level of violence in the commission of crimes which in and of themselves would not justify recourse; a possible crisis when exasperated citizens seek alternative and non-institutional forms of defense, these would already be sufficient motives for reconsidering the degree of attention and concern the phenomenology of wide-spread criminality [...].
Organized crime and petty crime, as two sides of the same coin, are of equal importance in the strategic choices for social defense, from the moment that the two phenomena coexist they are complimentary, they are perfectly integrated and functional in the same criminal world. [183]

De Gennaro refers to "increasing microcriminality," equates microcriminality with organized crime ("two sides of the same coin,") and fears that citizens will take justice into their own hands, but doesn't seem to suspect that the vigilantism — to which he alludes is actually fed by his superficial equation of "mafia" and "microcriminality."[184] The "same criminal world," mentioned here only exists in the imagination, or better, in the alarmist rhetoric of these specialists. In their role as experts, Violante and De Gennaro should know that the discrepancy between the steady and well-known decrease in thefts and robberies and the increased sense of insecurity (for which accurate data doesn't exist, but which is palpable on the streets and documented in the media) poses numerous questions, especially political questions. Is the problem of security independent from crime rates but dependent on other macrosocial factors? Is it connected to the crisis in the social state and the sense of precariousness that floods the populace as unemployment increases and job security declines? If the average citizen is unaware that the most severe crimes are declining, then why are

[183] De Gennaro, G. "Repressione democratic," *Micromega* 5 (1996): 56.
[184] Equating microcriminality with organized crime is based in "folk" perceptions, in a perception of "what people think" that has no supporting evidence or data. It is connected to the notion that "illegal immigration is controlled by organized crime," a notion that feeds the prejudice that immigration is the result of some criminal conspiracy. Thorough analysis reveals rather that organized crime is a normal, integral part of international economy.

political parties not working harder to publicize this information, since they have an obvious social responsibility? There is really one answer: the left-wing government, like the right-wing government before it, has preferred to legitimize the discourse of wide-spread microcriminality, based in anecdotal evidence and rumors fed by the press, in order to utilize it as a resource for forming consensus.[185]

Every form of deviance or threat perceived by the citizen is as serious as organized crime and microcriminality. The Minister of the Interior, Giorgio Napolitano, further extends the equation of organized crime with microcriminality and to "deviance" in general, thus illustrating the second exercise in translation that is necessary to the political rhetoric of legality. Minister Napolitano considers it ungrateful to even use the term "microcriminality," given that the acts included in that definition are "traumatic:"

> The use of the term microcriminality is unconvincing, because when citizens, families, and neighborhoods don't feel safe, when there are attempts on individuals and their property, these offenses are perceived as serious, even by those who were not directly threatened. The term microcriminality gives the idea of unimportance when compared to bloody, heinous crimes. We cannot indulge in the mistake of this undervaluation. It is important to distinguish because it's not merely the frequency of burglaries, muggings, thefts, or assaults that is so disturbing. Often it is something else, for example, drug dealing or organized prostitution that is visible and traumatic. [186]

---

[185] Beginning with the demonstrations in the autumn of 1995 (in which the political left participated) the left-wing government appropriated the buzz-words of "legality" and "regulating immigration." Together with the media campaign, this political message became the official "definition of reality," which contributed to increasingly more hostile reactions to foreigners. A good analytic model for the relationship between public discourse and general behavior can be found in Sasson, T. *Crime Talk. How Citizens Construct a Social Problem.* New York: Aldine De Gruyter, 1995.

[186] "Così libereremo le città dall'incubo della paura." F. La Licata's interview with minister Giorgio Napolitano in *La Stampa*, 22 February 1997: 15.

In a country with a recent history studded with "massacres" and heinous crimes which largely went unpunished (the terrorist bombings that resulted in the massacre of Milan, the massacre of Bologna, and the massacre of Ustica, for example), equating prostitution and drug dealing with terrorism is original, but not surprising. We have already discussed the irresistible tendency to parallel all the new "threats" – *clandestini*, window washers, prostitutes, drug dealers, and deviants of all kinds – with organized crime. On the other hand, this parallel has concrete effects when it justifies operations that normalize the daily life in the city. Initiatives of human *maquillage* took place in Milan and Bologna, where there have been attempts to distance actual and presumed deviants and immigrants from the historic and commercial downtown area. In Genoa, the downtown area is fiercely patrolled by multiple police forces to reassure citizens.

Immigration is the principal cause for the threat to citizens' security. At the same time that the government decreed the expulsion of Albanian refugees and prepared to send troops to Albania (March, 1997), the political initiatives against microcriminality to support urban safety increased. A revealing element in this campaign (promoted in part by the center-left) was that there was no difference between it and the traditional repressive style of the right-wing. Here is how *La Repubblica* with a perhaps involuntary malicious tone, represented one such initiative:

> "Guaranteeing responsible government regulation of security issues and still confronting everyday criminality with determination and necessary repressive structures." "We have always said that whoever breaks the law must be punished, stopped, or expelled. Nothing is more offensive to people concerned with their safety than to offer them solutions that focus on 'solidarity,' because that communicates a sense of powerlessness." Quiz: Who is speaking? Perhaps Teodoro Buontempo from National Alliance or Boso of the Northern League, or a general of the *carabinieri*? No, all wrong. Both statements were made yesterday at Living in Safety (Vivere Sicuri), a European convention about urban safety issues organized by the PDS.

The first statement was made in the opening remarks by the conference organizers. The second was made by Valentino Castellani, mayor of Turin and supportor of the Ulivo coalition. [187]

Castellani's references to "expulsion" and "solidarity" suggests that the use of terms such as "microcriminality" or "everyday crime" are intended as synonymous with the "criminality of immigrants." However, the figure of the "guilty foreigner" is hardly the invention of mayors from across the political spectrum who found themselves assailed by frightened citizens. The political culture of the "preventative suspicion of foreigners" is not due exclusively to the need to coddle an ever increasingly conservative public opinion, but is the product of an alarmist strategy that has long been pursued by the institutions responsible for security in the Italian State. Examining the police and military reports that the current administration gives to Parliament every six months, the leitmotiv of the "delinquent" or "dangerous" foreigner has been evident for more than ten years, the time at which immigration rates into Italy were paltry if compared to other European countries.

The Craxi report from September 1, 1985 speaks of

a high number of foreigners, particularly North Africans, Middle Easterners, Asians among whom we find a certain element that takes advantage of the favorable conditions offered by an especially liberal system to undertake terrorist activities."[188]

The De Mita report[189] confirms this notion, highlighting the

significant presence, mainly clandestina, of groups coming from countries at risk, which causes not only problems of social and public order, but represents a potential threat destined to increase the support of terrorism ...

[187] "Il 'Pds di governo' scopre la repression, *la Repubblica*. 23 March 1997: 8.
[188] Minister of the Interior. *Relazione al parlamento sull'attività delle forze di poliziae sullo stato dell'ordine e della sicurezza pubblica nel territorio nazionale*. Rome: 1985.
[189] De Mita report, Jan-June 1988: 25.

The alarmism of these reports justifies itself with data regarding immigration that is completely unreliable. The De Mitra report from the first part of 1989 refers to 1.2 million immigrants, "two-thirds of whom are without a *permesso di soggiorno*," while the Andreotti report places the immigrant population between 800,000 and 1.2 million.[190] When the administration changes, the tone of the reports do not: according to the Amato report from the second half of 1992,

> [...] the criminal expansion of citizens from an Asian country (the name of the country is not given, but the information indicates Iran [...]) makes us assume there is a network of logistical and operational instruments organized for the purpose of illegal trafficking" (p. 15).

Equally reckless is the Ciampi report (1993) which includes friends of immigrants as part of the threat and "fundamentalists," citing a

> significant capacity for certain communities of foreigners in Italy to organize and demand their rights, readily supported by talented activists that gravitate to pacifism and Islamic extremism.

During the Berlusconi administration that followed, the reports slavishly repeated the usual evaluations of *clandestini*, but then the Dini report (1995) and the Prodi report confront the problem of xenophobia:

> The need for security in our society continues to increase, as we are faced with serious problems due to organized crime, illegal immigration, Islamic fundamentalism, ideological subversion, and instability in the financial markets.[191]

> The persistent crisis areas near Italy, which have seen a marked demographic trend toward increase, have continued to feed illegal immigration. This phenomenon has

---

[190] The systemic inflation of the number of immigrants in Italy by the office of the Minister of the Interior has been occurring since the 1980s (in 1984, they estimated the number of immigrants in Italy to be an astronomical 1,400,000.)
[191] Dini Report, July-Dec. 1995, p. 5.

precipitated social tensions and reactions that could be characterized as xenophobic, especially in areas that display elements of urban decline.[192]

These texts represent what disrupts the social order according to ordinary citizens – "instability in the financial markets," "organized crime," "social tensions," "ideological subversion," "urban decline," and "Islamic fundamentalism." Also, these texts reveal that the political system considers these issues equivalent. It is no surprise that the security services exaggerate the impact of illegal immigration, invent the perils of terrorism when there have been no consistent traces of terrorist activities, and increase the alarm about foreigners. Evidently in this way they justify their own existence, which became more necessary since Italy lost its external enemy with the end of real socialism. More interesting is the fact that the central-leftist government has aligned itself with earlier administrations in accepting this fantastical version of reality. Even more significantly, the relationship between cause and effect has been inverted in attributing the "xenophobic reactions" to illegal immigration as if xenophobia were the consequence of a threat (which has never been demonstrated), and not a public style of defining reality which is divided between intellectuals, opinion makers, and political classes.

2 Left, Right, and Immigration

Between the mobilizations of the first citizens' groups in the early1990s (in Genoa this began in 1993) [193] and the events of the summer of 1997 when Italy decided to repatriate the Albanian *clandestini*, the "immigration panic" swamped Italian public opinion. For the first time since the battle against terrorism, many opinion makers and political leaders came on the scene defending society and its institutions from a collective threat, in this case, an

---

[192] Prodi Report, Jan.-June 1996.

[193] The first instance of an anti-immigration demonstration was in Florence in 1988 when groups of young locals went after immigrants on the streets of the downtown area. An earlier protest by local shop owners precipitated the expulsion of street vendors from the Ponte Vecchio area.

external threat. What is so original about this mobilization against foreigners is its consensual character, its unanimity, its "democracy." Not only the right-wing political parties such as the Northern League, Forza Italia, or National Alliance use the battle against criminal immigrants as a fundamental element in their political platforms, but a wide section of the left-wing parties as well. The era is now past in which that "battle" served a mediating function between separate social groups. The fundamental political problem this reveals is confirmed by the sort of rhetorical questions used by the left and exemplified in the following editorial by Ernesto Galli della Loggia, written during one of the recurring "immigration emergencies."

> [...] For the left, what is at risk in this problem is its social representability (and even the Church has the same issue). Because it's the weaker levels of the population--the urban lower-middle class, the elderly, women, workers in unstable industries, the at-risk segments of the urban population – these are the sectors of society that feel most directly and most negatively the impact from the indiscriminate arrival of waves of immigrants with all the accompanying issues of violence, crime, and insecurity [...] So, does the left still want to represent the weaker levels of society? Does the left represent them now?[194]

That there is no documented or demonstrated relationship between the "waves of immigrants" and the "relative violent phenomena" is irrelevant. As soon as public opinion establishes that such a relationship obviously exists (i.e. "common sense" Galli della Loggia calls it in this same article), then the left assumes ownership. If microcriminality is the concern of the man on the street, and immigrants and gypsies are considered responsible according to public opinion, then the political left, in the name of representing the common man or its electorate, demands that these problems be resolved by tossing overboard all "criminals" and *"clandestini."* This conscious, political – even electoral – strategy that has contributed to the success of the center-left coalition in some local elections by aligning itself with the Northern League has proved itself to

---

[194] Galli della Loggia, E. "Chi non vede gli immigrati," *Corriere della sera.* 18 September 1995.

be a mistake, at least in one instance. This is how the main leader of the Italian left justified the PDS's support for the Dini decree on immigration in the autumn of 1995:

> V. Parlato: "It is admissible to suggest that a crime committed by an *extra-communitari* carries heavier consequences than a crime committed by a native individual. The rule of law would go to the dogs. And in a country like Italy, which has historically been a country of emigration [...]. Also, you'll have to explain to me what the left has to do with the Northern League."
>
> M. D'Alema: "The Northern League has everything to do with the left, and it's no sacrilege to admit it. There is a strong social continuity between the two. The largest working-class party in the North is the Northern League, like it or not. We're cut from the same cloth. The ballots in the administrative elections confirm that there is a very strong tendency among Northern League supporters to vote for our candidates and an equally strong tendency for our members to vote for the Northern League."[195]

My purpose here is not to discuss political tactics[196] but to show how such tactics have perverse social and cultural reactions because they indirectly legitimize the political-ideological campaign of the Northern League. Aside from its role as political and moral avant-garde in the period of the end of the First Republic, the Northern League served a decisive function in mobilizing urban citizens against foreigners, promoting these mobilizations whenever possible and always assuming a political paternity. Supporters, members of Parliament, and senators of the Northern League are marked by racist declarations and their obsessive demands to "register," "expel," and "control" immigrants. But above all, the Northern League and the movements that fall in line behind it have carried out a wide-spread campaign of xenophobic propaganda that has not been ineffective even while its content has often been

---

[195] Interview of V. Parlato with M. D'Alema in *Il Manifesto*, 31 October, 1995.

[196] It took nearly two years before this leader would speak out about the "racism" in the Northern League, albeit with a certain reluctance. Even among scientific and neutral observers, the racism of the Northern League is frequently underestimated. One exception would be the work of A. Burgio. *L'invenzione delle razze*. Rome: Manifestolibri, 1998.

grotesque. Following are several telling passages from a political pamphlet that was distributed widely in the spring of 1997 by the party that D'Alema said was "cut from the same cloth" as the workers' movement.

> Let's examine this invasion as a whole and look at the strategy that promotes and sustains it. In general, an invasion of a people and its territory by another group is violent and occurs spontaneously, almost by accident. Invasions need generals, politicians, and enormous financial resources from the foreign land attempting the conquest. But the invasion we face has the strangest characteristics: it isn't violent, for the time being, but it has its own strategists who are not foreigners and also has immense financial resources.
>
> The strategists, don't you know, are our own mafiosi politicians, our own priests of a misguided clergy, the considerable financial resources are expended by our own government which extracts funds from its citizens [...] The final objective of this invasion is not to conquer a territory but to overthrow a society that has worked and sacrificed to take care of its own needs, a society which has for centuries been sustained by a liberal, Christian culture and wants to transform it into a multi-racial society, materially and spiritually impoverished, marked by hatred, tensions, and misery from the Third World, growing ever closer to Islam and further from Christianity [...] The greatest hope of these strategists would be to transform all of Europe along these same lines [...] The Italian Communist Party and PDS preach the basic doctrines of Marxism. They are priming future political leaders, sensitizing the *extracommunitari* to eventually vote for the communists. These efforts to sensitize *extracommunitari* are directed especially toward Muslims who are less resistant to becoming communists than their orthodox Catholic counterparts.[197]

In their rhetoric and their iconography, positions of this nature recall myths about Jewish conspiracies against "Christian civilization." As evident in Figure 21, such attitudes move toward an explicit demand to eliminate Albanians. They reveal a certain anti-Semitic, racist subculture that persists, reformulating and adapting itself according to the new Northern nationalism. This subculture tends

---

[197] SAL (Sindacato autonomista ligure). *L'invasione extracommunitaria e la sua strategia.* Genoa, April 1997: 2.

to gloss over the role of that anti-Semitic racism in our history, particularly in its desire to recast fascism as a fundamental component of our national heritage.

L'INVASIONE EXTRA COMUNITARIA
OBIETTIVI E STRATEGIA

Figure 20	Figure 21
Invasions and Conspiracies	Northern League Electoral Poster

The illustration in Figure 20 reproduces almost word for word slogans published in the fascist magazine *La Difesa della Razza* (In Defense of Our Race).[198] But there is something even worse, if that is possible. The same rhetoric used by the SAL in this pamphlet and the use of the term "strategy" (Figure 20) recall a famous apocryphal document, "The Protocols of Zion's

[198] See Centro Furio Jesi. *La menzogna della razza. Documenti e immagini del razzismo e dell'antisemitismo fascista.*

Sages," which has been used for over a century as "proof" of Jewish conspiracies to bring down Western society. Let the reader determine if the
following citation from this sham pamphlet doesn't bear a family resemblance
to the pamphlet published by the SAL, which represents, and I emphasize, the
official propaganda of the Northern League.

> The ends justify the means.
> In making our plans, we must pay attention not only to what is good or moral,
> but what is necessary and advantageous [...].
> We have a plan before us that outlines a strategy from which we must not
> deviate or we will destroy the work of centuries [...].
> We must educate all of Christian society along certain lines until they throw up
> their hands in despair when any undertaking requires individual initiative [...].
> By these means we can pressure Christians to the point that they will be forced
> to ask us to govern them internationally. When we achieve this position, we can
> assume the governing powers of the whole world and form a universal super-
> government. In place of the existing ones, we will set up one colossal government
> called "Super-government Administration." Its arms will extend like great
> tentacles and support an organization that will certainly bring about the
> submission of all nations.[199]

The xenophobic documents of the Northern League circulate widely in all
of the cities most sensitive to the "immigration emergency." Even if such
documents did not always translate into consistent actions, their symbolic value
is significant. Along with the "squads" against *extracommunitari*" and street
vendors, and other disturbing initiatives, such as the "reward" of one million
lire offered by the city council of Acqui Terme for illegal Albanian immigrants
in September, 1997, these documents express an extremist point of view in

---

[199] Citations are from "I protocolli dei savi di Sion." Published in an appendix of S. Romano. *I falsi protocolli. Il "complotto ebraico" dalla Russia di Nicola II a oggi.* Milan: Corbaccio, 1992. These apocryphal protocols were fabricated by the czarist police at the beginning of the twentieth century and formed a central part of the Nazi and fascist anti-Semitic propaganda.

local society that wants to defend itself against the threat of invasion that it has itself constructed.[200]

Actually, as will be shown at the conclusion of this chapter, the presumed panic about the invasion is shared by the political right as well as by the democratic intellectuals of the left, regardless of the different rhetoric they employ. This means that the left, while it has not sustained overt xenophobic campaigns, has nonetheless displaced or minimized them. Undervaluing xenophobia does not merely manifest a willingness to surrender principles to obtain votes, but reveals the traditional mistrust of labor parties toward immigrants. This mistrust deepens not only when the left vindicates the national political tradition with its inevitable *Realpolitik*, but that mistrust is shared by social sectors that had always seemed above suspicion of prejudice against immigrants. The following passage comes from a political pamphlet published by a new, rising star of the radical left:

> The Fourth World War with its process of destruction-depopulation and reconstruction-reordering causes the relocation of millions of people. It will be their destiny to continually wander, carrying their nightmares with them, and they will represent a threat to the job stability of workers in many different nations, a useful enemy to hide the silhouette of the bosses, and a pretext that gives meaning to the racist foolishness that neoliberalism promotes. Figure 3 [a circle] [...] is the symbol of the wandering nightmare of global migration, and is a roller coaster of terror that moves throughout the world.[201]

---

[200] In his foundational work on the extermination of the Jews, Raul Hilberg (*The Destruction of the European Jews, 3 Volume Set*, New Haven, CT: Yale University Press, 3rd Edition, 2003) shows how cultural irrationality and organizational rationality can coexist. A comparison between the persecution and extermination of the Jews historically and the current politics of wealthy Northern countries' exclusion of underprivileged foreigners of course cannot be propounded. However, the fact remains that the nationalist rhetorics used against the Jews a century ago find disturbing parallels in the current campaign against "*clandestini*," and "criminal immigrants," etc. As Z. Bauman shows, the exterminitaon of the Jews would not have been possible without the collaboration of "rational" structures. See Bauman, Z. *Modernity and the Holocaust*, Ithaca, NY: Cornell University Press, 2001.

[201] Subcomandante Marcos. *Our Word is Our Weapon*, New York: Seven Stories Press, 2003.

The significance of this passage is self-evident. The new leaders of the liberationist movements would do well to clarify the social contradictions promoted by neoliberalism. Migration is not necessarily a nightmare, or a "roller coaster of terror," and even less do migrants "represent a threat to the job stability of workers." Aside from the rhetoric, the fact emerges that the political culture represented by this text seems unable to resolve the contradiction between defending local culture against globalization (or "neoliberalism") and the fact that individuals who are forced to abandon their own cultures or those who freely migrate still constitute a group of workers, i.e. the proletariat (or are even more removed from the social fabric if they are separated from their children).[202] These new voices of the left are incapable of establishing the historical parallel between the current "wanderers" and those populations which have for centuries been forced from the land only to swell the ranks of workers employed in nascent industrial societies, like those dangerous classes criminalized by the law that Marx defined as "bloody." Let's review a passage from Marx that is ignored these days:

> The proletariat created by the breaking-up of the bands of feudal retainers and by the forcible expropriation of the people from the soil, this free and rightless proletariat could not possibly be absorbed by the nascent manufactures as fast as it was thrown upon the world. On the other hand, these men, suddenly dragged from their accustomed mode of life, could not as immediately adapt themselves to the discipline of their new condition. They were turned in massive quantities into beggars, robbers, vagabonds, partly from inclination, in most cases under the force of circumstances. Hence at the end of the fifteenth and during the whole of the sixteenth centuries, *a bloody legislation against vagabondage* was enforced throughout Western Europe. The fathers of the present working class were chastised for their enforced transformation into vagabonds and paupers. *Legislation treated them as "voluntary" criminals, and assumed that it was*

---

[202] This is not an isolated case. In a study on the working class resistance to Nazism, S. Bologna defines "working class xenophobia" as a form of protest against the loss of "civilization of the working class condition" caused by immigration. See Bologna, S. "Prefazione alla seconda edizione." *Nazismo e classe operaia 1933-1993.* Rome: Manifestolibri, 1996. 49-50.

entirely within their powers to go on working under the old conditionswhich in fact no longer existed.[203]

This passage, as the entire chapter from *Capital* from which it comes, shows the relationship between economic transformations and the legal conditions of people that today seem lost on the left. "The fathers of the contemporary working class were punished [...] for transforming into wanderers." Hardly a case of migrations as "a threat to the job stability of workers." Obviously, I am not attempting to establish a historical parallel between the criminalization of agricultural workers displaced from their lands at the beginning of the modern era and the criminalization of contemporary workers who have no civil rights. Rather, I am interested in highlighting how Marx evokes the horror of the double punishment of "free" labor (the factory and the gallows)[204] that resounds in the contemporary duality of "illegal labor/ repression of *"extracommunitari."* This offers an interpretive key for understanding what is at risk in the political and cultural conflict over immigration, and therefore the vice that closes over whoever attempts to flee from the political and institutional conditions of the capitalist labor market, both historically and now. The migrant who effects an actual secession from the labor market becomes a potential criminal and above all, a stigmatized entity by both the right and the left.[205]

The current alignment of some exponents of the left with the campaigns against *clandestini* and "immigrants who commit crimes" cannot even be praised for originality. It imitates events that occurred in France at the beginning of the 1980s when the French Communist Party disguised the "popular" initiatives

---

[203] Marx, Karl. *Capital: A Critique of Political Economy.* Vol. 1, New York: Penguin Classics, 1992. 896.

[204] As Marx noted, in every age, whoever attempts to avoid punishment not only is repressed, but becomes a criminal. M. Rediker examines the stories of seventeeth-century piracy in this light (*Sulle tracce dei pirati.*Casale Monferrato: Edizioni Piemme, 1995). For a parallel perspective, see Linebaugh, P. *The London Hanged. Crime and Civil Society in the Eighteenth Century.* London: Penguin, 1991.

[205] Moulier-Boutang, Y. *Le salariat bridé, Origines de la politique migratory, constitution du salariat et contrôle de la mobilité du travail.* Paris: Doctorate Thesis from University FNSP-IEP, 1997.

against immigrants. The words of E. Balibar decades ago regarding the party's about face on migration issues could easily be applied to the citizens' mobilizations occurring in Italy, as well as to the front that the left enjoys:

> This is abdication, this is surrender to racism and populism [...] that is suddenly laid bare by bulldozer operations, by the administrative "quotas" aimed at imposing a "limit of tolerance" where we have the power and by the risk we run without the least hesitation of equating every Maghrebi with a potential drug dealer! [...] The local community governments that are communist, or at least some of them [...] are tempted to find a new electoral base by exploiting the fears and prejudices that they believe they are unable to combat. [206]

3 The Intellectuals Enter the Field

In Italy, the adhesion of the left to the culture of "law and order" is not recent and has certainly been reinforced by the popularity of judicial solutions to political conflicts which began at the outset of the 1970s during our years of domestic terrorism, and has continued through the so-called "moral crises of the First Republic." It is equally true, however, that the demand for accountability from those who break the law (whether dealing with big-time corruption or small-time crooks) seems to dominate current public opinion, including that segment that would define itself as "democratic." The time is now past in which the intellectuals, either leftist or democratic, could discuss social deviance as a social phenomenon and not simply as criminality. An example of this frequent tendency among those intellectuals who have just rediscovered the fascination of the liberal culture of laws that are "severe but just," is a citation from an editorial about the death of Tarzan Suljic, the gypsy boy who was killed several years ago in the *carabinieri* compound:

---

[206] Balibar, E. "Da Charonne a Vitry," *Le frontiere della democrazia.* Rome: Manifestolibri, 1993. 31 and 33. Original article published in *Le nouvel observateur* 852, 9 March 1981, for which the author was immediately expelled from the French communist party.

Tarzan [...] was a professional burglar, the best of his gang, and so he had a good reputation [...]; if I can express my private opinion, and I say this with pity, Tarzan was killed because his reputation was too good: he had to make a great deal every day and never get caught ever. Caught in the act, inside an apartment, and taken to the official compound, he fought with everyone day and night and he ended up with a bullet in his head. *We'll never know if someone shot him on purpose, but the child was practically condemned to death by his relatives who had trapped him in this vice: forever stealing and forever escaping in order to continue stealing.*[207]

Probably no one will ever know if someone shot him on purpose or not. It is indisputable that in a civil society with an established juridical culture, the responsibility for the death of a child that was *alive* when he entered the compound, even though he was assumed to be guilty of burglary, rests squarely with the person who shot the bullet, and certainly not with the boy's "clan." This is not just bigoted rhetoric about justice that becomes lachrymose when describing the boy's funeral ("a meal among the lamentations, with the relatives seated around, hunched and bowed over").[208] What we see at work here is the unwritten but widely held notion that can be summed up in the motto: "They were asking for it." According to this motto, gypsies, refugees, legal and illegal immigrants, also thieves, drug addicts and any other kind of deviant, as Marx would have said, are all exclusively responsible for what befalls them, even if it is fatal.

This brand of ethics,[209] if we can call it that, implicitly reintroduces the death penalty and not just for those who have committed capital offenses but also for whoever falls outside of the moral order for which "normal" society has assumed moral authority. So, if a ship full of Albanians deluded by the mirage of

---

[207] Camon, F. "Veneto, La violenza è di casa," *La Stampa.* 4 September 1995: 9. (My italics).
[208] *Ibid.*
[209] This can be classified as a code of ethics (laying aside its questionable and repellent nature) in that it seeks to reason about "responsibilities." In her studies in cognitive anthropology, Mary Douglas demonstrated how rhetorics of "risk" and cultural contamination have a close connection to the strategic dilemas of contemporary western society. See Douglas, M. *Risk and Blame: Essays in Cultural Theory*, New York. Routledge, 1994.

prosperous Italy drowns off the cost of Puglia, or if "Africans" drown in the Tyrrhenian Sea (or were perhaps thrown into the water by the sailors), then "they were asking for it."[210] One would find him or herself accused of vacuous "solidarity" or "ideology" for bringing a court action to explain the context for these deaths, the patrols from the different branches of law enforcement, the fundamental human right to flee from starvation or to find a better life, or even the right to provide asylum that societies considered "civilized" should respect, and not forgetting the responsibilities of western nations toward those countries who freed themselves from communism, believing that they were participating in a vast celebration of free people. The morality of "they were asking for it" re-echoes with the executionary attitudes of the dominant classes at the time of Charles Dickens, yet it reigns now in western society, inaugurated by the neoliberal turn of Ronald Reagan and Margaret Thatcher.[211] It is aimed against every kind of marginal, underprivileged insider or outsider, but targets especially foreigners and migrants inasmuch as they epitomize who is "outside" but presumes to "come in." This morality, obviously, invokes "common sense" and "realism" but is not above utilizing questionable humor. For example, in expressing his support of assigning immigrants magnetic identity cards, Alberto Arbasino commented:

> The term "registration" will only shock those who are not already registered in multiple ways, with a social security card, a tax identification number, a driver's license, gun license and so on. And how can "magnetic cards" seem like

[210] On 1 December, 1995, fifteen Albanians who were trying to reach Italy in an inflatable boat drowned off the coast of Puglia. No one indicated the relationship between this event and the Italian military's patrols of the coasts. Instead, in commenting on the tragedy, a progressive MP suggested "more stringent measures [for the *clandestini* awaiting deportation] and regulations requiring proof of stable housing." "Boat people, un traffico inarrestabile," *La Repubblica.* 2 December 1995: 5.
[211] See the observations of G. Vidal. *The Decline and Fall of the American Empire*, Tucson, AZ: Odonian Press, 2002, and Ehrenreich, B. *The Worst Years of our Lives. Irreverent Notes from a Decade of Greed.* New York: Harper & Row, 1990.

freedom-destroyers when they are easily flaunted by opening your wallet and used with no embarrassment at the cash machine?[212]

Putting a state imposed, magnetic identification card – an electric collar – on the same level as a credit card, evidently renders the wearer more elegant according to this commentator who champions a national "aesthetic house-cleaning." Arbasino's articles, while they never miss a chance to cast migrants as criminals and to call those who are against expulsion "typical chicken Italians," are still tame when compared to the invectives of Guido Ceronetti, who is often hailed in the press as the proud opponent of facile clichés. On the front page of a national daily he published the following:

> Please explain to me, Mr. Attorney, or Honorable Prime Minister, why knifings, thefts, or scattered corpses are still considered punishable by law when these actions are committed by our dear co-nationals, but legal action, the due course of law, etc. regardless of how inadequate or tardy it may be, when dealing with Albanians, gypsies, and Maghrebi become lost in a fog that allows the guilty to get off with hasty prison releases and expulsion orders that exist only on paper? [...] The system remains a machine of prevention and repression that merely spins its wheels, spins them faster and faster, especially when dealing with undesirable foreigners. And they aren't stupid: they only would be if they didn't take advantage of such a situation [...] It would already be a relief to hear our grand guardians define immigration as savage, especially in its criminal aspects, to call it a social calamity, a flood [...]. No, *that*, that would be a social calamity: the arrival with no departure date of fanatics, the mentally imbalanced, predators and prostitutes, who build up walls and break down doors [...][213]

Charitable readers could attribute these tirades to the hypochondria of an intellectual who is ignorant of the reality of urban life, and therefore dismiss

---

[212] Arbasino, A. "Immigrati, una nuova commedia." *La Repubblica.* 24 September 1995: 16. A few years ago, Arbasino called the home cultures of immigrants "nomadic and parassitic." It has taken several years for intellectuals to distance themselves from this type of moralizing. See the cautious article of Tabucchi, A. "Intellettuali copritevi, ora piovono pietre." *Corriere della sera.* 1 April 1997: 6.

[213] Ceronetti, G. "L'invasione che nessuno vuol capire." *La Stampa.* 14 October 1996.

them as inoffensive. Nevertheless, such tirades are published at a steady pace by the major national papers and therefore, given the status of the authors, they literally form the dominant opinion regarding immigration, criminality, and urban problems. Letters are published daily in *la Repubblica, La Stampa, Corriere della Sera* and *l'Unità* that echo the same tirades of Arbasino, Ceronetti, and many others. The commentators of leftist radio programs are astounded because their own listeners seem to share what appears to be an actual mass paranoia.[214] Below is an example of one such letter. The attitudes expressed are revealing, not only because it was published shortly after a ship of Albanians was sunk, but also for the positive response it received from an authoritative journalist who writes a column with readers' letters for *la Repubblica*.

"Frightened People Accused of Racism"

[...] The demand for regulation is answered with conferences about "racism." What do you mean "racism!" These are legitimate manifestations of discomfort, fear, difficulty in sharing food, jobs, and homes with all of these new, desperate people. The Gozzini law allowed numerous murderers and terrorists out of prison. So what's going to happen now, and it's easy to foresee that it will, when the masses of armed, desperate people begin to steal and start gang warfare, as has already begun in Turin and not just in the San Salvario district? Should we start saying prayers in the Caritas headquarters? 85 % of crimes go unpunished. Poor Christians who are simply afraid are accused of racism. Actually, if bad faith didn't cloud the issue, it would be obvious that the real driving forces are the interests of the Vatican, the Green Party, the left, and International Islam which has huge economic resources, along with all the countries that benefit by dumping their starving, uncontrollable masses onto others. France, Germany, and England all had huge colonies, and even they're closing their borders. Italy, who usually tries to solve its problems by drowning them in a sea of talking, lets the unfortunate Manconi, Bertinotti, or Caritas determine our future and the future of our children by brainwashing our children about solidarity and anti-racism instead of giving them an education and jobs.

Franco Resta, Turin

---

[214] "Choc a Radio Popolare, emittente della sinistra doc. 'Microfono aperto': in onda l'intolleranza." *Corriere della sera.* 1 April 1997: 5.

"Barbara Palombelli Replies"

We keep talking about being invaded by destitute people. This letter, so sincere, and so harsh, was written in the name of "poor frightened Christians [...]." They are victims, too--everyone who has been mugged, robbed, or assaulted by the new barbarian hordes of all colors and races. It's true, the citizens of Italy are suffering from a lack of regulations: just look at the city streets that have been given over to rackets of prostitution, the intersections where window washers become more aggressive, parks that are out of control [...]. People are right to be afraid. It's not about racial hatred: it's a question of safety for everyone, including the honest immigrants who are in the majority. The fears expressed by Franco Resta are shared by many other good people who in their hearts do not feel they are racists.[215]

The original letter is not as shocking as the supportive response to its obsessive, persecutory perception of reality (the reference to "numerous murderers and terrorists released from prison" because of the Gozzini law, or the "interests" of the Vatican, the left, or International Islam with its "huge economic resources" [...]). This is not just an example of journalistic legitimization of the growing paranoia in public opinion, but seems to be an actual political standpoint that has been adopted by a significant sector of the mass media. Shortly after this revealing exchange of letters, an even more important journalist followed suit in expressing what was to be the political standpoint of the left regarding microcriminality and immigration:

The voluble debate over the presumed racism of millions of Italians continues [...]. The pretended left doesn't understand that Italy today is a country pressured by many problems, but one is decisive: the conviction that the State is unable to guarantee the safety of its own citizens from the effects of crime. On Tuesday, April 1, an article by Ernesto Galli della Loggia in *Corriere della Sera* and a letter from Franco Resta published in *La Repubblica* clearly outlined the situation.[216]

[215] *La Repubblica*. 1 April 1997: 10.
[216] Pansa, G. "Ma sì, guardiamo Televalona." *L'Espresso*. 10 April 1997: 56. After this, *L'Espresso* published a letter protesting Pansa's comments. "I would never have thought that I

It is irrelevant whether the residents of Turin determine the viewpoint of the media or if the media utilize the letters of neighborhood *imprenditori morali* to justify their campaign which mixes political motives with a paranoid perception of reality. The fact remains that a supposition devoid of any empirical evidence ("the invasion of delinquent foreigners threatens exasperated citizens in this crises of the State") progressively reinforces itself due to a cycle that is fed by politicians, citizens, and journalists – a cultural tautology of fear. Within this mechanism, journalists acts as politicians, citizens act as *imprenditori morali*, and these in turn act as journalists. Consider the admonitions that a high-level trade union functionary offers to the left regarding the politics of migration:

> The problem itself is simple: determine who is not a refugee, was not persecuted or evacuated due to a war, but crosses the border without documents and is therefore breaking the law. Referring to demographic imbalances and world-wide poverty as the motivating force every time some one tries to take illegal immigration into hand, while these are painful realities, merely offers an alibi, an ideological justification for covering up administrative inertia and ineptitude.[217]

Defining the clandestine entering of a country as an offense (and what type of offense? Criminal, political, or administrative?) ignores a priori the "painful realities" that expatriates carry and offers a grossly over-simplified solution to the problem. Inversely, bringing up those issues is "an ideological alibi." Notice that Bolaffi says the same things less directly in the *la Repubblica* article cited above. Unlike many progressive contortionists, Bolaffi clearly states that what happens outside our borders has nothing to do with us. Making *"clandestinità"* a crime confirms the inviolability of borders, and therefore of national space,

could feel so indignant about an article by Giampaolo Pansa as I was reading his Bestiario on Albanians and the left. The first reason is that it oozes that hypocrisy that has become a hallmark of the intelligentsia of the left that first demonstrated in support of marginal people and then decided to label them "mafiosi," and now prefers to ask for expulsion orders and regulations. The feeling I get is that when it comes to immigration, there is no difference between the left and the right." Romeo Aureli, Rome (*L'Espresso*, 17 April, 1997. 215).
[217] Bolaffi, G. "Diritto d'asilo all'italiana." *la Repubblica.* 8 October 1995: 9.

which has become a battle-cry of the democratic left and of influential public opinion generally.[218]

All this would be bad enough, but expected if it didn't clash against all the discourse of economic globalization, freedom and flexibility in the workplace, etc. which has become so common in those same sectors that call for draconian measures against those who do not expatriate unless "they are refugees, persecuted, or evacuated due to a war." But consider this: what is the difference between an individual who is a "war evacuee" and someone who is an "economic evacuee," between a Bosnian or Croatian or Serb fleeing ethnic cleansing from and Algerian who leaves his village because he's terrorized by the government or by renegade fundamentalist militants, or an Albanian who flees because he's starving to death? Who can forget the Vietnamese boat people and the international disdain that accompanied that tragedy at the end of the 1970s? Is it not equally true that the only crime of the Albanian or "Maghrebi" boat people is that they are fleeing economic death rather than political violence? The prejudiced (and therefore ideological) character of Bolaffi-style arguments remains that refugees are rejected at borders simply because they are inconvenient, even if they truly are "war refugees," such as the Kurds. Never once do these self-styled Catos provide data about the cataclysmic demographic dimensions that they threateningly evoke in their tirades. Once again, that task falls to those who call for solidarity, the Catholics, the volunteers, and the associations for the defense of civil liberties. "Tell us once and for all how much money do you really want?" Ernesto Galli Della Loggia severely asks in the front page of *Corriere della Sera*,[219] as if the problem were merely money and not the need for an unemotional response to the structural problem of the contemporary global economy, a problem that will certainly remain with us in the following decades.

---

[218] There are those who claim that xenophobia among Italians represents a way of reacting to a lack of national spirit. See Galli della Loggia, E. "La nazione che ci manca," *Corriere della sera*.1 April 1997: 1 and 8.

[219] See Galli della Loggia, E. "Chi non vede gli immigrati," *Corriere della sera*. 18 September 1995.

To read a balanced opinion in all this debate, we need a true liberal, and one that demonstrates true social sensitivity far more advanced than that of the Italian left (even more so of the center or right). In several recent interviews Ralf Dahrendorf has commented on how the globalization of the economy and the opening of new markets in Asia and South America has caused a certain segment of the population to grow richer but determines that a far greater segment of the population grows poorer. Furthermore, in these new regions, the development of businesses and competition doesn't bring a substantial democritization of society. The authoritarianism of the Malaysian, Chinese, Mexican, or Peruvian governments who are viewed positively by both conservatives and free-market supporters in the west, join the market economy to the violation of human rights. Under these new conditions, one could emigrate out of simple need or in order to flee a latent civil war. To think that wealthy states can isolate themselves inside a fortress is not only unrealistic given that economic circuits transcend national borders, but this explicitly violates the founding ideals of western democracy. I am not referring to the ideals spoken of by philosophers, but those formally incorporated in the democratic constitutions after World War II. Dahrendorf doesn't hide the problems that globalization raises for the weaker levels of western society, but with no verbal gymnastics he defines our rejection of workers that are not native to the west:

> Many of these "underprivileged" are not only economically marginalized: they are excluded for other reasons: they are "foreign" because of race, nationality, religion or for some other distinctive sign that is used as an excuse for discrimination, xenophobia, and often violence. The social groups that are in decline, that 40% of the population that over the last ten years has seen a constant decline in their income, are the fertile field in which these feelings take root. Borders, even social borders, are always clearest and most visible to those who are closest to them. Far from being a fad only in those areas ravaged by war such as Bosnia Herzegovina, the "ethnic cleansing" now in vogue threatens to overwhelm us all.[220]

[220] Dahrendorf, R. *Economic Opportunity, Civil Society, and Political Liberty*, Copenhagen: UNRISD, 1995, 35-36.

IV Scientists and Immigrants

He knows what he's talking about the way a blind man understands colors.[221]

1 Science, Opinions, Immigration

Contrary to common belief in our culture, scientific inquiry is less rigorous and untainted by methodological viewpoints than one would tend to think.[222] For example, theories are not necessarily abandoned when they cannot be proven false, as K. Popper advocates,[223] because, as in every other aspect of social life, an opposing opinion has grown up, and no one has taken the trouble to verify it completely, but it ends up burying hypotheses considered to be authoritative.[224] It is also debatable if scientific reasoning is always free from the deplorable methods of general, human reasoning (metaphors, analogies and other rhetorical figures, groundless hypotheses, circular explanations, self-referentiality, ad hoc arguments). In fact, scientific progress is often based on hare-brained ideas, notions and concepts from separate fields, spurious methods and methodological

---

[221] Hazlitt,W. *Sull'ignoranza delle persone colte.* Rome: Fazi, 1996.
[222] The scientific analytical practices to which I allude here are a specialized branch of sociology. See Elkana, Y. *Sciences and Cultures: Anthropological and Historical Studies of the Sciences,* Heidelberg: Springer, 1981.
[223] Popper, K. *Conjectures and Refutations: The Growth of Scientific Knowledge,* New York: Routledge (5th Edition), 2002.
[224] Bloor, D. *The Sociology of Scientific Knowledge,* New York: Routledge, 2008.

tricks.[225] This is not all bad, and in fact, the truth in scientific research often arises from creativity more than from scientific legalism. This is true for the exact or "hard" sciences as well as for the "soft" sciences, including social science.

Beyond epistemological dimensions, scientists' habits seem less free from taint than general opinion would hold. From plagiarism, fraud, and bias to personal battles that are often the basis for "scientific controversies," science is not immune from the problems experienced in any other symbolic sector in which human beings operate. Thus, even in the realm of science, ideology, material interests, passions and prejudices play a determinative role even if masked by the neutral, clinical language employed by scientists.

Science is not that image of the isolated, pristine world that is circulated by science's lawmakers, and taken up by its fans. Between science and normal everyday life there is no sense of continuity, but a terrain divided between everyday society of the man on the street and the scientists, even though scientists, too, live, converse, and work in the same terrestrial world. Science and the world of daily life in its innumerable dimensions are not distant and opposed, but interwoven and superimposed. Different spheres of scientific research are far more sensitive to pressure from the media, economic and political interests and even the shifting moods of the public than the detached, clinical, scientific mindset would have us believe.[226] It is worth noting that studies on the osmotic relationship between public opinion and science have concentrated more on the exposition of science within the real world rather

---

[225] For the use of metaphors in scientific discourse, see Hesse, M. *Models and Analogies in Science*, Notre Dame, INN.: Notre Dame University Press, 1967. One of the most brilliant analyses of the elasticity of mathematical methods of demonstration is found in Lakatos, I. *The Methodology of Scientific Research Programmes: Volume 1: Philosophical Papers*, Cambridge: Cambridge University Press, 1980, which is engagingly commented by Bloor, D. This perspective is not accepted by the more conservative epistemologists who study external influences. See Popper, K "Normal Science and Its Dangers," I. Lakatos and A. Musgrave, *Criticism and the Growth of Knowledge*, Cambridge: Cambridge University Press, 1970. See also Popper, K. *Conjectures and Refutations: The Growth of Scientific Knowledge*, New York: Routledge (5th Edition), 2002. The continued debate on these issues can be found in Hollis, M. and S. Lukes, eds. *Rationality and Relativism*. Oxford, Blackwell, 1982.
[226] Bucchi, M., *Science and the Media.* London: Routledge, 1998.

than how the latter is influenced by scientific rhetoric. In other words, research has focused more on how common reasoning influences science and less on science's capacity to direct common reasoning. Thus, a great deal has been written on persuasion, or the rhetorical and stylistic instruments used in written documents, and while these instruments are not scientific in and of themselves, thanks to them, some scientists have convinced their colleagues to adopt a scientific theory or point of view. However, very little has been written about the role that scientific discourse has had in forming the opinions of the non-experts, those people, such as politicians, who have in mind the cognitive and communicative horizon of the ignorant as their reference point.

To examine the relationship between science and the world of daily life, it is helpful to consider the osmosis that occurs between science and public opinion in its many articulations. Given that the subject of this analysis is the scientific discourse about immigration – a theme profoundly conditioned if not constituted by prejudices in public opinion that influence communications and decisions – it is necessary to focus attention on the relationship between social science, political systems, and the media. It is well-known that political systems do not operate based on scientific competence in the sense that no politician, either functioning within the institution as a minister or representative of a political party, is required to have any specific know how. True, if a government minister has had a specific career, such as judge, he or she might become the Minister of Justice, or a businessman or financial expert could become Minister of Finance, or an economist could be Minister of the Budget, or a university professor Minister of Education. But even in these specific offices, as with political offices in general, it is considered completely legitimate and acceptable for ministers to enter into office who are without any competence in that area. A minister's functions are essentially political, and no past professional experience guarantees the ability to fulfill the numerous and varied tasks required of a specific position. Government administration, companies, consultants, and ad hoc committees contribute to the practices a political leader supports (and who also makes decisions based on political considerations). The very nature of political considerations makes it so that expertise is called upon only ex-post to justify political choices, party strategies, and legislative provisions. This arouses irritation among experts who often ignore the practical everyday functions of political procedures and demand a more important role, asking to be consulted regularly.

However, the fact that experts are not assigned an explicit or official role in making political decisions or establish procedures does not mean that they do not exercise any influence on political processes. Often their influence, though indirect, can be decisive. An epidemiologist, a professor of commercial science, a public administration analyst, or an expert on electoral systems can't be ignored if the task is adapting the measures to combat AIDS or altering the income tax forms, the structure of the postal service, or the mechanisms of political representation. Outside of the experts' role as consultants in specific political issues – which sometimes leads the experts to enter politics, as has sometimes occurred in Italy in the so-called "Administrations of Technicians" – the experts still have a formidable instrument of influence: the media.

Unlike other countries such as the United States, in Europe and especially in Italy, the experts use the press, and for decades the television and radio, to make proclamations, expound points of view, or make comments, proposals, and invectives. According to their competence – either real or imagined – they actually replace the political commentators in the authoritative front-page articles as well as journalists specializing in specific issues. Frequently we see that no one casts their expertise in doubt, expertise that is often established by their success in publishing professional articles, or their writing ability, or their visibility from television exposure. Presumed competence and visibility reinforce each other in a circular way so that the same names attract attention and are disputed in newspapers, and invited on television programs for exorbitant fees. The result, and this is typically Italian, is that professors of political science, philosophy, or German write articles about domestic politics, art teachers comment on soccer, sociologists remark on advertising, not to mention all the others who modestly share what they know, or think they know, within the realm of their own area of expertise.

A politician generally has little time for reading books, but still has to look at the newspapers. And although politicians probably have little regard for the opinions of professors and experts, it is indisputable that the experts help create the cognitive background against which the politicians operate. As discussed in chapter 2, regarding issues of migration and information, it is the media, and particularly the press, that constitutes the cognitive background for the formation of what is considered to be "public opinion." The leader of a political party gathers information from many sources – private polls, surveys commissioned by specialized agencies, conferences, relations with leaders who are peripheral to "what the voter base is thinking." However, at every level, the principle cognitive filter is always constituted by the media. That the media feeds directly on the opinions expressed by politicians in interviews, official announcements, and press conferences, makes it so that the "facts" and opinions about those facts are created in a circular way in a process of interaction between public opinion and the political machine. In this way, social "emergencies" of all kinds are created, including the "immigration emergency." I submit that professors, experts, and intellectuals in general, because of the very role that they have acquired in the formation of public opinion, play a significant role, if not a decisive role, in this interaction. They contribute in a myriad of ways, since their viewpoints are transmitted via the press and the media, to the formation of the opinion that the political system draws upon in its decision-making processes. In a reflection on the public function of economists, Keynes alludes to this very sort of effective influence of ideas:

> […] The ideas of economists and political philosophers, whether right or wrong, are more powerful than is commonly believed. Actually, the world is governed by few things outside of these. Men of action, who believe themselves to be free from any external intellectual influence are often slaves to the ideas of some bygone economist. The insane who hold power hear an idea in passing from some academic scribbler and their frenzies distil around it. I am confident that

the power of traditional interests is highly exaggerated compared to the progressive affirmation of ideas.[227]

The legitimization of the experts in public debate, a recognized duty, depends above all on their "science." This is true mainly for those strategic sectors of public life such as economics and finance. In our numerical, pragmatic culture, oriented toward short-term or mid-range quantitative evaluations, the publication or diffusion of scientific "data" on any aspect of social or political life has in and of itself an enormous power of persuasion, particularly for specific, factual issues. Statistics, economic indicators, or electoral surveys, simply because they are formulated in technical language, are considered reliable. In a market society that depends directly on percentage-based variations (in inflation, unemployment, interest levels, fluctuations in the stock market, or exchange rates with foreign currency), numbers have an almost magical power of persuasion. This is even more true when our contemporary concept of communication demands the transmission of rapid, up-to-date information that is at the same time "objective," and not problematic, a demand that is satisfied far more easily by a language of numbers rather than by verbal communication.[228]

But the force of persuasion wielded by the magic power of numbers extends inevitably to the magicians as well, who are legitimized as authorities by concerning themselves with "technical" issues as well as with general prospective, strategic issues. In this arena, professors enjoy a special legitimacy based not only on their area of competency, but by the authority of their social role as experts, whether their expertise is called upon or not. In other words, the prestige of their role constitutes a privileged access to public debate. Thus, an economist could authoritatively comment on the political choice to reduce loans in the social state, or a geneticist could offer opinions on the public

---

[227] Keynes, J.M. *The General Theory of Employment, Interest and Money*, New York: Macmillan Publishers, 1936. For a brilliant analysis od the role of science in the production of social prejudices, see Gould, S.J. *The Mismeasure of Man*, New York: W. W. Norton, 1981.

[228] Ritzer, G. *McDonaldization: The Reader*, Thousand Oaks, CA: Pine Forge Press, (2nd Edition), 2006. This study analyzes how information in contemporary society is serialized in response to standardized and uniform consumption of the same goods.

definition of "race," or a pathologist or expert of AIDS could comment on the sexual habits of young people, a demographer discuss the reduction or control of migration trends, and a philosopher could expound on anything discussed publicly. Clearly, their authority is not damaged by the obvious consideration that in these debates the experts go beyond their specific area of competence: they are speaking "of something else," they are "doing something else," namely opinionating rather than doing science. But they are speaking in the name of science, and that gives them the right to be listened to.

That they can speak "outside" of science, and yet remain scientists for all intents and purposes means that they can appeal to "extra-scientific" discussions (such as papers do with the "man on the street" interview), and yet continue to implicitly maintain the pretence of expressing themselves scientifically. Just as certain sociologists or psychologists untiringly debate about love or the attitudes of young people, and say the same things that we who have no expertise say to our friends over dinner or at the bar, but they are consulted and listened to because they are sociologists and psychologists, so scientists can transmit their obvious, non-scientific arguments with the security that their arguments will still be authoritative. In this way, they offer a formidable contribution to reinforcing obviousness, "what everybody knows," and what "everybody" has confirmed by hearing the opinions of the scientists. Thus obviousness, which is born from the natural need to have practical and non-problematic viewpoints about the world, actually ends up dominating debates on the most difficult and controversial social issues.

We can define these "extra-scientific" arguments, tempered in the fire of scientific authority, as "rhetorics," practical systems of thought in which common, non-problematic opinions somehow become authoritative and un-assailable.[229] By "rhetorics," I do not intend the analogous concept of lie or fiction, as if some objective scientific truth existed that professors would betray by diffusing their non-scientific opinions. Very often, in the political dimension

---

[229] On the concept of rhetoric in the social sciences, see McCloskey, D.N. *If You're So Smart: The Narrative of Economic Expertise*, Chicago: University of Chicago Press, 1992.

of public life, there is not *one* truth, but *various* truths, relative to the relationships that we humans institute with values, choices, viewpoints, preconceived moral positions, and in which there are no true and false.[230] At the outset of this study, I maintained that the issue of immigration involves value judgments with a political and moral basis relative to questions of humanity, equality, civil rights, that depend ultimately on subjective opinions and should be subject to political dispute. In the following pages, I am not pretending to expose the rhetorical discourses of immigration, but rather simply to demonstrate how discourses that wish to be scientific are actually arguments of common knowledge that betray, as does any other discourse, assumptions and subjective opions that are more or less transparent. I do not counter these with *one* truth, but highlight the need to return the debate over immigration to honest political opposition. Ultimately, it does not seem decisive that some of these rhetorics are complex and articulate while others are so coarse as to appear as manifestations of racial or cultural prejudice disguised as scientific declarations. To me, it seems important that such declarations seem authoritative and influence political debate, creating and reinforcing current opinions and decisions that politicians base on what they believe to be public opinion.[231]

Among all of the current issues, the "immigration problem" most easily invokes scientific rhetoric because it is laden with strategic implications (i.e. what is the nation, what are human rights, what is "the future of our society") as well as presuppositions, anxieties, and common interpretive viewpoints that the scientist shares completely with the average citizen – presuppositions that include everything from racism to the simple phobia of the foreigner to questions such as "the safety of our cities" or the fear of invasions coming from the Third World. Thus the debate over immigration in which scientists participate on an

---

[230] Given the current positivistic models, this is an aspect of Weberian epistemology the social sciences now tend to overlook.
[231] As Callon and Latour would say, these scientific rhetorics do not describe or explain the world, but "increase" and "produce" it. See Callon, M. and B. Latour. "Unscrewing the Big Leviathan: How Actors Macrostructure the Reality and How Sociologists Help Them to Do So." *Advances in Social Theory and Methodology: Toward an Integration of Micro- and Macro-Sociologies.* Eds. K. Knorr-Cetina and A.V. Cicourel. London: Routledge & Kegan Paul, 1981.

equal plane with other opinion makers reveals what is fundamentally most disturbing and unrecognized in our society. My thesis is simply that some scientists more effectively than others nourish that particular aspect of public opinion that I defined earlier as "official state thought," with reference to A. Sayad, and which I attempted to trace through local public opinion, citizen mobilizations, political-media campaigns, and in some examples from newspapers. This "official state thought" hinges on a construction of the Other – the foreigner, the migrant – as enemy, either actual or potential, both implicitly and explicitly.

What other social actors, both influential and less so, discuss merely in terms of public opinion, scientists discuss in a far more elaborate way. And while they still move within public opinion or "official state thought," accepting its pretexts and discourses, scientists offer more authoritative and reasoned positions, thus contributing to the construction of official state thought not just as a simple disguise for economic, political or symbolic interests, but instead as a complex and intricate vision of the world. Obviously, if state thought and public opinion were linear, transparent phenomenon, then a study such as this one would be unnecessary.

2 The Rhetorics of Immigration

I will delineate the rhetorics of immigration based on their continuity with public opinion without citing and describing each one of those rhetorics in an exhaustive way, but will rather choose several examples representative of each rhetorical style, and current or dominant opinion. I wish to examine examples of *moral* rhetoric (which debates the rights and responsibilities of migrants), *demographic* rhetoric (which accounts for the quantitative evaluation of migration phenomena), and *cultural* rhetoric (which discusses the threat and the impact that migration presents to our culture). I emphasize that I do not consider these examples as representative of the sciences to which their authors or professors belong. Rather, these are arguments that *some* scientists or experts appropriate and propagate thanks to their authority. I will further emphasize that I am not motivated by any particular problematic theme or interpretive line, but simply desire to understand the hidden, implicit mechanisms that legitimize public opinion and official state thought. Therefore, I will limit my analysis to those rhetorics that express positions of public opinion previously discussed in this study and will not examine those extreme rhetorics that are openly xenophobic. For the reasons listed at the end of the second chapter, I am unconvinced that ideological racism (which appears in "scientific analyses" more often than one would think) is the real problem. I am more interested in those *reasonable* rhetorics that litter the immigrant's path with difficulties and misunderstandings. And like the sensationalistic media reports and historical and political double-mindedness cited earlier, scientific rhetorics give the impression that it is actually possible to say everything there is about immigration, and thus imposes as objective and scientific hypochondriacal outbursts or prejudices *tout court*. I have nothing against science in the vast sense, which would also include philosophy as do the Germans, but I am opposed to certain scientists or experts giving in to pure and simple current opinion.

We are the ones being discriminated against. This rhetoric represents the quintessence of "what everybody thinks." It appears on both sides of the Atlantic, in the Po Valley or on Wall Street. The following citation comes from an authoritative expert in finance. In his title, *Alien Nation: Common Sense about America's Immigration Disaster*, the author, P. Brimelow, promises to wed the American "perspective of common sense" about immigration, especially the fears that "the people" (the decisive force on that continent as well) feel about "aliens." Though Brimelow's text is richly provided with tables and statistics with the obvious intent to demonstrate the author's scientific perspective, his thesis reinforces the opinion shared by Italians that talking about discrimination against foreigners masks the "real" discrimination that is faced by "real" Americans who are overwhelmed by "aliens" unable to speak English, protected by irresponsible lawmakers, and who are trying to steal jobs and the future from our children.

My son, Alexander, is white male with blue eyes and blond hair. He has never discriminated against anyone in his little life [...]. But public policy now discriminates against him. The sheer size of these so-called "protected classes" that are now politically favoured such as Hispanics, will be a matter of vital importance as long as he lives. And their size is basically determined by immigration.[232]

It would be useless to emphasize that this reasoning is subject to opinion, and that entire libraries are dedicated to the fact that "new Americans" are always discriminated against by "old Americans," and that young whites enjoy a privileged position in terms of educational and employment opportunities (not to mention their lower statistical likelihood of ending up unemployed or in prison, as compared to their minority counterparts, particularly black youths).[233] It's more amusing to reveal how similar positions are presented as typical expressions of American pragmatism, and particularly that Brimelow wants to convince us that his progeny (who is, after all, the son of an influential financial analyst) will be discriminated against by protectionist laws favoring Hispanics. The eventuality seems remote when we consider that some states, such as California, pass laws against social assistance and free schooling for immigrants.[234]

We will accept them, but only if they stay lower than us. This element of current opinion is widely accepted in various forms among "scientists" who study immigration. Unlike the previous alarmist rhetoric, this avails itself of refined political and moral justifications. These justifications are interesting because

[232] Brimelow, P. *Alien Nation. Common Sense about America's Immigration Disaster.* New York: Random House, 1995. 11.
[233] The bibliography in this area is enormous. For an example, see West, C. "La razza conta." *The War Against the Poor. The Underclass and Antipoverty Policy.* Ed. H. Gans. New York: Basic Books, 1995. For a first hand ethnographic description of the factors that make young African American males the most frequent clients of the American penal system, see Kotlowitz, A. *There Are No Children Here: The Story of Two Boys Growing up in the Other America.* New York: Doubleday, 1991.
[234] One of the more amusing aspects of this book is the author's attempt to prove that those who are most hurt by immigration are African Americans. Davis, M. *City of Quartz: Excavating the Future in Los Angeles,* New York: Vintage Books, 1992, and "Who Killed Los Angeles? A Political Autopsy." *New Left Review* 197 (1993): 23-28 and 198 (1993): 29-542.

they confer on public opinion and reasoning the lofty duty of establishing the "rights" and "responsibilities" of immigrants. Before elaborating further, it will be necessary to define the concept of "responsibility" and its function. Though the moral philosophy dedicated to social responsibility has been amply studied for over two centuries, that has not necessarily found a parallel application in the laws that govern society. Both Kant, who considered accepting the categorical imperative as the ultimate expression of human freedom, and Hegel, for whom the "ethical State" was an expression of "the Divine on Earth," were often ignored by constitutions, if for no other reason than the fact that in liberal states, few people wanted ethics or the Divine to become involved in issues of the market or free trade. Even a sociologist like Durkheim who believed in consensual society limited the "collective conscience" to a narrow group of imperatives present in nearly all human societies, such as "do not kill," "do not commit incest," and so on. And for those individuals who violate these and many other precepts, modern societies do not offer eternal damnation or philosophical condemnation but prisons and punishments.

The moral concept of "duty" has a controversial normative capacity in our culture. Although numerous lawmakers and political philosophers try to "reconstruct" the foundation of the moral state based on that very concept, the ethics of duty is applicable only if we accept that ethics of our own free will.[235] Across the centuries, constitutional order and western lawmakers have reduced the role of "duty" in public and private life. What the law often defines as "duties" are mainly legal limitations, distinct from the moral ideal or ethical concept of "duty." For example, citizens have the "duty" to pay taxes, but is unlikely that a tax evader would unanimously be considered an immoral citizen. The law, which takes account of the changes in what we will call the

---

[235]Georg Simmel, one of the most fascinating Kantian philosophers, makes this objection regarding the normative theories of morality. See Simmel, G. *Einleitung in die Moralwissenschaft. Eine Kritik der etischen Grundbegriffe*. Frankfurt a.M.: Suhrkamp, 1989. For Simmel, Kant's categorical imperative was an example of "moral fanaticism." Of course, when I speak of the "de-moralization of society" I am not including the debate on "republicanism" or "communalism" or "constitutional patriotism," which are all beyond the purveys of this study.

morality of a culture, tends to provide administrative rather than criminal sanctions for infractions like tax evasion. Analogously, a father has specific legal obligations to his spouse and children (financial support, providing education), but he is under no legal obligation to see that they dress well or even to love them. The de-moralization of western society, as unpleasant as it may seem to someone old-fashioned, or to some philosophers or certain religious believers, nevertheless conforms to the typical modern principle that no one is obligated to obey any norm not expressly dictated by the law.

But our society's progressive tolerance on moral issues is immediately revoked in every moral reflection as soon as we depart from the implicit "us" to the "them," that is, when ethics encounters foreigners. Naturally, there are numerous *philosophical* positions regarding foreigners or "guests," that criticize the western pretensions to regulate foreigners and reduce them to convenient stereotypes, but rarely do those philosophical positions call for an accounting (as is frequently the case with philosophy) of our interactions with actual foreigners in the flesh, such as migrants and refugees.[236] On those few occasions when there is an accounting, the tolerance that contemporary philosophy often exhibits toward foreigners leaves ample room for far less liberal and open-minded points of view.

Several years ago in the course of a debate regarding the reduction of the rights of political asylum in German, the philosopher Agnes Heller outlined ten theses on immigration that form the "duties" that immigrants and foreigners in general must respect in order to enjoy the "rights" of the host society.[237] The first thesis provides the essential presuppositions of the relationship between host society and its guests:

---

[236] There are exceptions. Derrida, J. *Cosmopoliti di tutti i Paesi, ancora una sforzo!* Naples: Cronopio, 1997 confronts the issue of the right to exile, abandoning the terminology "Foreigner" and the "Other," so common in philosophical discourse currently. While I disagree with Derrida's views, I appreciate the commitment of philosophers in this field.

[237] Heller, A. "Zehn Thesen zum Asylrecht." *Die Zeit* 46 (1992): 60.

First Thesis: Emigration is a human right, but immigration is not. This concept is merely the legal and international extension of ancient domestic order (*Hausordnung*). If an individual wishes to leave home, we cannot prevent him or her from doing so with violence. If a person expresses the desire to stay in our home, the members of the household (*Haushalt*) determine if he or she may remain or must leave.

This thesis relies on the obvious analogy between society and domestic order, and while this parallel is widely utilized in journalistic, political, and literary rhetoric ("Our Home – the European Union") it has no legal or ethical basis. The analogy presupposes that the immigrant is not an individual with recognizable rights (such as the right to leave home or emigrate) but a guest to whom we offer benefits or, as will be discussed, an individual that vacillates between the non-entity of foreigner and infant. Above all, this analogy depends on arbitrarily equating the sphere of public right and collective social life (which obviously includes immigration) with the sphere of private rights and family relationships.

Evoking the "humanity" of the immigrant based on an analogy between *oikos* (the indigenous community) and the public sphere conflicts not only with the universalist concept of western ethics (which a moral philosopher like Heller should take into account), but also basic "common sense," which is far different from public opinion. No immigrant knocks on our front door, but rather comes to our borders asking to live in our society. And clearly, the *oikos* has nothing to do with that, given that the ideal immigrant for the "indigenous community" had no connections with the community's past. I am not suggesting that Agnes Heller wants to deliberately de-humanized immigrants, but simply point out that her arguments against "the rights of immigration" are based on a faulty analogy that is scientifically invalid and from which the de-humanization of immigrants implicitly derives.[238]

[238] In other words, Heller applies three principles outlined in the 1948 "Universal Declaration of Human Rights," which explicitly provides for the "right to leave and return to any country," (article 13, paragraph 2), as well as "the right to seek and obtain aslyum in other countries to flee persecution," but without the corresponding proviso for another country to grant asylum (article

Beginning with this faulty analogy in Heller's theses, and other even more unfortunate ones, the immigrant is systematically established as coming *after* the members of the household, i.e. the members of the host society. If they are "fugitives," then they *are allowed into the home after relatives* (*Second Thesis*). Even if they were "angels," irrespective of "race" or "culture," they would need to respect the "law of Abraham's tent" (*Third Thesis*). This reference to the bible is disturbing. The "law of Abraham's tent" contrasts the hospitality of Abraham with the violence and the wilfulness of the citizens of Sodom, and refers to the fact that Abraham honours his guests (he remains standing under a tree "while they take refreshment,") while Abraham's relative, Lot, offers his own daughters to the inhabitants of Sodom in order to save the guests that found refuge in his house. The inaccuracy of Heller's references to religious law and the ancient customs of hospitality[239] become more evident in her definition of domestic order:

14, paragraph 1). In addition, this Declaration provides for the right for "everyone" to move freely within the borders of a state without specifying if "everyone" needs to be a citizen of that state (article 13, paragraph 1). In other words, this Declaration, which responds to the conditions of the Jews under the Nazi regime, is far more open regarding the rights to "emigrate and immigrate" than Heller's reading gives us to believe. Obviously, declarations or pacts of this nature have virtually no power over states in the formation of migration legislation. The entire text of the Declaration is available on the website of the United Nations. J. Rawls, not unlike Heller, has a reductive conception of human rights, dependent on the consensus of "the people," i.e. the people in charge. See Rawls, J. "The Law of Peoples" *On Human Rights (Oxford Amnesty Lectures)*, New York: Basic Books, 1994.

[239] As demonstrated by H.C. Peyer, *Viaggiare nel Medioevo. Dall'ospitalità alla locanda.* 3rd Ed. Rome and Bari: Laterza, 1997, ancient hospitality is defined by the supremacy – temporary supremacy – accorded to the foreigner by the host. Heller refers to various places in Genesis, but inverts the meaning of those passages. Abraham is a *foreigner* in Canaan when he welcomes the "messengers of the Lord," accommodating and caring for them, while the inhabitants of Sodom wand to "abuse" the guest of Abraham's relative, Lot. The inhabitants of Sodom protest because Lot, a foreigner, makes himself their judge. The law of the "tent of Abraham" is the law of hospitality, not subordination of the foreigner to the host family. See also Ginzberg, L. *Legends of the Jews*, Philadelphia, PA: Jewish Publication Society of America, (2nd Edition), 2003.

is: [...] What does domestic order mean? First: guests or those
ıg asylum are required to obey the laws of the State, even when they
om countries in which the laws are different.

ɔ would disagree with the fact that it is necessary to obey the laws of the
So why is it necessary to define this as "domestic order"? For the
ımental reason that without the initial analogy, the entire *pathos* of this
al rhetoric would vanish, and Heller could not longer require that immigrants
ıo "are living in a society" follow its "precepts of hygiene and courtesy" (*Sixth
hesis*). This is not the only place that we see a double juridical standard for
family members and foreigners, but there is a further extension of other ideas: no
member of a society can be legally or morally punished for infractions of
"courtesy" and "hygiene" (unless we are dealing with a child). Unfortunate
ethical formulations such as these reconfirm the absolute difference between "us"
and our "guests" who are *secondary, infantile, and subordinate*. In fact, "the
owner of the home, who always has the position of superior power, is the one
who allows or refuses asylum, establishes domestic order, and understands the
implications. Therefore, from an ethical point of view, his obligations are
enormous." (*Seventh Thesis*). The burden of the home owner allows for the
ethical non-existence of the immigrant-infant, and Heller magnanimously
accords to them the "right to know the truth" of their own condition, and accords
to the home owner the obligation to ease the sufferings that derive from being
admitted into a new family (*Tenth Thesis*). Ultimately, immigrants are nothing
more than children:

Tenth Thesis: A child from birth through the first year of life is the ideal
example for universalists. In a literal sense, every child is the universal
individual. If one smiles at any infant a few months old, her or she will react in
the same identical way whether the child is black or white, male or female,
regardless of cultural milieu or background.

This analogy renders immigrants infants in two ways: a) they are infants
because they still do not know the language of the "home" and therefore b)

they require education. The "universalism" that Heller supports here is that of the educator who out of personal goodness ignores differences of color and knows that the child can be taught "regardless of cultural milieu or background." Heller quickly resolves any problem of "multiculturalism" in a manner that would appeal to any Romantic theoretician of forced assimilation, like Herder. The point is, by espousing a highly idiosyncratic notion of "universalism" (which is merely the assimilation or cultural homogenization of migrants and refugees), Heller supports a discriminatory statute for foreigners as such, thus rendering them nothing more than servant-children.

I wish to note that Heller's concept of education contains authoritarian and discriminatory elements when we remember that the object of these domestic attentions are mainly foreign adults. Her viewpoint seems contradictory, given that she herself was a refugee who fled to the United States where she has a successful teaching career. This professor of moral philosopher who landed in New York excludes herself from the class of foreigners, thus contradicting her own condition, which often happens to those who leave the realm of pure thought and enter into concrete issues. A few years before publishing her theses about foreigners, and perhaps because she was confining herself to moral reflections, Heller seemed more sensitive to the needs of "others," and less interested in "dominion," such as parents' dominion over children or autochthones dominion over foreigners:

> The recognition of all needs whose satisfaction does not in principle imply the use of others as means to an end must be exercised. This may be due to virtue (the attitude) of radical tolerance. Excluded from this recognition are those needs whose satisfaction necessarily implies dominion.[240]

Another case that is far removed from the archaic moralizing rhetoric of Heller but analogous in its results is that of those scientific arguments which weigh the rights and responsibilities of foreigners and natives with the purpose of blunting the inevitable "racial," cultural and any other kind of conflict

---

[240] Heller, A. *Beyond Justice*, Malden, MA: Blackwell Pub, 1990.

sparked by the arrival of immigrants. These arguments are not only more sophisticated, but also well intentioned, and behind them the sincere attempt to combat racism is perceivable. However, they are based on a pessimistic view of public opinion in which racism is intrinsic to the human condition in as much as it is an expression of that hatred for anyone who is different from the rest of the group, equalizing any "other" from women to foreigners:

> Nearly all forms of racism are part of the State. By this I in no way intend to relate the immigration debate to the absurd notion that an inherently benevolent civil society exists and that the State constructs morality. Quite the inverse; *I believe that racism is a natural condition of the human soul.* Humans mistrust difference and they distain it. Just consider the how the most fundamental of all racisms has been generalized across time and space: the invention of feminine nature and its concomitant devaluation. In our democracies, there are far more women who are beaten, tortured, and killed by men than there are immigrants who are victims of natives, or natives who are victims of immigrants. And yet this fact does not seem worthy of being considered a political issue, but instead remains hidden behind the walls of the home, or relegated to the crime pages of the papers, downgraded to the private realm.[241]

Immigrants are grouped in the class of "different," that also includes women, and similarly, are assigned a certain "nature." This text suggests that immigrants and women are both parts of a wider homogenous subclass that is the target of the racism that is "the natural condition of the human soul." That racism should be considered an element of the "soul" rather than the definition of certain specific social behaviors aimed against specific people is obviously a debateable question. The interesting part of this argument is that immigrants, dissolved into the class of "different," no longer exist as social and legal subjects, but only as the objects of an indiscriminate racism. And strangely, this racism is simultaneously "part of the State," and also the natural condition of the human soul, something that seems utterly senseless unless one were to

[241] Zincone, G. *Una schermo contro il razzismo. Per una politica dei diritti utili.* Rome: Donzelli, 1994. 7.

postulate that the state is the natural condition of the human soul, which seems highly debateable. It would follow from this argument that in order to reduce racism generally, or to avoid arousing it, it is best to avoid talking about "universal rights," of immigrants, especially in reference to social rights[242] but rather extend specific, limited rights, being mindful of the reactions of natives who, feeling discriminated against, could protest and then give into their "natural racism," which brings us back to a more elaborated and euphemized version of Brimelow's thesis.

It goes without saying that the balance that carefully weighs out the "rights" of immigrants is firmly in "our" hands, just as Heller would have it. Once again, in Zincone's book, immigrants are merely the recipients of our initiatives and they have no say in the matter. This is a theory based on "common sense" and appears to be quite reasonable, except that it neglects to account for the idea that on principle the "us," (women and men) and the "them" (women and men) are equal. It's rather like the Cheyenne, who called themselves, "the people of men," but called all others by their tribal names, implying that the Sioux or the Arapahoes were not really humans (though I wish to add that according to experts on the tribes of the Plains, the Cheyenne were extremely tolerant and welcoming toward the "non-humans.")

All people are equal (but some are less equal). To illustrate this thesis, I refer to a scholar who has scientifically refuted the current justifications about the concept of race. In an article published in a scientific journal, L. Cavalli-Sforza demonstrates how the differences between "races" are more or less irrelevant in genetic terms, and to use the most obvious example, the pigmentation of the skin is determined by the fact that in Africa those who carry the gene FY-O are resistant to a certain parasite that spreads malaria. In other terms, dark skin indicates the adaptation of a given population to its environment through the process of natural selection, and nothing more. Therefore:

[242] See "The Powerful Consequences of Being too Weak. The Impact of Immigration on Democratic Regimes." *Archives Européennes de Sociologie* 1997.

The differences between the "races," [...] are actually limited and quantitative rather than qualitative. Within the same continents, the average number of differences is even fewer. Seen in this light, the confusion, terrible tragedies, and cruelty caused in the world due to racial differences are, in the words of Macbeth, "a tale told by an idiot, full of sound and fury, signifying nothing."[243]

Thus, "race" is nothing more than a conventional way of defining superficial differences, mere variations in appearance and not indications of differences in human beings, just as height or degree of suntan are never interpreted in terms of superiority or inferiority, except by Nazis or Lombrosians. Cavalli-Sforza does not seem far removed from those biologists and geneticists who have for years struggled to cleanse our culture of racial prejudices that exist both in science and common opinion, and even more from the improper or ideological uses of genetics.[244] However, the problem remains that, having abandoned the field of racial ideology, scientific analysis does not negate all the old clichés about the cultural inferiority of foreigners:

Racism is another social disease that we do not yet know how to prevent or cure. In fact, one could say that it is getting worse, because we have encouraged and nurtured it by carefully avoiding finding any answers to the problems that racism is creating. We have maintained a foolish tolerance for immigration, permitting masses of people to enter our society who are unprepared to live here among us, who are so different from them [...].[245]

That immigration causes racism is a recurring idea, and I regret to say, an idea that bears significant resemblance to the views of "moderate" Germans who opposed the entrance of Jews into Germany at the end of the nineteenth century. The presupposition remains that immigration is foolishly "tolerated" even though

---

[243] Cavalli-Sforza, L. and F. Cavalli-Sforza. *The Great Human Diasporas: The History Of Diversity And Evolution*, New York: Basic Books, 1996.
[244] See, among others, Lewontin, R. *The Genetic Basis of Evolutionary Change*, Irvington, NY: Columbia University Press, 1974, and Rose, S. *Molecules and Minds, Biology and Social Order*, New York: John Wileys and Sons, 1991.
[245] Cavalli-Sforza, L. and F. Cavalli-Sforza. *The Great Human Diasporas*, op. cit.

immigrants are individuals "unprepared to live here among us, who are so different from them." As we have seen, this presupposition in common social belief is shared by some moral philosophers and political scientists but still has no empirical foundation. First, the "diversity of society" is a highly generic formulation that does not take into account what "our society" and "their society" hold in common (from economic fluctuations to the circulation of consumer goods). Second, this notion ignores the fact that a relatively high percentage of migrants exhibit a higher level of education than the average educational level in the country to which they are migrating, though they are not able to find employment befitting their education. Third, it ignores the historical fact that between the nineteenth and twentieth centuries, as in previous critical developmental periods,[246] immigrants have formed the base for the economic and cultural development of Europe[247] and the United States (the country in which, incidentally, the Italian Cavalli-Sforza happily lives and works). The same things that Cavalli-Sforza writes about Latin American migrants were said at the beginning of the nineteenth century about Italian and Polish migrants, and before that, about Irish migrants, and before that, about the Jews. What is most interesting in this position is that the objective inferiorization of foreigners is transferred from the racial-biological sphere, which is unsustainable, to the cultural-educational sphere.[248] In other words, the "difference" that cannot be justified based on genetics, or even less on I.Q. as Rose, Lewontin, and others

[246] Trevor-Roper, H. *The Crisis of the Seventeenth Century. Religion, the Reformation and Social Change*, New York: Harper & Row, 1968 is a critique of Weberian theory in the context of the role of Calvinism from the birth of modern capitalism. Among the decisive factors in the economic development of Europe at the beginning of the seventeenth century, Trevor-Roper cites immigration and the circulation of entrepeneurs. See also Sassen, S. *Migranten, Siedler, Flüchtinge. Von der Massenauswanderung zur Festung Europa.* Frankfurt a.M., Sassen: Fischer, 1997, and Noiriel, G. *Le creuset français. Histoire de l'immigration XIXe-XXe siècle.* 2nd Ed. Paris: Seuil, 1988.
[247] Livi-Bacci, M. *Storia minima della popolazione del mondo.* Bologna: Il Mulino, 1998. 159, estimates the number of transoceanic European migrants to be 50 million between 1846 and 1932. Italy alone sent 8 million emigrants between 1861 and 1961.
[248] For further analysis of these transformations, see Stolcke, V. "New Boundaries, New Frontiers of Exclusion in Europe." *Current Anthropology* 36 (1995).

demonstrate, but can be attributed to the differences between "incompatible" cultures.[249] This paradigm shift which attributes the inferiority of migrants (or some of them) to cultural factors is explicitly claimed in an interview with Cavalli-Sforza in which the eminent scholar of genetics does not shrink from using common clichés about criminal foreigners and applying the concept of "selection" to the non-biological field of migration politics:

"Cavalli-Sforza: Migrants Should Be Selected before Leaving"

We should follow Australia's example, says the scholar, a country that has in comparatively few years accepted something like a million Italian immigrants across its borders: this was a wave of migration that was organized from the start to the finish, with a careful pre-selection […]. *Even Japan, a country not lacking in expressions of racism, has allowed in Korean immigrants, but after having selected them, and awarded them scholarships (an excellent way to avoid paying them too much), then taught them marketable, specialized skills that then many of them took back with them when they returned home* […]. We need to try to bring people into the country who have some education, adds Cavalli-Sforza, and not just criminals, prostitutes, and thieves, as often happens […].[250]

Immigration is an unstoppable wave the will drown us. Over thirty years ago, in an incisive study that caused a great stir, A. W. Cicourel criticized the use of statistics and quantitative measurements in the social sciences generally. Independent of the formal validity of the measurements and calculations, Cicourel noted that frequently social sciences do not verify if the categories into which the data was divided were free from the classifications used commonly by non-experts in the area of describing social phenomena. In other words, the scientific categories themselves incorporated presuppositions and

---

[249] The most radical expression on this paradigm is found in Huntington, S.P *The Clash of Civilizations and the Remaking of World Order*, New York: Simon & Schuster, 1998.

[250] *Corriere della sera.* 4 December 1997. 3. (My italics). It could be sarcastically pointed out that the genetic concept of selection is now being applied to cultural differences. Notice the sincerity with which Cavalli-Sforza admits that the real reason for this selection-formation of foreigners is "so that we can pay them less."

prejudices from commonly held but unsupported beliefs, which then acquired scientific status in the statistical elaborations. Demography in particular played a specific role in this scientific legitimization of common, public opinion:

> Demographers prefer to work with data they often know have drawbacks but with which they feel "at home." This is often the result of having easy access to information assembled by local, state, national and international agencies which is already "packaged" in quantitative or quantifiable form. The data come from sources over which the demographers seldom have any control and their packaged character precludes breakdowns and assimilation of new information which would permit more theoretical alternatives. Careful study of the conditions which surround the construction of a given distribution is necessary if the data's value is to be estimated effectively. The drawbacks to such studies are due to distortions of records by common-sense conceptions of personnel who must record the raw data according to some set of rules.[251]

Cicourel's observations target demographers' uncontrolled use of data from government sources, and the unquestioned trust that sociologists traditionally give to demographic analysis. This problem becomes even more relevant when sociological and demographic analyses deal with the more controversial aspects of social life, such as deviance and criminality.[252] This becomes even more important in the case of scientific discourses on migration, because these tend to include not only categories and data drawn from commonly held beliefs that are then combined with pseudo-issues (such as the "migrant's tendency to commit crime") but then legitimizes them in public opinion in that circular autopoeitic process that characterizes the perception of migration phenomena generally.[253] In the case of migration, the methodological questions assume a different and vaster import than those outlined by Cicourel. It could be said that the contribution demography has made to the production of rhetorical common

[251] Cicourel, A.V. *Method and Measurement in Sociology.* New York: The Free Press, 1964, 138-139.
[252] Kitsuse, J. and A.V. Cicourel. "A Note on the Official Use of Statistics." *Social Problems* 2 (1963).
[253] The critique of scientific-methodological *doxa* initiated by Cicourel and others in the 1960s is now continued by a group of mathematicians and statisticians in the journal *Pénombre*.

opinion regarding immigration is expressed on three levels, two are scientific, and one is rhetorical in the literal sense:

1. Construction of a model of standard previsions based on the population increases in countries of emigration (for example, the countries off the southern and eastern coasts of the Mediterranean) that would create a tremendous imbalance compared to the countries of immigration on the northern coast (i.e. between 1985 and 2020, "of the population increase of 192 million, 9 million are attributable to the northern coast as opposed to the 183 million attributable to the southern and eastern coasts.")[254]
2. Automatic transformation of this hypothetical imbalance into a flow of population from south to north (the "plumbing model" of migration).
3. A call to the informed and "responsible" parties of society to prepare for these events.

As Livi-Bacci, a demographer highly attuned to what Cicourel would term scientific limitations, has warned, the first and second hypotheses contain two evident pitfalls. The standard long-term projections (25 years or more) cannot account for economic, social and demographic variables that are contingent by nature; economic development, political transformations, urbanization, increased literacy and educational level, not to mention the degree of female emancipation in countries to the south, which are all factors whose exact future influence is unpredictable but that can influence fertility rates and frustrate projections, so that the exponential population increase in "poor" countries remains hypothetical. Second, the "plumbing model" that translates an eventual imbalance between the populations on the northern and southern sides of the Mediterranean into a push for migration is an obvious case of metaphorizing quantitative predictions. Even if such an imbalance should find empirical confirmation, that would not necessarily justify a proportionally higher – much less catastrophic – variation in the

---

[254] Livi-Bacci, M. and F. Martuzzi Veronesi, eds. *Le risore umane del Mediterraneo. Popolazione e società al crocevia tra Nord e Sud.* Bologna: Il Mulino, 1990. 24.

migration flows between south and north: the alterations in the labor market and political policies, as well as the economic development in countries of emigration constituted the obvious hurdles to the "push" for migration. More generally, the "plumbing model" ignores the presupposition that migrations are not a "thing," but the result of a great number of individual choices which in their turn are based on factors influenced by perception, decisional processes, social conditions, and cultural representations, all factors that demography cannot account for, as Cicourel suggests. It is probably the impossibility of including all of these elements in predictive models that causes demographers (unless they adopt the precautions suggested by Livi-Bacci) to fall into tremendous errors in calculations. Consider for example the myth in the 1960s that hinged on the prediction of a catastrophic demographic increase in southern Italy, with its consequent appeals to control the birth rate and other considerations that were both implicitly and explicitly racist regarding the fertility of those southern Italian "rabbits." Italian demographers did not foresee the population decline that became unstoppable after the mid-1970s. And yet, after recovering from this accident, some demographers still do not hesitate to predict new catastrophes, this time due to the new *"terroni"* from the countries south of the Mediterranean.[255] A colorful example of this "demographic propensity for exaggeration" is found in the predictions that have to do not just with the "plumbing model" of migration, but the consequences of several political crises on the southern coast.

> Certain political situations exist that derive from specific economic relationships
> or treaties which involve individual European countries as well as the European
> Union as a whole. *Forms of political pressure follow that will be difficult to resist.*
> *One can imagine, for example, that the growth in Islamic fundamentalism in*
> *Algeria could incite those sectors of the population to leave who do not share or*

---

[255] Objective demographic predictions can easily be employed by political platforms. Recall the Nazi's use of the demographic myth of "overpopulation" in its foreign policy. See Heim, S. and U. Schaz. *Berechnung und Beschwörung. Übervölkerung-Kritik einer Debatte.* Berlin: Schwarze Risse-Rote Strasse, 1996.

accept forms of religious fundamentalism, or that their own home country could exile them. Would Italy be able to stand up to these kinds of pressures?[256]

The answer to this question is obvious. In fact, Italy has had no significant problem with Algeria. After the outbreak of the civil war in Algeria, the population of that country was not the protagonist of a significant level of migration due to political or religious motives. In Italy, the population of Algerian migrants numbers in the thousands and has not exhibited significant variations since the beginning of the 1990s. My purpose is not to condemn in hindsight hypotheses that are faulty by definition. I wish only to note that their mechanisms ("non-fundamentalists there will want to flee here") is based on the presupposition that the citizens of a country caught in the turmoil of civil war will be able to flee and pressure us, rather than resist, even under extreme conditions, the dissolution of their society. These "analyses" reveal the more or less tacit presupposition that "others" are different from us, mechanical or living beings that are without any capacity for individual choice, political initiative, or sense of freedom. One could object that in a few cases, populations of significant numbers have had no alternative other than exodus to avoid complete destruction, such as the Kurds. But this case is qualitatively different, for it has to do with "people without a country," as Hannah Arendt would say, people whose political freedom was destroyed by the conniving of those very governments who then did nothing to save them from their fate.

In general, the catastrophizing of demographers and others is not without consequences. Once the predicted invasions of biblical proportions fail to materialize, the next alarmist prediction is cheerfully undertaken because the issue in question is not a scientific analysis but sustaining an alarmist model that is shared by scientists and politicians alike. This model clearly appears in some of the comments made by Romano Prodi regarding immigration and crime:

[256] Golini, A. "Tendenza e proiezioni demografiche." *Antropologia urbana e relazioni interetniche. Città nuovo, nuove città.* Ed. P. Chiozzi. Florence: Angelo Pontecorboli Editore, 1991. 25. (My italics). It is analyses like these that form the basis for terming any arrival of hundreds or thousands of refugees a phenomenon of "biblical exodus."

When the Berlin Wall fell, we all predicted tremendous waves of migration from the East, these didn't occur. The East held on because its societies are strong, even if the economic disparity and poverty in many countries prompted immigration. And though there were emigrations from Poland, Russia, and the Ukraine, these were not on the "biblical" level. *The "biblical" migrations have all been from the south, they impact Italy and Spain and along these borders, we must react for all of Europe [...]*[257]

Immigration is an ethnic problem. Migrations, like any other social phenomenon, are the sum of innumerable individual stories, contingent decisions, "projects" that are only partly conscious, existential trajectories that, based on the accepted scientific rhetoric, are fused into collective processes and therefore transformed into abstractions. Human beings reacting to different motivations (looking for a job or better salary, hunger, fleeing from religious or political persecution) "decide" to abandon their home country or national state, cross the border and enter into another national state (or society, or labor market) based on a multitude of circumstances. Sociology has highlighted the different social perceptions and conditioning that contribute to the formation of the so-called "migration projects." The migration experience of one's elders or peer group, the availability of information, accurate or not, about the country of destination, the circulation of consumer goods, but also the diffusion of universal symbols and images are all generic cultural factors of attraction that orient individual toward "migration projects." Nevertheless, the migrant remains essentially an individual who completes an actual secession from his or her own economic, political, and social context (not to mention personal and familial), as Moulier-Boutang reminds us.[258]

If all of this is true, we should expect that the "science of migration" attentively examines the transformations and vicissitudes that create the "identity" of migrants. The classic studies in this area highlight the cognitive and cultural shock that accompany the "migrant's career," as well as the

---

[257] Prodi, R. "Intervento conclusivo." *Presentazione del rapporto annuale, 1997, sui problemi della sicurezza in Emilia-Romagna.* Bologna, 1 December 1997. 17. (My italics).
[258] Moulier-Boutang, Y. *Le salariat bridé, Origines de la politique migratory, constitution du salariat et contrôle de la mobilité du travail.* Paris: Doctorate Thesis from University FNSP-IEP, 1997.

plurality of levels on which the migrant's identity necessarily reflects. Migrations show how the highly abused concept of cultural or social identity is virtually useless for describing the life style changes and self-perceptions that migrants are not only subjected to, but that they sometimes accept with dizzying speed, as if individuals who are by definition "mobile," (or "migratory birds" according to the famous formulation of R. Priore) eluded the various distinctions that different social sciences apply to pin them down. By definition, migrants find themselves in a "bastardized" condition,[259] in the sense that "they are no longer and they are not yet." They have left their social space but have not yet entered into the new social space in which they can insert themselves, except in a marginalized or subservient way. This is reflected in the highly variable forms of social and cultural networks that migrants create or adapt to in the host country. Purely individual and utilitarian forms of adaptation coexist with informal networks, often derived from family ties or other ties from the country of origin. And not only that: there are different adaptations on the level of choices, or professional, social, and economic necessity, which do not exclude maintaining cultural or other ties, such as religious, with society of origin. Thus, overall, no collective, cultural, ethnic, or religious identity exists *of the migrant as such*, but rather there are as many plural identities as there are subjects who transform in the course of their experience, which is by definition, transitory. It is only conventions, or rather the opacity of the language of public opinion and the social sciences in the host countries (once again, all united in agreement) that waves a magic wand and transforms this multitude of singularities into a single new wave of "culture," "community," "ethnicity," or "religion."[260] As E.R. Wolf has stated,

---

[259] Bourdieu, P. "Préface." *L'immigration ou le paradoxe de l'alterité*. A. Sayad. Brussels: De Boeck-Wesmael, 1990.

[260] Naturally, I am referring to contemporary migrations. See Piore, M. *Birds of Passage*. Cambridge: Cambridge University Press, 1979. The relationship between the original cultural heritage and of migrants and the transformation of their identity in the destination culture has been studied, and the majority of the work has been done in regards to migrants in the United States. See Thomas, W.I. *Gli immigrati e l'America. Tra il vecchio mondo e il nuovo*. Rome: Donzelli, 1997 and Thomas, W.I. and F. Znaniecki. *The Polish Peasant in Europe and America*,

It is a mistake to consider the migrant as the carrier or protagonist of a homogenous, integral culture that he can maintain or reject in its entirety. We have learned enough about cultural models to know that they are often inherently contradictory, and at the same time, capable of being integrated with models coming from other countries. It is no more difficult for a Zulu or a Hawaiian to learn or unlearn a culture than it is for a person from Pomerania or China. What is important for a migrant is the position at which he is inserted, his relationship with other groups, from the moment he arrives. This positioning determines which among the resources he brought with him can be used, and which new resources he will need to acquire.[261]

It is this manualistic, "normal" knowledge in social sciences[262] that reveals the procedure of transforming individuals into expressions of a collective, homogenous reality (which inevitably impinges upon identity).[263] We're not dealing here with an emotional rhetoric that charms the whims of public opinion, but a "clinical," "neutral," and therefore "scientific" rhetoric. In a recent, popular sociology manual, there is a section entitled, "Immigration into European Countries, particularly Italy," in the chapter, "Races, Ethnicities, and Nations,"[264] thus suggesting rather overtly that immigration is a "racial, ethnic, and national" issue, which as we have seen many times may be true, especially in the nexus of images and perceptions that are produced in the countries of immigration in reference to migrants, but this is not equally the case for the migrants themselves who (leaving aside the concept of "race," which no one uses any more in sociology) do not constitute an ethnicity or a nation but are individuals who have a passport, i.e. citizenship, that is different from that of the majority of the

Champaign, IL: University of Illinois Press, 1996. As is typical with the Chicago school, these works show the tendency to overestimate the importance of the migrant's community identity.
[261] Wolf, E. *Europe and the People without History*, Berkeley, CA: University of California Press, 1997.
[262] I refer to the concept of "normal science" from Kuhn, T.S. *The Structure of Scientific Revolutions*, Chicago: University Of Chicago Press (3rd Edition), 1996.
[263] For an insightful critique of the construction of identity in other cultures and the resulting conflicts, see Bayart, J.-F. *L'illusion identitaire*. Paris: Fayard, 1996.
[264] Smith, A.J. cited in A. Bagnasco, M. Barbagli, A. Cavelli. *Corso di sociologia*. Bologna: Il Mulino, 1990. 414-417.

population to which they have moved. In other words, "race, ethnicity, and nation," are identities artificially constructed by the countries of immigration and are not original sociological characteristics of the migrants. My observations may seem sweeping, unless one reflects on the fact that immigration, more than any other social phenomenon, is also a political, economic, geographic, and legal "fact." Why then should it be sent down an essentializing funnel of race, ethnicity, and nation? The typical rhetoric of the racial, ethnic, and national construction of migration phenomena becomes evident in the definition of ethnicity. According to the manual mentioned above, an ethnic group consists of:

1. The members of a group designating themselves, or designated by other members by a name that distinguishes them.
2. A mythology of common origin or descendent.
3. A community that shares certain collective memories or traditions and is concerned with their transmission to future generations.
4. Has a common culture [...]
5. Has a territory [...] that the group members consider to be their own [...]
6. Develops bonds of solidarity among members of the group that do not extend to members of other groups.[265]

Setting aside the openly problematic, conflictual concept of "ethnicity," which has led many scholars to interrogate the validity of that concept, the possible applications of this definition are so vast as to dissolve into indeterminacy. According to this definition, any territorial group, from a neighborhood gang to a group of soccer fans, could be classified as an "ethnicity." For example, the members of an ultra-group define themselves with a specific name, they delineate myths about their origins, transmit communal memories to future generations, desire exclusive control over a specific territory, share a culture, and develop bonds of solidarity among members of the group. With all due caution, one could apply this definition to the Crips and the Bloods

[265] *Ibid.* 418.

in Los Angeles, or to that difficult problem of the Northern League, and so on. But beyond these superficial objections, it is evident that here the concept of ethnicity is generically and inattentively being superimposed upon the definition of culture or subculture with one critical addition: while the term "culture" is currently being used carefully in anthropology,[266] underlining its developmental, self-referential, and interactive aspects, as Geertz[267] points out, citing Weber, culture is fundamentally a network of symbols in which humans are drawn together. The term "ethnicity," however, carries the idea of a fundamental cultural reality, invariable and rigidly deterministic, that would orient the actions of certain social groups, as has occurred with the concept of "race." A truly revealing example of this apparent confusion between "race," "ethnicity," "culture," and "nation," and any other type of determinism is evident in the following recent attempt to "analyze" the new Italian capitalism:

> This is the only explanation [the decline of the traditional working classes] for the tragic shift at the end of the twentieth century from the struggle between the classes to a *battle between the races, actual conflicts as seen in ex-Yugoslavia or simulated and invented conflicts, as in Italy today. I am not saying that we are in the midst of a racial war*. Threads of identification and belonging to "other" groups from the *ethnicity-based according to Heimat (homeland of place, traditions, of the known and familiar), identities different from the local as a resource for competition, still exist in the self-awareness that crosses the ambiguous identity of the producers.*[268]

Ethnicity, culture, civilization, religion, community and nation tend to be used synonymously in ordinary language and in the social sciences when referring to

[266] For a debate on this tendency see Clifford, J. *The Predicament of Culture: Twentieth-Century Ethnography, Literature and Art*, Cambridge, MA: Harvard University Press, 1988, and Clifford, J. and G. Marcus, eds. *Writing Culture. The Poetics and Politics of Ethnography.* Berkeley, CA: University of California Press, 1986.
[267] Geertz, C. *The Interpretation Of Cultures*, New York: Basic Books, 1977.
[268] Bonomi, A. *Il capitalismo molecolare. La società al lavoro del Nord Italia.* Turin: Einaudi, 1997. 148. (My italics). The war in the ex-Yugoslavia was really a racial war? Which: Bosnian, Croatian, or Serbian? Notice in this text the ease with which the author conflates issues of race, ethnicity, homelands, etc.

who lives outside of the economic and cultural space of the wealthy northern or western parts of the world, particularly when defining migrant or refugee individuals who live, or try to live, among us. The rhetorics of immigration cited here share something in common, that is an implied but rigid asymmetry. Rights are natural (universal) for "us," but applied (specific) for "them." They are equal to us by nature, but not by culture. They are children, and we are adults. They are mechanical, "unprepared," entities while we are reasonable and flexible. We could add that their music and food are "ethnic," while ours are not, etc. An asymmetry that few would admit but that corresponds completely to the prevalent public opinion and to the presuppositions of migration politics. (Notice how the "rhetorics of immigration" appropriate the language of the "logic of common sense" discussed in chapter one, with various levels of sophistication in the various sciences).

This fundamental asymmetry expresses itself in the contrast of our culture to theirs on several planes. With this, we have reached the actual location of the conflict, or rather the war between cultures, ethnicities, and civilizations which constitutes one of the most widely played intellectual games of our day and which has uncorked a flood of textual production in books, newspapers, and media reports. Immersed as we are in this forest of images of war and conflict, it is no small task to untangle the unstoppable floods of migration, invasions of refugees and ethnic wars, decline of western civilization, the end of history, the wearing of the chador, and Islamic terrorism and fundamentalist extremism. Let us focus the discussion by formulating a basic question. Isn't it possible that today's growing "war between cultures," or whatever name is being applied (together with "racial," ethnic, and cultural tensions), *does not exist except in the rhetoric of scientific discourse?*

3 Culture Has Nothing to Do with It

To begin, notice that the theoretical panorama of supposed conflicts between cultures, ethnicities, and civilizations is extremely varied and also includes positions favorable to accepting immigrants into "our culture" as members of another culture, civilization, or "ethnicity." This is evident in the overwhelming use of terms such as "multicultural," or "intercultural" in many publications dedicated to migration phenomena. The implicit presupposition in the use of this language is that immigrants represent their culture *within* our culture. Consequently, our culture is no longer singular, but multiple, no longer unitary, but fragmentary, which would create identity problems for them and for us. There are those who would label these problems inevitable, talking about an actual cultural conflict between cultures (the "prophets of cultural conflict"),[269] or those who claim they are under control (the "reasonable, realistic, responsible multiculturalists"),[270] and those who view our society in a positive way as multicultural (the "happy multiculturalists").

Common to all of these positions is the idea that culture is something rigid and closed, like a skin that different social identities can sew around themselves. We tend to talk about ethnicity in referring to the roots of identity, of nation, in order to identify its political-governmental expression, of community to define the essential unity, and civilization to express specific intellectual or religious ideas. It is evident that all these definitions have a metaphoric value and above all, are dependent upon the rhetoric that is being employed. If applied to specific situations, they appear generic labels, containers that cannot take into account transformations, cultural exchanges, the multiple transitions that occur between the generic cultural "unities." For example, these days can one say that a "European" culture or civilization exists as opposed to other cultures or civilizations? Perhaps it does, but in such a general sense that it does not consider what other cultural unities have in common. In terms of communication, economic exchanges, aspects of daily life and numerous other physical or

---

[269] This position is typified by the works of S. Huntington. See also Eibl-Eibesfeldt, I. "Der Brand in unserem Haus." *Süddeutsche Zeitung.* Feuilleton Beilage, 8/9, 1993. In Italy, the prototype of these positions that are hostile to "multiculturalism" or "multiethnicity" could be considered M. Losano. On the success of these positions, see Leante.

[270] I have already discussed the position of G. Zincone. See also Cohn-Bendit, D. and T. Schmid. *Heimat Babylon. Das Wagnis der multikulturellen Demokratie.* Frankfurt a.M.: Hoffman and Campe, 1991, and Todd, E. *Le destin des immigrés. Assimilation et ségrégation dans le démocraties occidentales.* Paris: Seuil, 1994. Habermas, J. *Morale, diritto, politica.* Turin: Einaudi, 1993.

symbolic aspects, the culture of a European country such as Germany has more in common with the United States, Japan, or Singapore, than it has with some European countries.

And what about "civilizations" or "universal religions"? The civilization of western Christianity is nothing more than a vocabulary term if we consider the differences in sects and denominations as well as the differences in practice (from ritualism to the prevalent lack of belief in traditions of various kinds) that would all have to fit into the same container. On the other hand, only the defenders of European traditionalism, whether secular or religious, or the followers of Huntington can believe in or preach that Islam is one unified religion or civilization, when this label covers a vast accumulation of tendencies, interpretations, political representations, and contaminations from philosophy and other non-Islamic ideas – religious and secular – that perhaps make Islam an even more pluralistic and diverse universe than its Christian counterpart.[271] Basic understanding of history suggests, rather, that labels such as "civilization" or "culture" hide and even falsify the incessant exchanges in practices, knowledge, representation, conceptual models, symbols and beliefs that have made religions, as well as civilizations, into nebulous entities that coincide and diverge but most of all, are mutable. To combat the complexity of these crossovers and inter-weavings the princely counsellors take up their pens, thinkers on the level of Fukuyama, Allan Bloom, Huntington, or Brimelow followed by legions repeating clichés with differing levels of sophistication, to contend that religions or civilizations have little in common. Indeed, a common place in these positions is that there is an "irreconcilable" difference between native cultures and their internal minorities that cannot be assimilated into white civilization.[272]

---

[271] Partner, P. *God of Battles: Holy Wars of Christianity and Islam*, Princeton, NJ: Princeton University Press, 1998, and see also Tibi, B. *Krieg der Zivilisationen. Politik und Religion zwischen Vernunft und Fundamentalismus.* 2nd Ed. München: W. Heyne Verlag, 1998, which discusses the position of Huntington, albeit in a more problematic way.

[272] The most illustrious precedent of this tendency is Glaser, N. and D.P. Moynihan. *Beyond the Melting Pot. The Negroes, Puertoricans, Italians, and Irish of New York City.* 2nd Ed. Cambridge, Mass: MIT Press, 1970, which proclaims the end of the "melting pot" model in the United States.

These arguments reveal their prosaic nature when they are applied to the case of migrants, individuals who by definition resist the use of religious, cultural, ethnic, or communal containers. Migrants come from countries (societies, cultures, religions, etc.) that are different from that of other migrants: therefore, they do *not* constitute *a single* culture, nor is it written in stone anywhere that they *represent* their own culture respective to the host country. To say that a culture has become multicultural due to the presence of heterogeneous migrants does not mean 1) seeing a fez or chador on our city's streets, not to mention mosques, or 2) redefining individuals by assigning them a cultural, religious, or ethnic identity apart from their specific relationships with their cultural heredity.[273]

Actually, the culture or ethnicity of migrants exists more as the effect of society's process of label construction which transforms migrants into ethnicities, communities, or subcultures to the degree to which the society would like to identify, stratify, and control them. When we speak of "multi-culturalism" whether in negative or positive terms, the false presupposition has already been accepted that migrants constitute fragments or the avant-garde of different cultures, so their difference is hypothesized, and the divide between "us" and "them" is drawn with the somewhat paradoxical result that often, cast into their cultural, religious, and ethnic containers, migrants end up identifying themselves in that way, similar to how deviant youth subculture becomes the fulfilment of what the society that excludes them has expected.[274] This is a typical differentialist process that western societies with long histories of migration (the United States, France, England, Germany) know well, and that societies new to migration, Italy first of all, have happily begun to practice. Aside from the specific national forms of redefining the "ethnicity" or

---

[273] A surprising example of this tendency can be found in Cohn-Bendit, D. and T. Schmid. *Patria Babilonia. Il rischio della democrazia multiculturale.* Milan: Theoria, 1994. This text examines multicultural society in terms of its problems, i.e. risks of conflicts and their results, greater hesitation about accepting migrants and granting them citizenship rights, etc.

[274] See Appiah, A. "Identity, Authenticity, Survival, Multicultural Societies and Social Reproduction." *Multiculturalism.* 2nd Ed. Ed. C. Taylor. Princeton, N.J.: Princeton University Press, 1994.

"culture" of migrants (segregating the Turks in Germany, the allocation of "other cultures" to the lowest rung of the social structure in England, the urban marginalization in France or the US, the criminalization of migrants in Italy), cultural differentialism appears to be a process that mirrors the political, legislative procedures of controlling and rendering migrants inferior.[275] This is even more true when migrants are assigned to the lowest levels of the work force (in the "old" migration countries) or into the poorest segments of informal economy (in the "new" migration countries). Frequently, "multiculturalism" is invoked to reinforce the impossibility of integrating migrants, and their civil and social equation with autochthons. As a German theoretician of multiculturalism observes,

> I believe that, in the future, integration and assimilation will no longer be possible because the majority of those who decide to come to this country have no intention of assimilating or renouncing their own cultural identity, also because they come in ever greater numbers from different cultural contexts.[276]

In multicultural or differentialist theories, as is common in the economic relations between rich and poor countries, the existence of migrants' work is tacitly ignored, which emulsifies inequalities and specific conflicts into battles between civilizations or worse, between races.[277] Migrants exist only inasmuch

---

[275] For a comparative analysis of these processes in Europe and the United States, see Bryant, C.G. "Citizenship, National Identity and the Accomodation of Difference: Reflections on the German, French, Dutch and British Cases." *The New Community* 2 (1997) and Todd, E. *Le destin des immigrés. Assimilation et ségrégation dans le démocraties occidentales.* Paris: Seuil, 1994. On theoretic differentialism and its results, see Taguieff, P.A. *La forza del pregiudizio. Saggio sul razzismo e sull'antirazzismo.* Rome: Il Mulino, 1994. On the dialectic of integration and segregation in Germany, see Benz, W., ed. *Integration ist machbar. Aüslander in Deutschland.* Müchen: Beck, 1993.

[276] Geissler, H., cited in V. Götz. "Multiculturalismo e valori costituzionali in Germania." *Cittadinanza e diritti nelle società multiculturali.* Bologna: Il Mulino, 1994. 194. Geissler is considered to be the person who first used the term "multiculturalism" in the German discussion of these issues.

[277] See Wallerstein, I. "Culture is the World System: A Reply to Boyne." *Global Culture. Nationalism, Globalization and Modernity.* 6th Ed. Ed. M. Featherstone. 1995. 63.

as they are "other," fragments of other cultures or religions, but not as subjects who act in determinate conditions. Assigning rigidly deterministic "ethnic," "racial," or "cultural" categories to migrants (which become the category of "criminal" when there are "problems") is subject to an inflexible dialectic that mainly involves their visibility. If they can be rendered invisible in the corners of the illegal labor market and non-regulated economy, accepting its rules and subjecting themselves to that subordination, then their existence is tolerated and ignored. If they make themselves visible, by the nature of their work (irregular and marginal, but public) or because there is an emergency, they are ethnicized and culturally segregated.[278] This is true not only for public institutions but also for cultural or "intercultural" social services (in Italy and in other countries of "new" immigration these are frequently volunteer organizations) that seek to deal with the problems of migration on a practical level. The direct link between ethnicization and control appears in the following interview with a social worker that deals with the area of "multicultures."

> Thank you for asking about the problems of terminology [...]. It's very important that we understand each other. From a cultural point of view, there's a modern interpretation of migration phenomenon in terms of "mutual enrichment between cultures." An organization whose main goal is to educate could have this objective. Our directives accept integration and interaction: foreign students, including those here illegally, are encouraged to learn their own mother tongue. [...] But we have to face many practical problems. *We are dealing with 134 distinct ethnic communities.*[279]

The revealing confusion between "nationality" and "ethnic community" says a great deal about the daily procedural, unaware dealings that transform a

---

[278] On the political use of "cultural differentialism," see Meyer, T. *Identitas-Wahn. Die Politisierung des kulturellen Unterschieds.* Berlin: Aufbau Verlag, 1997. On this same theme, there are also interesting points made in Menzel, U. *Globalisierung versus Fragmentierung.* Suhrkamp, 1998. This author still maintains, however, that migrants must accept western "culture."

[279] Cited in Barbesino, P. "Talking about Migration: the State Monitoring System in Italy." *Délit d'immigration. La construction sociale de la deviance et de la criminalité parmi les immigrés.* Ed. S. Palidda. Brussels: Cost A2/ Migrations, 1996.

passport ("nationality") into an ethnic and cultural marker. This is even more true when the private social sector functions as a substitute for the state, which up until now had limited itself to external controls and repression of migration phenomena. Now the culturalization and ethnicization of migrants is seen as completely compatible with the official non-racist language of "democratic exclusion," and has the function of erasing the essential aspect of the *universal* rights of migrants in the work place as well as in public life and for institutions. This is not only because cultural particularism is incompatible on principle with legal and political universalism, according to which all people have equal rights independent of their origin or nationality. On the stage of cultures or multicultures the reality of any concrete relationship between migrants with the economic, institutional, or political powers has been obliterated. The "right to one's own culture" is not being questioned here;[280] it is logical, and is equal to any other right such as practicing one's own religion or sexual orientation or the right to privacy, when these are rights extended to everyone and are therefore recognized as universal rights, not alternatives to them. In this sense, "culture has nothing to do with it," but only legitimately enters into the debate on migration when the necessary legal and political clarifications have been made. As an American scholar affirms:

> The multiculturalism of our time has helped us to recognize and appreciate cultural diversity, but I believe this movement has too often left the lines of shape and color.[281]

[280] See also Appiah K. and A. Gutman. *Color Conscious. The Political Morality of Race.* Princeton: Princeton University Press, 1996.
[281] Hollinger, D. A. *Postethnic America. Beyond Multiculturalism.* New York: Basic Books, 1995. x.

V Albanian Campaigns

And what if all the ragged beggars in the old, rotten Mediterranean headed to Italy? Throw them into the sea! (Statement made to the press by Irene Pivetti, former President of the Chamber of Deputies, March, 1997)[282]

1 Stadiums, Camps, and other Accomodations

According to prevailing public opinion, the new migrations were a mainly a spontaneous and unforeseeable phenomenon, a calamity to be dealt with rationally and without complicating things with optimistic or emotional conceptions about universal human rights. The previous chapters discussed how this negative image is the cumulative result of interactions between the media and the political system, and how scientific discourses contribute to its legitimization. We also saw how this presupposes a fundamental asymmetry between "us" and "them," that "official State thought" still maintains "their" inferiority as opposed to "our" rationality despite its refined expressions and new myths of "ethnicity" and "multiculturalism." A culture of inferiorization is not the inevitable product of a strategy or intentional plan, but a complex system of symbolic references and material, economic, and political presuppositions that develop slowly and adapt to the contingencies and real or supposed fluctuations in migration "flows." And this culture operates not just on the level of media, general public opinion or views of intellectuals, but on the more mundane level of police measures and border patrols, that is, the control of aliens within and

---

[282] *Il Giornale.* 15 August 1991.

outside of "our" national space. While unintentional, the culture of inferiorization demonstrates consistent characteristics over long periods of time.

Various "politics of migration" aside, the Italian State has held firmly to the principle of migrants' inferiority, which is evident in the presupposition that they should be dealt with *exclusively* as a function of Italian interests, either real or imagined. Naturally, this formulation has found explicit formulations – consider for example the definition of migrants as "legally non-existent beings." More often, this principle manifests itself in the form of automatic procedures which just "work by themselves" and which public powers have rarely felt the need to justify, except when employing the rhetoric of "emergency," as if the objects or targets of these procedures were unworthy of the slightest interest in their motivations or their needs, much less their rights. The way in which Italy, at different times, has dealt with "the Albanian emergency" is a revealing illustration of the ability to put into practice an absolutist culture of inferiorization toward "others."

The "Albanian problem" exploded as a national emergency between March and September of 1997, the period from the crisis in the Berisha regime to the repatriation of migrants and refugees. And though the relations between Italy and Albania seem weak and infrequent, they are of ancient date. Beginning with the long communist regime of Hoxha (and the arrival of Albanians by boat in 1991, to which I will return), Italy has had dealings with Albania at critical historical moments. In 1939, the Kingdom of Albania was annexed by Italy, an episode that does little to enhance the honor of the "nation" of Italy, but moreover marks the beginning of a series of military mistakes during the Second World War (the disastrous Fascist attack on Greece the following year was launched from Albania). For obvious reasons, the events from the early months of 1997 have remained in the shadows. During this period, the debate over "nation" raged in Italy. Many voices called for the antifascist elements of the constitution to be eliminated so that honor could be restored to those young soldiers who had lined up in support of Mussolini and the Republic of Salò. In our *Historikerstreit* the Italian contribution to anti-Semitism is always downplayed, and we glide past the use of poison gas during the war in

Abyssinia, not to mention the massacres and deportations organized by Rodolfo Graziani in Libya, because we are Italians and *"brava gente."* Our military now assigned to peace-keeping missions in Lebanon, Bosnia, and Somalia has to deal with the scandal over soldiers who tortured Somalis. National honor is at stake, so perhaps it is best not to go on too much about the annexation of Albania in 1939.

Over sixty years of calamities separate us from that last imperial adventure. Looking at Italy's annexing of Albania reveals something about the persistence of a certain culture, an attitude that is "naturally" colonial and paternalistic toward the Albanians, and says more about today's rejections than yesterday's colonial endeavors.[283] That moment displays grotesque elements typical of fascism, as seen in the newsreels of the time.[284] On April 13, 1939 Mussolini as "founder of the Empire," announced from Palazzo Venezia the deposition of King Zogu[285] and proclaimed Vittorio Emmanuele III the sovereign of Albania. "Italy will show the world and the people of Albania that with its men and its weapons, it is capable of enforcing order, social progress, and respect for every religious faith," stated Mussolini.[286] On April 16, 1939, a delegation of Albanian collaborators offered the crown of Albania to Vittorio Emmanule III. On May 9, a guard of Albanian soldiers commanded by Italians swore their loyalty to the king of Italy (in Italian). In keeping with fascist diplomatic style, the annexation had in reality already occurred on April 7 with the arrival of a military unit at Valona and the following painless occupation of the Albanian

---

[283] The present considerations become part of the ongoing debate over the persistence of colonialist discourses in the so-called era of post-colonialism. See also Prakash, G., ed. *After Colonialism. Imperial Histories and Postcolonial Displacements.* Princeton: Princeton University Press, 1995; Weimann, R., ed. *Ränder der Moderne. Repräsentation und Alterität im (post)kolonialen Diskurs.* Frankfurt a.M.: Suhrkamp, 1993; Weibel, P and S. Zizek, eds. *Inklusion/Exklusion. Probleme des Postkolonailismus und der globalen Migration.* Wien: Passagen Verlag, 1997.

[284] Caracciolo, N. *L'Albania dal Duce a Prodi.* Video distributed as a supplement to *L'Espresso*, March 1997. The video was produced by the RAI in collaboration with the Istituto Luce, and contains footage from 1990, 1997, and the fascist era.

[285] King Zogu came to power in 1924 with help from Italy. Albania was already an Italian protectorate from the moment of the annexation.

[286] My transcription of *L'Albania dal Duce a Prodi.*

territory. At any rate, some shots were fired. According to the newsreels of the time, average Albanians did not oppose the "peace keeping forces," but opponents were from "armed gangs of former prisoners who had been set free in an attempt to halt Italy's intervention."[287] The same expression was used in March, 1997 to define the "maniacs" who threatened Italians. Even sixty years later we talk about prisons being emptied out, gangs and "former inmates" out on bail who this time are attempting surreptitiously to mingle with the thousands of "*clandestini*" trying to land on Italian shores.

Of course recently there has been no shortage of contacts between Italy and the picturesque "land of eagles." Since the death of Enver Hoxha in 1985 media interest was limited about this communist "agropastoral" dictatorship that was considered hostile to both the west and the USSR (and even China, and in fact, the entire world), a "mysterious," backwards country, that was trying to cope with a new international order. Then, after 1990 we sensed a confused awakening, a growing interest in anything that came "from here," from consumerism to the market, television, and freedom. Public opinion in the west was still euphoric in the wake of the fall of the Berlin Wall and eagerly hailed any cracks we saw opening in this last bastion of communism. In July of 1990, Italy was among the first to organize refugees who opposed the regime and who wanted to cross over into Europe, seeking asylum in the embassies of western countries (800,000 in the Italian embassy alone). The press gave tremendous coverage of the offers Italian mayors made to welcome refugees, the television showed Albanian fathers landing in Italy, lifting up their children and crying, "Free, you are finally free!"[288] The historically bonds with Albania were discovered with enthusiasm, which had always been a bastion of Christianity against the Turks, and in Italy then there were over 100,000 citizens of Albanian origin and who spoke Albanian.[289] In March, 1991, more Albanians set sail for Italy, this time under their own initiative. Apparently, the

[287] *Ibid.*
[288] *L'Albania dal Duce a Prodi.* Video distributed as a supplement to *L'Espresso*, March 1997.
[289] *La Stampa*, 12 July 1990, cited in Vehbiu, A. and R. Devole. *La scoperta dell'Albania. Gli albanesi secondo i mass media.* Milan: Paoline Editoriali, 1996.

welcome for these freedom-starved brothers never materialized. Instead, they were annexed, shall we say, by the west, or rather, the north, thanks to the distinction between those that were coming to "be one of us" and those others who were just coming, which was beginning to irritate us (and the symptoms of the "immigration emergency" began to spread):

> Why would you welcome these Albanians without standing there laying down the rules and regulations, but when it comes to the people coming from Africa and the Third World, you want to count and control each one? [...]. First, because there is an Adriatic homeland: the people who live across the sea from us have never stopped feeling that they were the children of the same sea, even in times of war; and second, we feel a certain affinity for other Adriatic peoples [. . .][290]

However, it only took a few days for Albanians to be pushed back across the line. The fluid frontier that had included them when there were only a few hundred and they were choosing freedom (and when their flight had been organized by "us") moved backwards rapidly to establish a bridgehead on the "limes," our territorial waters. The Gulf War had just ended and the west feared reawakening the "Islamic menace" with the terrifying military humiliation in Iraq. Won't the Albanians be motivated to "rediscover Islam?" worried F. Venturini.[291] Wasn't Valona the port from which Mahomet II in 1480 launched his successful attack on Otranto, the very city that Albanians are pouring into today?[292] These melodramatic references to distant events translated suddenly into a definite panic of invasion, and not just an invasion of "ugly, dirty, and evil men," but an invasion of "trash," of "Asian" epidemics, of unimaginable diseases including "the mange." Consequently, the mayors of Brindisi and Otranto called upon the state authorities to aid in their disinfection efforts. The

---

[290] Bocca, G. *La Repubblica,* 10 March 1991, cited in Vehbiu, A. and R. Devole. P. 48. The main difficulty with these considerations is the riemergence of the ancient rhetoric of "mare nostrum," which smacks of the "Italy's Dalmatia," propaganda. The same discourse expands to include the rhetoric of "our Mediterranean" and the cultural roots of "our vital interests," etc.
[291] *Corriere della sera,* 7 March 1991. It was already evident that Islam had nothing to do with the flight from Albania, a pluri-religious country.
[292] See *L'Europeo,* 12 March 1991.

image of the Albanians, who were seen only eight months earlier as the proud inhabitants of the "land of eagles," people beside themselves with the joy of freedom and who opened their "blue eyes" wide toward a country that saw them as similar, now became the image of destitute beggars who needed to be aided, fed, and cleaned up.

The basis of political, economic, and cultural relations between Italy and Albania was laid and soon became established in the years from 1991-1997. Actually, the perception of the Albanians as dangerous beggars and the consequent measures of social defence did not deter hundreds of commercial ventures, coming mainly from the area of Puglia and other Adriatic regions, which saw tremendous commercial possibilities in Albania. These two processes are definitely not in contradiction. The fundamental idea (thanks to which the Albanian case was incorporated into Italian and European migration politics, along with Tunis and Morocco) is that between "us" and "them," there should be an open traffic in goods, but not people. Or rather, while the exchange of goods can be bi-directional, the exchange of people can only be uni-directional. Entrepreneurs, politicians, military personnel are free to go there, but none of them are free to come here. If they do, it becomes an "illegitimate wave." In March, 1991, a redefinition occurred, first in the sense of actions, and then in the sense of rights, or actions of the state, as was demonstrated dramatically a few months later with the horrific events when refugees were enclosed at the sports stadium in Bari, which no one ever mentions any more (similar to how we no longer discuss the annexation of 1939).

Although a great number of the refugees from March, 1991 have returned to Albania, disappointed and angry for the reception they received in Italy, thousands more have arrived. In August, 1991, a migration immediately defined as "a biblical exodus" became an international emergency. A photo circled the globe of a boat in the port of Bari filled far beyond capacity, with young Albanians trying to jump from it into the sea or sliding along the moorings, and thanks to the multiethnic industry of Benetton, this image has become a *Zeitbild*, a poster that represents our time, worthy of being considered alongside the serial images of Andy Warhol (Figure 22).[293]

Figure 22

[293] Cover of *Colors* 2 (Summer 1992): The Albanian *Zeitbild*. The cover reads, "Immigration brings new blood, new food, new music, new words, new film, new concepts of the world, new romantic possibilities, new excuses for parades … in an old world."

This time, under scrutiny from the entire world, Italian authorities were not taken by surprise. The Albanians were promised work papers and jobs, taken to the stadium in Bari where they remained for more than a week with no provisions for hygiene, washed down by police-held hydrants, and provided with food dropped from helicopters. The stadium was surrounded by law enforcement officers, and visited by Italian citizens who wanted to take their children "to see the Albanians." On August 14, the stadium was emptied by police, some of the Albanians were taken to refugee camps, while several hundred (including those who had deserted from the army, and so represented a potential danger) were dispersed to various Italian cities and finally sent back to Albania on military aircraft. The deception perpetrated against the Albanians was justified as a necessity for national security, as some officials of the operation admitted years later:

> Orfei (from "*Limes*"): It seems clear to me that the problem of the Alba mission hangs on the rules of engagement. Under current procedures, can a commander impede or discourage an exodus toward the Italian coast?
> General Caligaris: Absolutely not. Not because he doesn't have clear duties, no one told him that he has to stop the departure of refugees. Under what regulation would he stop them?
> General Angioni: It would be devastating, because women and children are involved. It's an order that can't be carried out, and if it were, it would cause problems. Remember what happened in Somalia. What would happen if our men open fired? The refugee problem has to solved on Italian soil. [...]
> General Pedone: I concur with what General Angioni has said. The refugee problem has to be solved in Italy. I directed our response to the "Albanian emergency" three times as vice-commander of the Pinerolo Brigade. The last time, when thousands of Albanians were locked in the stadium at the port in Bari, we managed to divide them up through various parts of Italy, and then, in a coordinated effort with the police, they were repatriated [...]
> General Angioni: I would like to mercifully draw a curtain over the whole affair! It was an embarrassment that I have no wish to repeat.[294]

---

[294] "Tavola rotonda. Le missioni di pace secondo i militari." *Limes* 2 (1997): 290-291.

To delineate the dimensions of the episode, it becomes necessary remember that a sports center was used as a detainment center. Many commentators in the national and international press immediately indicated parallels between this and other such episodes, dramatic examples in historic memory: the internment of the Jews in Paris at "Vélo d'Hiver," in July 1942,[295] or the stadium-lager in Santiago, Chile, in the autumn of 1973. Terms such as "lager" and "cages" are tossed about, and even if used ironically, still directly suggest that Albanians are subhuman or bestial. The savage crowds, like magma ready to flood into the streets of Bari if not contained by police, were considered dangerous (the crowd contained "ex-inmates," as in 1939) and armed (after the stadium was emptied, thirteen pistols, three old rifles, and one sub-machine gun were found). Albanians always simultaneously incite pity, disgust, solidarity and fear.[296] But the spontaneous parallel seen between this and other different internments masks the inability to define the innovative political significance of this action.

Aside from the emotional but superficial analogies to internments in Paris and Santiago (the purpose in both those cases was to *annihilate* respectively the Jews and the opponents of Pinochet),[297] the internment in Bari in 1991 was only the preparatory and theatrical phase of a mass expulsion. Actually, it fits neatly with the measures that western democracies assume nowadays toward migrants and refugees. The assault of the church of Saint-Bernard (summer, 1996) the expulsion of the *sans papiers*, the expulsion of foreign women and children from Germany (spring, 1997), the repatriation of *"clandestini"* organized by Italy in accord with the governments of Tunis and Morocco (summer, 1998), are all examples of the same kind of politics: police actions aided by the military undertaken under the satisfied eye of public opinion in

[295] See Hilberg, R. *The Destruction of the European Jews*, New Haven, CT: Yale University Press (3rd Edition), 2003.
[296] See Vehbiu, A. "La nave della follia." *Derive e approdi* 14 (1997): 13 for a description of the Albanians as primordial horde.
[297] For a discussion of the typology of the camps, see Agamben, G. *Homo Sacer: Sovereign Power and Bare Life*, Palo Alto, CA: Stanford University Press, 1998.

collaboration with the governments of the countries of origin or departure of those to be expelled (to whom we deign to offer some economic or practical assistance), and conclude the episode to international satisfaction.

In this context, the stadium acts merely as the *trash dump*, a non-place[298] parallel to the *terrains vagues* where gypsies camp or the "*campi di permanenza temporanea*" that today "welcome" those foreigners awaiting repatriation. The cultural extra-territoriality of the stadium, a place usually intended for amusement, sport, or concerts, transforms into a space of juridical extra-territoriality. Given the objective is to contain a few thousand refugees, nothing better can be found that an animal pen. As people of uncertain status (were they "*extracommunitari*," "immigrants," "*clandestini*," or "refugees"?), the Albanians in Bari were treated as animals, not only because the Italian State had become fiercer but simply because immediate legal categories were not available that allowed them to be treated as men and women. The Albanians thought they had arrived in Italy, but they were actually somewhere else, in an extra-territorial space, whose sole function was provisional containment. If dealt with as an indistinct, dangerous mass, they are treated as animals, imagined as nothing better than a zoo – sprayed down with water, food thrown over the bars, open-air defecation, and even Sunday visitors. It is because they represent the unthinkable: *a crowd that believes it is human, but it is not.* No satisfaction, then if the stadium in Bari doesn't fit with the typology of the "Vélo d'Hiver" or Santiago. The stadium in Bari documents a new modality in the historical mechanics of the dehumanization of human beings. Only a few years later, in the summer of 1998, Italy would have the chance to refine this model.

2 At the Bottom

The history of the relationships between Italy and Albania has seen different stages, but they are all unified by a common denominator: the *inexistence* of

---

[298] Augé, M. *Non-Places: Introduction to an Anthropology of Supermodernity*, Brooklyn, NY: Verso, 1995.

the Albanians as human beings: the annexation in 1939, the acceptance that was purely rhetorical and instrumentalized in 1990, the elimination of the refugee problem by interring them in the stadium at Bari in 1991, the incredible media campaign about the "Albanian danger" when the government of Sali Berisha dissolved in the face of popular uprisings at the beginning of 1997. The inexistence is obviously *political* and has never excluded individual activities to aid and support Albanian refugees, which are usually the work of volunteers. My point is that this politics of inexistence has had tragic consequences: on the night between March 28 and 29, 1997, the Italian sloop *Sibilla* collided with the Albanian motorboat *Kater I Rades*, sinking it and causing the death of nearly 90 Albanians, mostly women and children, who drowned without arousing in Italy any outcry to investigate the meaning of this "fatality." If the reasons are sought, they can be framed within the broader context of the relations between the world of the rich and the world of the poor.

Before analyzing this episode and the disconcerting manner in which the Italian government and public opinion handled and internalized it, some preliminary considerations are necessary. At the time that this study was being completed, little more than a year after the "Albanian crisis" and the sinking of the *Kater I Rades,* the issue had disappeared from public discussion. Too many other events occurred that prevented the episode from arousing sustained reactions. In April, 1997, Italy sent a peace-keeping mission to Albania, which was concluded with no incident of note. The Fatos Nano government that followed the Berisha government attempted to normalize things in the country. In September of 1997, the repatriation of *"clandestini"* began, while numerous other boats arrived and quickly disappeared from media attention. Italy finally became provided with a law about immigration, was accepted by the Schengen group and entered triumphantly into the European Union after years of painful economic sacrifices. The Albanians, as had previously occurred with the Moroccans and gypsies, became the leading actors in daily crime dramas that have "made our cities unliveable": we only heard of them when a prostitute was arrested by the police, or maybe killed by a client or a pimp, or when some form of illegal trafficking brought attention to the existence of the "Albanian mafia."

It has become clichéd to point out that public memory in societies of mass communication are notoriously short. It is less obvious that during the period of the Albanian tragedy, *inasmuch as they were "refugees" or "immigrati clandestini," they were already dead, either drowned or living it Italy, because they didn't exist.* The most dramatic example of this non-existence, and something that caused quite a bit of stir at the time of the ship's sinking, was the absence of the government or the state in the symbolic location in the tragedy, the ports where the survivors landed. No representative of the government was present in Brindisi, there was no ceremony organized to recognize the women and children who would not have drowned if the Italian navy had not patrolled the coasts of Puglia with the explicit order to prevent anyone from landing.[299] Silvio Berlusconi alone, trying to ride the populism of the new right, appeared in tears in Brindisi only to later ignore the entire issue. The only reaction of the Italian government was given by Romano Prodi sometime later during a visit to Albania in which he promised to remunerate the victims' families. In short, today's silence is only the extension of yesterday's silence about the true victims of the whole affair.

The fact that the Italian press ranted on about the Albanian question for the entire Spring of 1997 should deceive no one. Actually, as represented in the media, Italy does nothing but talk about itself, give voice to its own anxieties and form to its own ghosts, scream its own obsessions, and watch over its own political affairs (and this would be the "specular function of migration phenomena"). Rereading the news articles from the spring, 1997 creates an impression today that could only be termed "grotesque." But beyond that, the ways that the media constructed the "Albanian emergency" and especially the Otranto tragedy are the product of a powerful logic. First was the *consensual construction* of the Albanians as a threat. Second, the *consensual performance* of a script that concludes in the climax of the ship's sinking. Third, the *removal*

---

[299] It was not until 5 April, 1997 that a representative of the government, vice-president Veltroni, met with a delegation of victims' family members. In March, 1998, exactly one year after the ship went down, procedures began for opening a court case against the officials who were responsible. There was no significant public response.

or rather redirection of the significance of the event. In other words, the media's analysis of the Albanian crisis at the time demonstrated how a country prepares the conditions of a tragedy, stages it in a certain way, and then uses it to talk about something else.[300]

"Consensual preparation" of an event does not equal *intentionality*. Clearly, the government cannot be accused of having *wanted* the ship to sink. Rather, given certain prerequisites, the probability that an event will occur is very high. In the case of the *Kater I Rades*, there were two fundamental prerequisites: first, using the media to label the Albanian people a horde of criminals ready to attack us, thus transforming refugees into *"clandestini"* with a wave of the magical legal wand, and second, the resulting order to the navy to prevent them leaving their boats.[301] These prerequisites manifest an absolute synchronicity between the media construction of the Albanian danger and the government's actions. Indeed, the government appears subordinated to the reality constructed by the media. The drowning of the Albanian refugees is only the cruel and highly visible result of the "tautology of fear" whose various workings we have already seen.

The analysis offered by the Italian press in the early spring of 1997 shows how, with few exceptions, all the major national dailies shared the same paranoid image of the Albanian issue, beginning with the representation of Albania as a boil infected by the communist virus. Mario Vargas Llosa, though he admits he "has never set food in Albania," is convinced that,

> The Albanian tragedy [...] didn't begin with bank fraud. What we are seeing is nothing more than the bursting of a pustule filled for decades with the pus of despotism and oppression."[302]

---

[300] I am indebted to M. Maneri (*Lo straniero consensuale*) for the articulation of these concepts, which I am applying to in a different context.

[301] See the decree of 20 March 1997, n. 60, which abrogates special powers to the Minister of the Interior and authorizes prefects and police commissioners to expel every foreigner whom they believe to be undesirable. This decree was preceded by numerous declarations by government leaders who insisted that Albanians no longer be considered "refugees," but *"clandestini."*

[302] "La barbarie sempre in agguato." *La Repubblica.* 26 March 1997.

A boil or pustule that swells with the crisis of the Berisha government and the dissolution of the Albanian state explodes, infecting us with its virus, its refugees, as soon as they begin to touch our ports. To give an idea of the role of the media in the crisis that ended with the drowning, I include here several representative headlines from the two weeks that preceded the tragedy on March 29, 1997:

March 14: "Civil War, Flight from Albania, Italy's Coasts under Siege" (*l'Unità*).

March 15: "The Pugliese Mafia Enlista Refugees (*Il Giornale*); Invasion by Desperate People" (*la Repubblica*); "Italy Is Invaded by People in Flight" (*la Repubblica*).

March 16: "Refugee Emergency. Now It's an Exodus: Ship Full of Children, Thousands Arrive, Brindisi Port Is Closed" (*la Repubblica*); "Refugees, There's No Room Left. Thousands of Them, 50 Children Flee on a War Ship" (*la Repubblica*).

March 18: "Vigna: Red Alert, Risk of Criminal Invasion" (*Corriere della Sera*); "Albanian Refugees a Danger To Neighborhoods. Some Escape from Refugees Centers and We Fear They Will Take Over Empty Houses on the Adriatic Coast" (*Il Giornale*); "An Ocean of Refugees in Puglia. Beyond the Limit of 9,000, It's an Emergency" (*l'Unità*).

March 19: "The Most Desperate Ones Are the Ones from '91. Six Years Ago Starving Families Landed, Now They Are Derelicts with Cell Phones. One Restaurant Owner Says, 'Back then They Needed Food, Now They Need a Good Beating.'" (*Il Giornale*); "They Use Their Children as Passports. Albanians Find Orphans for Easy Visas" (*Il Giornale*); "Hotel Owners: Do We Choose Refugees or Tourists?" (*la Repubblica*); "Four Teenagers Arrive in Termini in Rags and Starving – The First of an Unstoppable Wave" (*Mattina*, insert in Rome's edition of *l'Unità*); "Refugees and Criminal Gangs" (*Il Messaggero*); "Refugees – Crime Alert" (*La Stampa*); "Warning! Albanian Criminals" (*Il Gazzettino di Venezia*).

March 24: "Judge Vigna Tells Minister Del Turco, 'Yes, Criminals Have Infiltrated'" (*Corriere della Sera*).

March 25: "Naval Blockade to Halt Albanians. Government Takes Hard Line. They'll Be Sent Back Because They're '*Immigrati clandestini*'" (*la Repubblica*)

March 29: "Albanian Boat Overturns. Craft Dragged to Puglia's Coast by Naval Unit" (*l'Unità*)

The different newspapers, regardless of political orientation, large or small, local or national, all share the same rhetorics, the same sensational language and especially the same alarmism that became violent on March 19, the day before refugees were transformed into *clandestini* by means of a governmental decree. A certain uniformity corresponds perfectly between the content of the news articles and the comments that fill the inside pages. Below are comments from Alberto Arbasino that synthesize the press' entire campaign about the "criminal emergency:"

> Our Balkan guests came with Kalashnikov, with their ethnic habit of pillaging, which historians tell us has existed for centuries before communism [...]. Our guests sell packets of drugs and lead groups of kids down the road to addiction, they line up swarms of ragged, hungry, abused children at stop lights [...]. Our guests fight at knife point with gangs of other guests to gain control of "their" territory, in accordance with the African customs described by anthropologists and seen again and again in television to make us feel guilty [...].[303]

It seems almost superfluous to mention that at no point during the entire crisis and up through the expulsions in 1997, was any consistent proof ever found for these accusations made against Albanians (that they use their children as human shields, that criminals had infiltrated them en masse, etc.) Evidence is gathered ad hoc in the news stories that all follow the same system: shocking headlines, reliance on the basest of stereotypes, distortion or exaggeration of insignificant details in order to reinforce stereotypes and so on. Within this framework,

---

[303] Arbasino, A. "Ma armati di mitra." *La Repubblica.* 15 March 1997.

anything goes, even inventing details, like "submachine guns floating in the port" as in the story below:

"Warning!"

Their features are baked by the sun and furrowed with early wrinkles, the faces of destitute farmers with a clever look. Their faded sweaters stink of the stable […]. These escaped criminals from Valona are from the past […] yesterday in the waters of San Cataldo there were Kalashnikov submachine guns that had been thrown from the boat when a unit from the San Marco division arrived. (*La Stampa*)

This same style was adopted by nearly all of the daily papers, and could make Eugène Sue blush with its absolute disdain for human beings who, according to the descriptions of journalists and observers, are frightened animals or potential murderers. The fact remains that the 15,000 Albanians who arrived in Italy in March, 1997, thanks to this label of subhuman, were deprived yet again of any human aspect and could not advance any claim to human rights. Their presence constituted the pretext under which Italy could give voice to its obsessions: the Northern League called its mayors to resist the Albanians, the owners of tourist based businesses on the Riviera protested any asylum that would damage the summer tourist season, mayors from Romagna proposed accepting Albanian women and children because they are "inoffensive" but wanted to refuse men, etc.

After an event in which all the victims were Albanians, only volunteers insisted (unsuccessfully) on reviewing the politics of the programmatic refusal of refugees. The drowning of 90 innocent victims, a fact that any civil society in a modern democracy should be deeply ashamed of, became the occasion for a provocative debate on the "goodness" of Italians, while the institutions could do nothing more than quibble over the legal definition of the navy's intervention. Following are excerpts of a television report from April 1, 1997, two days after the Albanian boat was sunk:

Gad Lerner: Monsignor Di Liegro, do you think that in and of itself, the patrol, the idea of dissuading them from entering Italy while they were already in the middle of the sea could have been the cause of the risk, was is something that could have been avoided or …?
Luigi di Liegro: Well, I believe that the volunteers have been unanimous in raising a cry that has been important on the international level. I'm referring to the United Nations High Commission for Refugees […]. So this naval cordon certainly impeded those who wanted to come to Italy asking for asylum, humanitarian rather than political, it kept them from accomplishing their desire, their aspiration […].
Admiral Angelo Mariani: I completely disagree with what the United Nations commissioner said. He referred to this as a blockade […].
Lerner: He said that this form of patrol strongly resembled a blockade.
Mariani: And I believe he is completely mistaken.
Lerner: Why is that?
Mariani: A blockade is an act of war between two enemy nations, an action carried out with force […] and against the will of one of the governments. This patrol was the result of collaboration between two friendly nations, such as Italy and Albania, who decided to put this action into place to prevent illegal actions and to keep individuals from placing themselves at risk.[304]

So the drowning of women and children caused by a "patrol" whose assignment was "to prevent people from putting themselves at risk" was merely a daily occurrence along the way that carried no great weight in the "Albanian threat." As mentioned earlier, the "fear machine" sets into motion anytime an "immigration emergency" arises, and is an absolutely irrational reaction respective to the nature and dimensions of the phenomenon. And although the reaction is irrational, it is not without logical motivations. Liquidating refugees as "*clandestini*," preparing for a portion of them to filter into the interment camps, mobilizing *carabinieri* and police to contain these new *metoikos* obviously costs far less in terms of political intelligence and planning than activating the procedures and utilizing the public services for accepting and integrating them socially. Above all, the fear reaction allows a redefinition of the relations between a developed country and a poor one in terms that would

---

[304] Transcription of *Pinocchio.* 1 April 1997.

be economically advantageous. Considering the relations between Italy and Albania before the crisis of March, 1997, reveals some of the positive economic and geopolitical pay backs that arise from the panic of invasion.

3 **Minding Our Own Business**

On February 4, 1997, the journalist Gad Lerner dedicated an episode of his successful television program *Pinocchio* to the Italian businesses operating in Albania, which was televised from that nation's capital. The program's title, "Tirana, Italia," could not have been more appropriate. For more than two hours, a cast of euphoric *Italian* entrepreneurs, silent Albanian workers, Lerner, Mayor Bassolino of Naples, a representative of the government from Tirana, a union representative, and other guests, including the MP from the Northern League Borghezio (who has instigated patrols against "*extracommunitari*" and is known for having proposed in the past that the police take the footprints of all "*immigrati clandestini*" in order to be able to identify them) discussed the economic prospects of small *Italian* businesses in Albania, the bureaucratic tangles and insupportable labor costs that strangle businesses in *Italy*, and the unemployment in *southern Italy*. They claimed that an Albanian worker in a shoe factory costs his *Italian* employer less than $120 a month as opposed to the $2,000 a month that a worker would cost in *Italy*, that *Italian* business in Albania have found their Eldorado, or rather, their Far East, and that these entrepreneurs would be happy to see *Italian* salaries be competitive with Albanian ones. As the program's title infers, there was no discussion about the social situation in Albania, and what attracted these businessmen there. Only one volunteer from a religious institution pointed out that these salaries were low even for Albania, and alluded to the difficult work conditions imposed on the young Albanian workers.

Two months before the collapse of Berisha's government, the "invasion of the *clandestini* and delinquents" and the sinking of the Albanian boat (events which all appeared on the front pages of Italian newspapers between February and April, 1997, and also in two more episodes of *Pinocchio*) Tirana was

"Italian." This small country, having escaped from the Hoxha and Alia regimes, aided by Italian generosity (operation "Pellicano" in 1993), enlightened in every sense by the RAI and Fininvest, was becoming an Italian protectorate: politically, in that Ministers flew to Tirana to stipulate accords in the battle against crime and the *"clandestini;"* economically, with more than 600 active Italian companies; and cultural (one of our Ministers lamented in this episode of *Pinocchio* that the government is not generous enough with the Italian Cultural Institute in Tirana where Albanians are "hungry" for our books). Just as Italy was getting ready to join the European Union Club, it finally seemed ready to expand its sphere of geopolitical, geoeconomic, and geocultural influence. And when the fairy tale ended in tragedy, it was taken for granted that Albania was "our problem." "Albania, an Italian Emergency," was the title of an issue of the geopolitical journal *Limes* dedicated to the Berisha regime and published a few days after the sinking of the *Kater I Rades.*

Geopolitical analyses were unnecessary in order to create an immediate and general consensus that the crisis in Albania was essentially an Italian problem and only incidentally Albanian. As soon as the news spread in the first days of February, 1997, that the inhabitants of several cities were revolting against the Berisha regime, and after accusations of having covered the financial groups and organizing the so-called "pyramids," the crisis in Albania immediately was interpreted in an Italian key: "A death wish, that not just Albania, but all of Europe, and especially Italy, will have to deal with," warned one pessimistic editorial in *la Repubblica* from February 12, 1997. For nearly the entire month of March the editorials of the major Italian papers repeated the same theme. Paolo Garimberti spoke of "Europe Unarmed."[305] Enzo Bettiza demanded, "A Firm Hand in the Balkans."[306] In accordance with its northern leanings, on March 6, *Il Giornale* sounded the alarm, "The Statistics for a Venetian Company are in Danger," as processing this important document had been entrusted to an Albanian company. Franco Venturini reaffirmed that we are

[305] *La Repubblica.* 3 March 1997.
[306] *La Stampa.* 4 March 1997.

talking about, "Our Own Business."[307] Enzo Biagi discussed the possibility of a military intervention in "When Our Men Arrive."[308] "An Italian Problem," was the title of an editorial by Sergio Romano in which the former ambassador cuts right to the heart of the problem:

> The Italian workers who moved to Albania to utilize the local labor and produce goods at a lower cost will bear the costs [for the collapse of Berisha's government.] And the immigration laws will also bear the costs, destined as they are to be swamped by *clandestini* who are looking for jobs – either legal or illegal – on this side of the Adriatic.[309]

Faced with a purely domestic interpretation of the tragedy that was taking place only a few kilometers off of our coasts, the temptation arises to speak of neo-colonialism, even if this term can seem inappropriate. During the entire period of this crisis, from the beginning of the revolution through the elections in June, no colonial troops appeared on the streets of Albanian cities, but there were old police vans donated by Italy to the government, its "friend," and the tracked vehicles for the United Nations peace keepers were coordinated by the Italians. Colonialism had faded decades ago, we know. And yet, it is difficult to overcome the suspicion that a new form of domination was imposed by the rich and powerful North upon the poorer countries that "besiege" it on the south and east. It is a domination that has no need of a colonial rhetoric, but that makes use of every available economic, political, and military instrument to keep down the poor and hungry who are too close to us.

During the Golden Age of colonialism, domination was enacted by sending weapons and troops overseas, deposing petty kings or sultans (as in the film *The Wind and the Lion*) and annexing territories. In exchange, the subjected populations received some form of western administration, at times they were obligated to abandon subsistence economies to enjoy the advantages of

---

[307] *Corriere della sera.* 4 March 1997.
[308] *Corriere della sera.* 5 March 1997.
[309] *La Stampa.* 2 March 1997.

modernization, and they were granted the privilege of providing troops for European and international wars.[310] Colonialism, which is now dreadfully out of style, was based on the presupposition that natives, squeezed by colonies, needed to be integrated into an imperial territorial system. This lead to the dislocation of civilian and military personnel, the maintenance of costly administrative apparatus overseas, and an extension of limited benefits to the elite.[311] On the other hand, decolonization, which is usually interpreted as a product of western generosity, cost the lives of millions in the colonies as well as the political decline of Europe. Furthermore, for decades, European governments have had to deal with the backlash of colonial reflux, worry about ex-colonials who demanded naturalization,[312] maintain local governments that continued to defend European interests under the guise of independence (consider the histories of the Congo, Rwanda, and Burundi, rife with massacres and genocides that have been dragging on for ages).[313]

Nowadays, we are spared all of these difficulties. With the decline of political colonialism, no European government would dream of wasting resources to maintain troops in distant lands (with the obvious exception of peace keeping missions). The role of benefactors and educators, the "white man's burden," in the words of Kipling, has been assumed by entrepreneurs on the condition that the individuals being aided will accept lower salaries and that

---

[310] Italy's position is unusual in the global phenomenon of decolonialization. Italy was one of the last nations to become a colonial power, and Italian domination was brutal to the point of genocide in Eritrea, Ethiopia, Somalia, and Libya (1880-1945). While Italy's colonial past was quickly swept under the rug, thanks to works such as Rochat, G. and A. Del Boca. *Gli italiani in Africa orientale.* Vol I *Dall'unità alla marcia su Roma.* Vol II *La conquista dell'Impero.* Vol III *La caduta dell'Impero.* Vol IV *Nostalgia delle colonie.* Milan: Mondadori, 1992 and Rochat, G. and A. Del Boca. *Gli italiani in Libia. Tripoli bel suol d'amore 1860-1922.* Milan: Mondadori, 1993, and *Gli italiani in Libia. Dal fascismo a Gheddafi.* Milan: Mondadori, 1994, awareness of Italy's colonial past has reemerged. I am unaware of research that links the events of this period in history to current Italian attitudes toward migrants.

[311] For a meaningful description of these processes, see Panikkar, K.M. *Asia & Western Dominance,* London: George Allen & Unwin, 1953.

[312] See Nair, S. *Le regard des vainqueurs. Les enjeux français de l'immigration.* Paris: Grasset, 1992.

[313] Braeckman, C. *Ruanda. Storia di un genocidio.* Rome: Strategia della lumaca, 1995.

their governments will not concern themselves with unpatriotic issues such as workers' rights or union relations. This idea was reinforced on the episode of *Pinocchio* by an Italian entrepreneur with businesses in Albania:

> Gad Lerner: [question for an Italian entrepreneur in Tricase, Lecce, who at the time of the transmission owned a factory that manufactured shoe soles in Albania]. Yes, could you please explain one thing to me [...], is Albania still attractive for you, or has it become more expensive, as your colleague was saying earlier, as the lifestyle changes, and salaries will increase, then will you relocate to another country, one that is farther East?
> Entrepreneur: Mr. Lerner, there is labor available in the world, you can use the labor in Albania, as we do, which costs even less. That's the bottom line, and I'll let you draw your own conclusions. How much does it cost, does it cost less and so on: it's not that it *can* cost less, it *does* cost less.
> Lerner: Indeed, you've already opened locations in India, if I'm not mistaken?
> Entrepreneur: Exactly! And if Albania isn't competitive in the future, then of course we'll relocate to India, we'll relocate to Rwanda, where there are a lot of people who need to be given jobs.[314]

Naturally, no one can expect that, in addition to attractive production conditions, governments will always be supportive and willing or that police will always take a hard line against laborers as in Singapore, India, Indonesia, or Thailand. Often the work force is large and inexpensive and in turbulent and insecure countries. In this case, as in Albania, the entrepreneurs are forced to act:

> Lionello Polesel, a native of Venice, is a contractor building a section of the aqueduct financed by the World Bank and when all of Albania took up arms in March and the looting began, he hired 20 thugs armed to the teeth to guard the work and act as his body guards. Eight hundred dollars a month to each (while the workers on the aqueduct are paid $150 a month). On April 12, when the boats [from the Italian peace mission] were ready to slip the moorings in Brindisi, he fired everyone. That was too easy. They took him hostage, explaining that for the

[314] Transcription of "Pinocchio." 4 February 1997.

two days they worked, they had to be paid through the month of May. And why was that? Because they said so.[315]

The mass media reported, beginning in February 1997, that there were several cases of entrepreneurs who practiced armed self-defence, as if the reasons were obvious. In June of 1997, an Italian killed three Albanians who tried to attack his factory, and he suffered no legal consequences. To appreciate this entrepreneurial spirit, imagine if an American or German factory owner financed a private militia in Sardinia to protect himself from the danger of being kidnapped. It's true that Berisha's police force was disbanded, but few people questioned the legitimacy of this businessman's actions, just as few questioned that an international financial organization awards contracts for public works to entrepreneurs without checking on the salaries and work conditions. While entrepreneurs claim that they bring development, it seems they are allowed to do anything. The interesting aspect of the self-defence in this entrepreneurial culture is the *obviousness* with which it is presented. The question arises dramatically in the second episode of *Pinocchio* dedicated to the "Albanian emergency" televised from Brindisi on March 18, 1997. The Albanian "civil war" had already reached its climax, boatloads of "*clandestini*," or refugees in Italy continued to arrive, more than 8,000 at the time of the program's transmission. The episode, which included several entrepreneurs, two undersecretaries of the Foreign Affairs Department (Fassino and Sinisi), and other guests, the main issue of discussion was controlling "*clandestini*." In addition, the defence of Italian factories in Albania was also discussed:

> Lerner: [to an Italian entrepreneur] Your factory produces ....what?
> Entrepreneur: We have factories in Scuatari, Albania [...]
> Lerner: In Scutari. What are conditions like there?
> Entrepreneur: The situation is [....] one factory was attacked and they stole everything, including the windows, the bathroom tiles, the doors, everything [...]
> Lerner: So you lost this factory.

[315] *L'Espresso.* 24 April 1997. 56.

Entrepreneur: Yes, I lost the factory. For a second factory, its agroindustrial, we managed to make some private agreements, and we're managing to defend it, [...] day by day.
Lerner: What do you mean by "defend it"? Have you had to hire armed guards?
Entrepreneur: Yes, we've hired armed guards who are stationed inside [...]
Lerner: And they are not, sorry to say, but perhaps not very trustworthy?
Entrepreneur: Maybe, I don't know, but anyway, they're there on the inside with our factory foremen, and the workers are trying to defend the factories, so we're surviving.
Lerner: So the situation is rather like [...] 1943 in Italy, the workers are defending their factories [...].
Aloisi: Yes, their factories, exactly. From these hoards of [...] locusts.[316]

It's a strange situation when the economic actors hire the very gangs that are threatening them in order to defend themselves. Thanks to the entrepreneurs' openness, we discover that where there is no state, they don't hesitate to make themselves into one, if they feel that is necessary. But what exactly are they defending, other than their "property"? And what do the Albanians think? Who were the attackers? Were they hardened criminals or desperate starving people that were trying to get anything they could in the general confusion (like "locusts"?) It's difficult to know, because we've rarely had the opportunity of hearing the Albanians speak for themselves – workers, factory guards, the "locusts," the members of gangs. The entire issue of Italian-Albanian relations has been framed in criminal terms, and therefore from the standpoint of the *natural need to defend* Italian interests both there (where *our* factories are attacked by their gangs) and here (where boatloads of *clandestini* come to *our* beaches, and there are connections between their organized crime and *ours*). Rarely has there been some small tear in the image of what is happening "over there" through which the viewpoint of the Albanians appears, they who so suddenly found themselves involved in our disinterested economy. A peephole behind the curtain opened (and quickly closed again) in the second episode of *Pinocchio*:

[316] Transcription of "Pinocchio." 18 March 1997.

Lerner: So, [...] you, too, are Albanian?

Albanian youth: Yes, I'm just another Albanian [...]

Lerner: [...] and this logo means that you are here in Italy as a volunteer?

Albanian: Yes. I've been in Italy for 6 years and I'm part of a volunteer organization in [...] Otranto. And I would just like to say one thing to the gentleman here who says that only criminals and that kind of people are coming: *in Albania, every time I go, I see Italians, lots of Italians, and they go around loaded with money, and they're making that money off of the poor Albanians, and we are all under the eye of God, and the truth hurts.*

Lerner: Cataldo Motta [temporary director of the anti-mafia investigation division of Brindisi], this is an interesting point that this young Albanian man has made: is it true that there are Italian criminals who organize crime rings on the other side of the Adriatic, 80 km from here, sedition, etc.?

Motta: Well, we have no proof [...], no proof of this at all, nothing to affirm this [...]. *And I have the impression that this young man was referring to something else, to another kind of person, to those who make their money in a different way, through exploitation. I have the feeling that he's not talking about alliances between our organized crime and Albanian organized crime.*[317]

Even now very little is known about the work conditions in the Italian factories or about the "exploitation" that this young Albanian man mentions so candidly. The "emergency" that Italian entrepreneurs have tried to respond to individually is now past. In the very moment that the western lifestyle seemed in danger, the Italians (and then the Americans and the English) hurried up and called for support forces. It seems that these operations were not at as improvised and painless as television reports gave us to believe. One military expert reveals what the wider public ignored:

"What the News Doesn't Say: Secret Military Operations in Albania"

The sudden worsening of the crisis in Albania didn't come as a surprise to the western military commands and secret service organizations, contrary to popular belief. For some time, secret service agents have been operating in Albania with the two-fold mission of monitoring the development of the political situation

[317] *Ibid.* (My italics).

and laying the groundwork for an eventual evacuation operation of its own citizens. When the situation degenerated, small groups of special operations officers had already infiltrated the areas and determined the landing zones for the helicopters [...] In addition to their assignment as pathfinders, these nuclei carried out many other covert operations [...]. Because Brindisi is the seat of the NATO command for special operations in Bosnia, for several years helicopters, other special aircraft and naturally special operations officers had been stationed at the Italian airport there. *All of them had been under enemy fire at some time, and in every case the procedure was the same: neutralize as quickly as possible (i.e. eliminate) the aggressors or force them to desist and seek refuge.*[318]

After information about the actions of the UN's mission to Somalia, no one should be so naive as to be surprised if some reckless Albanian youth or "armed thugs" are "neutralized" ("i.e. eliminated") in their contact with the peace keepers. It would be more surprising to learn that there was no connection between the defense strategies of the factory owners and the covert operations in Albania. An Italian entrepreneur is tacitly allowed to hire local mercenaries just as our troops are permitted to "neutralize" them when they are not in the service of our business interests. The underlying idea that legitimizes this particular style of international relations is that "we" can do whatever we want to in their country to promote or defend "our" interests and "they" just need to collaborate. It's not an idea that can be proclaimed publicly but it is influential enough to guide political choices, military strategies, economic programs, demographic politics of immigration, and even influence popular television programs. Does anyone remember that quiz show, *Who is the Most Italianized Foreigner*? Pippo Baudo would ask an Albanian who had been blindfolded with an Italian flag to guess which Italian specialty he or she had just tasted.[319]

The relations that Italy has undertaken with Albania starting in 1990, the time at which refugees first arrived on the coasts of Puglia, can be summarized with the expression, "minding our own business." It's so very "ours" that it's taken for granted that Albanians are happy to work for us in Albania, but at the

---

[318] Nativi, A. "I retroscena militari della crisi." *Quaderni speciali di Limes.* March 1997. 51-52.
[319] Cited in Vehbiu, A. and R. Devole.

salaries we set, and they accept our private and national military, but they Italianize themselves "naturally" by speaking our language and appreciating our national cuisine. In addition to being an Italian protectorate economically and potentially culturally, too, Albania is included in the popular imagination as "our" social problem, equivalent to any run-down suburb or underdeveloped area in our own country.

There is however, a significant difference. Unlike the "*terroni*" during the 1960s or the southerners nowadays (according to a certain group north of the Appennines) we are not forced to consider the people of Albania as fellow citizens, and therefore obligated to "keep them," but we can free ourselves of them because they don't have Italian citizenship. The 15,000 refugees (or "*immigrati clandestini*") who had arrived in March, 1997 were forced to leave. On July 6, 1997 the Italian government declared its willingness to extend an exit bonus of 300,000 lire.[320] The hope was that these ragged beggars would stop being a problem on our soil but would try to go home and keep their problems there, with all the economic, political, and cultural advantages available that we outlined above. Thus Albania, precisely because it is our neighbour from across the road, embodies the concept that the rich societies of the world are developing about their closest, underprivileged neighbors.

---

[320] News reported in Italian newspapers from 7 July 1997.

VI **Non-Persons**

I am an invisible man. No, I am not a spook like those who haunted Edgar Allen Poe; nor am I one of your Hollywood-movie ectoplasms. I am a man of substance, of flesh and bone, fiber and liquids – and I might even be said to possess a mind. I am invisible, understand, simply because people refuse to see me. Like the bodiless heads you see sometimes in circus sideshows, it is as though I have been surrounded by mirrors of hard, distorting glass. When they approach me they see only my surroundings, themselves, or figments of their imagination – indeed, everything and anything except me.[321]

1 **In Limbo**

Consider the following dialogue that I transcribed in March, 1996 just a few days before the deadline for the illegal migrants to become legalized under the Dini decree. An Albanian citizen turned in all the necessary documentation for legalization to a functionary at the *questura* in an Italian city:

Albanian citizen: I have all my documents here […].
Functionary: I already told you that you still need the form for the social security number. Why don't you have it?
Albanian: Because my boss doesn't want to pay first.
Functionary: Look, I can't accept it this way. You have to have a receipt first. […]
Albanian (slightly agitated): I have all my documents in order. Why isn't everything all right?
Functionary (losing patience, after the exchange continues in a similar vein for several minutes): You have to stop being such a pain […]. Either bring me the receipt or take your application and get out. If you don't have everything back here and complete by the 31st, you'll be deported.

There are several things to point out in this exchange, beginning with the functionary's use of the informal "tu," which Italians in general and especially civil servants use with immigrants. I also feel compelled to point out how a mere

[321] Ellison, Ralph. *Invisible Man.* New York: Vintage Books, 1980. 3.

receipt can decide a foreigner's fate, even if he or she has no power to obtain it. During this period of legalizing migrants, civil servants could be polite to applicants or not, and the threat of being expelled could be carried out or not.[322] But the fact remains that from the moment he or she loses the possibility of making a complete application, the foreigner becomes "deportable."[323] He or she enters into the limbo shared by those who can be removed from the Italian territory because they are *"irregolare," "clandestino," "illegittimo,"* or *"abusivo."* In addition, even a complete application doesn't necessarily allow a foreigner to leave limbo. He or she could have all the documents in order, have a job and an employment card, and yet the final decision lies with an authority who of course decides based on the documentation, but that decision is influenced by the pressures of public opinion, and the good will and human sensitivity of individual functionaries. Theoretically, based on the Dini decree and the following decree of March 20, 1997 aimed at holding back the "Albanian invasion," as well as the immigration law of 1998, a foreigner can be expelled from Italy (for example, if suspected of a crime) even if he or she has a legal, steady job. In certain cases, if a foreigner has worked only intermittently or for short periods, as with seasonal work, his or her application will not be considered. But even foreigners who have been "legalized" can't expect a promising future. Italian law offers only temporary *permessi di soggiorno* and as soon their time is up, foreigners are back to where they started from in that absurd, endless game that our legislation has forced them to play.

Obviously, a foreigner could be in a condition of *"irregolarità"* even before applying for legal status. This uncertain condition does not prevent him or her from having some kind of employment, from living and entering into social relations. This condition can come to an end independently of the immigrant's social identity, who he or she really is. I define migrants who find themselves in this condition as "non-persons." They are alive, they conduct an existence

---

[322] According to the Minister of the Interior, in 1996 just over 5,000 foreign *"extracommunitari"* were expelled from Italy, while 34,000 were told to leave.

[323] For an elaboration of this concept, see Sayad, A. *L'immigration ou le paradoxe de l'alterité.* Brussels: De Boeck-Wesmael, 1990.

more or less analogous to that of "nationals," or the Italians around them, but against their will, they can slip from the condition of being individual persons. They continue to be alive anyway, but they no longer exist – not just for the society in which they live as "*clandestini*" but also for themselves as individuals in the sense that their actual existence will end and a different one will begin and they will have no choice in the matter.

That individuals pass from the condition of being "persons" to the condition of "non-persons" should in no way surprise us. If this were not the case, if the issue of expelling foreigners was of no interest to public opinion, it is because we free citizens, on whom no one would dare to impose a provision that limited our freedoms, it is because we have been blinded by enjoying our rights. Suppose that one of us, an Italian, had a close friend with a "deportable" foreigner. At any moment, that friend could be stopped by the police and expelled from the country and we would be unable to do a thing about it. In fact, we are in a completely different legal situation from that person: we can live the way we want to in our country, thanks to our status as citizens, while the foreigner can live physically and socially as we do, but has no stable future in our society. He or she is a slave to nationality, to being a foreigner, even if that person speaks our language and lives in our society. Here the artificial character of nationality becomes evident, but also its capacity to suppress the reality of concrete social relations, work, friendship, emotions. In short, the norms relative to citizenship make a person, not the reverse. This might appear obvious or "natural," until we reflect that those norms do not depend upon any meta-social necessity, they did not fall from the sky, nor are they written in some kind of natural code of law, but they are set in motion by our society. There is an extraordinary intrinsic contradiction to the idea of norm when applied to the case of foreigners: some one, a human being, is a person only if the law allows him or her to be, independent of the individual as a person. How is it possible that in the heart of western society which grew up on the culture of rights and legal universalism, this contradiction is considered admissible? Some considerations about the formation of the concept of person could prove useful.

2 **Persons and Non-Persons**

In the principal European languages, the noun "person" denotes essentially an individual as "living being," belonging to the human race and therefore mortal (in German *Mensch als lebendes Wesen*, in French *etre mortel*, in Italian *essere vivente*). More specialized terms can applied: social, legal, moral, psychological, theological, grammatical, theatrical. Thus "person" could indicate the exterior aspect of an individual, his or her conscience, identity, the concrete manifestation (or the hypothesis) of divinity, a legal entity, a theatrical role, the subject of a predicate. Undoubtedly, the concept of person refers to some conceptualization of humanity. Intuitively we know what "person" means: an individual of the human race, but more than just the biological manifestation, a being that is essentially social. In French, *personne* suggests the "human face," or in other words, how a person is seen by others, part of a network of looking, of relations, of sociality. This last term carries the riches connotations of the idea of "person." Inasmuch as people are more than biological entities, but social beings, "person" carries with it moral significance. If an individual is not necessarily a person, then he or she at least in ordinary language, must still be an individual. An individual reduced to a purely biological level of existence, for example some one in a coma, ceases to be a person except in the attentions of his or her loved ones or for the medical procedures or in the inevitable fiction of official documents. But a person exists only inasmuch as his or her humanity is not revoked or annulled.[324]

A person is therefore a combination of attributes sufficient to render a human being an individual among other individuals. Belonging to the human race is a precondition for being part of it. The implications of the concept of individual or person become especially evident when social and institutional practices are dehumanizing. Under totalizing institutions, the absolute control

---

[324] An excellent analysis of the practices of transforming sick individuals into "non-persons" can be found in Sudnow, D. *Passing on. The Social Organization of Dying.* Englewood Cliffs, NJ: Prentice Hall, 1967.

of human beings is accomplished by destroying them as "persons," treating them as mere biological entities. Only saints, aesthetics, or a Job manage to still be persons when their natural humanity is limited or wounded. Attacking an individual via the person or attacking the person via the individual corresponds to two different strategies of dehumanizing the human being. The former is the ordinary, normal, legal method of social control in totalizing institutions. The latter is the extreme and destructive form of war, concentration camps, large scale torture and organized extermination.[325]

In prison, human beings are maintained as such purely in vital terms, while the "person" is limited and at times destroyed by the recourse to practices that aim to dissolve social space and time. The different rituals of initiation and subjugation in prison or other totalizing institutions, such as insane asylums provide for the inmate or patient to be inserted according to disciplinary procedures that destroy respect for the person: humiliating body inspections, alterations in waking and sleeping times, containment, reduction of the space between individuals, elimination of intimacy, blind obedience to regulations without explanations or meaning. On the other hand, torture and extreme practices of detention aim at destroying or altering the living support of a person, to attack through the painful manipulation of the body. Although both practices share many empirical aspects, an essentially social difference exists between the two.

In the prevalent moral rhetoric of western society,[326] at least after World War II,

---

[325] I refer here to the work of Erving Goffman on totalizing institutions (see Goffman, E. *Asylums. Essays on the Social Situation of Mental Patients and Other Inmates*, Garden City, NY: Doubleday Anchor, 1961), and on the interpersonal practices of stigmatization (see Goffman, E. *Stigma: Notes on the Management of Spoiled Identity*, New York: Touchstone, 1986). See also M. Foucault, *Discipline & Punish: The Birth of the Prison*, London: Vintage, 1995. The fundamental text for connection between control and "biopolitics" implicit in my study is indebted to Foucault, M. *The Birth of Biopolitics: Lectures at the College de France, 1978-1979*, Basingstoke: Palgrave Macmillan, 2008.

[326] By "rhetoric" I include all the arguments and discourses employed in the debate surrounding the moral criteria of a society. I use this term to refer to, not fundamental social "values" but rather the tacit accord between the fundamental criteria of social action, even if these are already realized. My work distances itself from that of Habermas and Apel, and the sociologist Talcott Pareson, who tend to attribute a substantial significance to "collective conscience." For the concept of the "banality of evil," or the notion that extreme evil can be committed by societies

the strategy that aims to control the body by way of the person is socially legitimate and legally admissible (even if considered painful or unpleasant) while the strategy that aims to destroy the person through the painful manipulation or destruction of the body is considered illegitimate, with the exception of war. No post-war democracy officially and formally legitimates torture, the arbitrary execution of civil or military prisoners, or the starvation of inmates or reducing them to objects, all typical practices in totalitarian regimes, Nazi extermination camps, or Stalinist prisons. Furthermore, in our society, few consider the following practices inherently illegitimate: life imprisonment, the explicit humiliation of prisoners, the arbitrary reduction of personal freedom regulated by the police, the repeated administration of suppressive drugs, or all practices in which the person is controlled by the institution according to a mandate from society.

In these institutions, extreme practices are admitted, though quantitatively incommensurate with those of totalitarian regimes, in which the alteration or destruction of the person accompanies the alteration or destruction of the body: the death penalty is legal in many countries, the interrogation of civil and military prisoners, psychological practices such as electroshock or lobotomies are considered admissible in torture cases. Notice how in public discourse and debate these practices are questioned, and considered marginal or hardly legitimate. The death penalty, though legalized by numerous penal systems, tends to justify itself with embarrassment as a necessary practice for the supreme requirements of society, but in principle, it should not compromise the "person" of the condemned. It is maintained that those condemned to death still have the right to personal respect in the time before their execution (visits from relatives, psychological and spiritual assistance, sufficient food, etc.) These practices are horrible tricks according to any point of view, similar to the pretext that executions are "painless," "humane," etc. But these practices reveal the impossibility of a society to verbally deny its moral standards or conventions, which paradoxically are based on respect for the person even in

that are intellectually highly developed, see Arendt, Hannah. *Eichmann in Jerusalem: A Report on the Banality of Evil*, New York: Penguin Classics, 2006. See also Bauman, Z. *Modernity and the Holocaust*, Ithaca, NY: Cornell University Press, 2001.

the extreme case of destroying that person's body. Analogously, the tortures practiced during police interrogations, the "accidents resulting in death," the killings at roadblocks, are not legitimized, or rather, they are only legitimized when considered means employed in the name of a higher purpose. The practices that aim to destroy the person tend to fall into a different moral category than those practices which aim to destroy the body. During a war, no one aims to destroy the civilian population (which is composed of people, as opposed to the military, which is composed of soldiers, i.e. bodies) in order to destroy the enemy's resistance. If this does occur, it is called an inevitable "error," blamed on the fallibility of pilots or artillery or technological defects. But if soldiers deliberately kill and torture civilians, as occurred during the Vietnam War, they can be tried and condemned (even if the results of their "error" are infinitely inferior to a mistake in aim).

The spaces of the practices that destroy bodies and the practices that destroy people intersect, and are therefore controversial, the object of conflicts in interpretation where the limits of a society's morality become defined (debates over the death penalty, the admissibility of extreme psychological practices, the purpose of incarceration and punishments). This space, with different explicit moral, philosophical, or legal positions aside, is the object of cognitive practices of neutralization that allow us to side step the moral dilemmas and political conflicts. The widely accepted justification for the destruction of people in a society that wants to be rational and humane in the name of higher social needs is already a means for neutralizing moral dilemmas. In general, the neutralization takes effect by shifting concrete dilemmas and placing them in a wider and more generic framework that permits the avoidance of urgency and the responsibility of making decisions.[327]

[327] By "neutralize" I intend the processes by which the moral debates falsify certain realities. As we will see, "neutralization" plays a vital role in the "painless" transformation of individuals into non-persons. On the social mechanisms that render the neutralization of pity possible, see Boltanski, L. *La Souffrance à distance. Morale humanitaire, médias et politique.* Paris: Metaillié, 1993. 215. By way of comment, I add that the debates about "justifiable wars" are merely manifestations of the same rhetoric which they fail to recognize as such. See Walzer, M. *Just And Unjust Wars: A Moral Argument With Historical Illustrations*, New York: Basic Books (4th Edition), 2006.

The neutralization procedures are organized by theme: they can be the product of deliberate strategies or "objective" circumstances, but the operant in terms of an implicit shifting of meaning. This shift is accomplished by categorizing, abstracting, amplifying, and cognitive restructuring that do not silence the processes of destruction, but rather allows us to speak about those processes in terms that are literally depersonalized.[328] Elaine Scarry has discussed these procedures in detail in her research on the language of war, killing, and torture.

> The main purpose and outcome of war is injuring. Though this fact is too self-evident and massive ever to be directly contested, it can be indirectly contested by many means and disappear from view along many separate paths. It may disappeaer from view simply by being omitted: one can read many pages of a historic or strategic account of a particular military campaign, or listen to many successive instalments in a newscast narrative of events in a contemporary war, without encountering the acknowledgment that the purpose of the event described is to alter (to burn, to blast, to shell, to cut) human tissue, as well as to alter the surface, shape, and deep entirety of the objects that human beings recognize as an extension of themselves.[329]

Linguistic censoring is one of the most common forms of nullifying people. On the discursive plane it corresponds to the social invisibility of some human beings who are treated as non-persons. One of the most traumatic occurrences of our century is the fact that the victims of extreme persecution have not been recognized, as if the enormity of the crimes committed against them could not be represented by language, or the witnesses and their posterity were not able to bear remembering. This was the case in post-war Germany with the repression of information regarding the extermination of the Jews, which Hannah Arendt has

---

[328] I am indebted to Boltanski, L. and L. Thévenot. *De la Justification. Les economies de la grandeur.* Paris: Gallimard, 1991 for their analysis of the procedures of neutralization and the different dimensions in which they operate. See also Boltanski, L. *La souffrance á distance. Morale humanitaire, médias et politique.* Paris: Metaillié, 1993. The processes of neutralization belong to the field that ethnomethodology defines as ad hoc methods of justification.

[329] Scarry, E. *The Body in Pain: The Making and Unmaking of the World.* New York: Oxford UP, 1985. 63-4.

written about extensively.[330] But frequently the repression assumes more subtle and indirect forms. An example of this *a posteriori* repression appears in the autobiography of Albert Speer. While former Minister under Adolf Hitler admits his "errors," he remembers *Kristalnacht* without mentioning one word about the victims of this first mass persecution of the Jews:

> On November 10, 1938 as I was going to my office, I passed by the ruins of the Berlin synagogue, which were still smouldering. This was the fourth of a series of great events that marked this last year of peace. Reliving this time by remembering is one of the most depressing experiences of my life. *At that time, what disturbed me the most was the image of disorder in the* Fasanenstrasse, *the disorder of burned beams, crumbled walls, burned furniture, the image that shortly after would come to dominate Europe for the rest of the war.* It bothered me to see the piazza, the masses politically roused: all those shattered windows wounded my bourgeois sense of thrift.[331]

Elimination is not unknown in our democratic societies in which freedom of thought, criticism, and memory is practiced, at least theoretically. R. Wagner-Pacifici[332] has shown how extreme police procedures are rendered acceptable through metaphorical language that does not make reference to events or to their consequences to individuals. In the same way, the majority of the press did not reveal that in the outset of the first Allied offensive against Saddam Hussein in January, 1991, tens of thousands of Iraqi soldiers were buried alive by a division of caterpillars, followed by tanks and ground troops. The press did not even attempt to describe the sufferings, writhing, and agony of those dying underground, but used neutral expressions like, "The Iraqi front lines were

---

[330] Arendt, Hannah. "The Aftermath of Nazi Rule", *Commentary*, 10.10.1950, pp. 324-353. This is an extreme case. Arendt's purpose is to demonstrate how the annihilation of individuals can be part of the normal functioning of a democratic, developed, rational society. As outlined in the important work of Halbwachs, M. *On Collective Memory*, Chicago: University Of Chicago Press, 1992, we know that remembering and forgetting historical facts result from current conflicts between powers and interests.
[331] Speer, A. *Memoire del Terzo Reich*. Milan: Mondadori, 1997. 134-135. (My italics).
[332] Wagner-Pacifici, R. *Discourse and Destruction. The City of Philadelphia versus Move*. Chicago and London: The University of Chicago Press, 1994.

eliminated without losses of troops from the offensive." The press never mentioned that in the final offensive against Iraq, tens of thousands of soldiers in Saddam Hussein's republican guard were burned alive in their armored vehicles, but instead stated, "the Allied air force rapidly neutralized the armored division of the republican guard."[333]

The Gulf War demonstrated how the super-powers can manipulate information in order to guarantee that the conflict can be managed without any political interference as well as providing a reassuring, neutral perception of the military events for the public, aside from the virtuous need to defend popular western sensibilities from the spectacle of war which they have authorized, but don't fight in themselves. Thanks to the neutralizing procedures of communication, hundreds of thousands of military and civilian people have been "eliminated" or "removed" as if they constituted a purely theoretical problem, a residual cognitive category. These practices of physical elimination and linguistic repression are hardly limited to the sphere of war. They are also evident in cases of executions, accidental deaths, emergency police procedures and extreme practices in prisons. And they are used in a vast adjacent social area – less bloody and truculent, but just as diffused – whenever it would be too problematic to treat human beings as people, either in terms of actions or in legal and cognitive terms.

This is the moral and social space of the non-persons, those human beings who we know intuitively are individuals like us (living human beings with a social and cultural persona), but whose qualification as a person and its relative attributes have been revoked in word or deed, explicitly or implicitly, in ordinary transactions or in public language. This space is rarely explored and difficult to explore, for any exploration of it calls into question a multitude of social dimensions – political, legal, linguistic, and cognitive. My point is that foreigners who are legally and socially "illegitimate" (migrants whether legally in the country or "*clandestini*" as well as nomads or refugees) are the category that is

---

[333] Details regarding the atrocities committed during the Gulf War remained hidden until the *New York Times* did an investigation in 1991. Baudrillard, J. *The Perfect Crime*, Brooklyn, NY: Verso, 2008 discusses our inability to comprehend how the powers of mass communication produce atrocities and at the same time hide them from the inhabitants of the western world.

most susceptible to be treated as non-persons. Consider for example the limits that language imposes on the representation of the categories of human beings. For example, the image of migrants in the press and in the media generally, time and time again will be presented as the foreigner who is *"extracommunitario," "immigrato," "clandestino," "irregolare,"* categories which never refer to the autonomous characteristics of the individual, but only what he or she *is not* in relation to our categories: not European, not a native, not a citizen, not legal, not one of us. Beginning with this linguistic opacity which corresponds to a total social invisibility, certain presuppositions are made so that this individual cannot be considered a person and therefore may be literally neutralized.[334] Before restricting the analytical field of these processes, it will be useful to examine the concept of non-person, its genesis and its implications.

3 The Genealogy of Non-Persons

The English term "non-person" doesn't find a perfect parallel in other European languages. Webster's Dictionary defines "non-person" as "a person that usually for political or ideological reasons is removed from recognition or consideration." In English, the term is frequently used for a variety of social situations. To treat someone as a "non-person" means acting as if that person didn't exist or were invisible. A poor or bankrupt person is negligible as "economically non-person." A "non-person" is considered as such not because of any intrinsic or natural characteristics, but because he or she is socially considered as such due to an exclusionary process of social repression.

The social nature of a "non-person" is clearly correlated to its opposite, the public and relational meaning of "person." Facing us is an intuitive fact that a "person" has characteristics that have been acquired and are not dependent on the nature of the individual as a generic being. In other words, the person is a result of

---

[334] This is the cultural and linguistic space in which the presuppositions of racism occur. See Van Dijk, T.A. *Communicating Racism. Ethnic Prejudice in Thought and Talk.* Newbury: Sage Publications, 1987.

cultural and social processes that modify the image of the individual as a single, generic being, while presupposing its individuality. Typically, we don't refer to a newborn as "that person," in the sense that a person denotes a human being with confirmed and recognized social characteristics (an adult, socially inserted, etc.). In fact the attention given to a newborn presupposes an asymmetrical relationship between us and the infant, not completely unlike our relationships with our pets. The infantilization reserved for certain categories of people is a sure sign that we are treating them as non-persons or as sub-persons. Personhood, then as a social and cultural role of a human being, is not a fixed, invariable attribute, even less is it an anthropological universal, but a variable of the social condition provided by a specific history. An examination of this history, beginning with the fundamental study by Marcel Mauss, shows that behind events that present a linear and reassuring image of personhood, the constant possibility exists for human beings to slip into the condition of non-person.

The Latin term *persona*, probably of Etruscan origin (*phersu*), originally denoted the mask worn ritually as part of a sacred dance. The *persona*, at first made from animal skin later evolved into a mask that reproduced the image of an ancestor, and came to represent the clan or *gens*, the image, the emblem of a family. This then became confused with the *cognomen*, the nickname-image that came to identify a family line (Naso, Cicero, etc.) The Latin *persona* implicated broader meanings of belonging. It was the synthesis of the sacred name (*nomen-numen*) that defined the legitimate inclusion of a citizen in a family and that family into the community; therefore, the actual citizenship that an individual wore as a badge. The juridical character of the person clearly results from the exclusion of those who do not have this right:

> Moreover, the rights to the *persona* had been established. Only the slave is excluded from it. *Servus non habet personam.* He does not own his body, nor has he ancestors, name, *cognomen*, or personal belongings.[335]

---

[335] Mauss, M. "A category of the human mind: The notion of person; the notion of self", *The Category of the Person: Anthropology, Philosophy, History*, by Michael Carrithers (Ed.), Cambridge: Cambridge University Press, 2008, p. 17. From a political point of view, Hobbes

Marcel Mauss summarized the evolution of the modern significance of "person" beginning with the Latin root and its ritual-legal origins. From an individual with a legitimate status, the concept of person extended to mean individual in general and even a manifestation of divinity. (The Trinity is *unitas in tres personas*, just as Christ is *persona in duas naturas* according to the Nicean Creed). But a person, inasmuch as divine and human nature coincide (*substantia rationalis individua*) represents what we could call the specific identity of the human being, a spectrum of meanings that include the "self," and self-consciousness. True, parallel to this noble evolution, the Latin concept of person branched out, as did the original meaning of mask to include the "role of the actor" and the theatrical part (and from this the legendary etymology according to which the mask is the object through which the *personat* manifests itself). The original concept of mask dissolved into the notion of "member or representative of the human species," according to which the universalizing philosophical categories apparently define western thought. If we wish to believe the popular philosophy of rational humanism, and particularly that philosophical school of thought based in Catholicism called "personalism," then every human being on the earth is a person and is therefore sacred.

But this conception cannot offer any legal protection, much less social protection, to "persons." The generic concept of person that alludes to a common substance of humanity, waffling between common usage and philosophical or theological acceptance, has not found any recognized codification or specific application in conventional systems that regulate the relations between human beings. This is evident in the controversy that juridical formalism has been maintained against jurinaturalism. Kelsen especially has defended the exterior and formal character of the notion of "person:"

made the most elegant articulation in which "person" is the legal "representation" of individuals, collectives, or organizations. Hobbes, T. *Leviathan*, New York: W. W. Norton & Company, 1996. In other words, only those individuals who exist legally may also exist socially and be instructed. This leads us to question the structurally asocial condition of foreigners who have not been instructed.

The sum total of subjective rights and responsibilities, that is, the total of legal norms considered here which constitute a physical person, is due to the fact that it is the behavior of that individual which forms the content of these rights and responsibilities, which is the very behavior that is determined by these legal norms: *the so-called physical person is not a person, even though the total of the legal norms attributes rights and responsibilities to that very individual. This is not a natural reality, but rather a legal construction created by the rule of law, an auxiliary concept in the description of the legal relevant case in point. In this sense, the so-called physical person is a legal concept.*[336]

Kelsen insists that the legal person is artificial, a normative construct that can be applied to people, businesses, or institutions. To maintain that "the physical person is not … a person," but exclusively the object of legal norms is equivalent to limiting the environment of positive right in regards to generic definitions of "humanity." Despite their differing doctrinal presuppositions, this viewpoint is shared by a theoretician who is the polar opposite of Kelsen, Carl Schmitt. Consider the citation below in which Schmitt discusses an essentially analogous concept of person as "equality between what wears the human face," and negating that this could constitute the foundation for political procedure:

The equality between "that bears a human face" is incapable of providing a foundation for a state, a state form or a form of government […]. Nothing distinctive, either in religious or moral terms or in political or economics ones, may be derived from the fact that all persons are human.[337]

Though the reference to morality and religion is made merely in passing, the essence of this position, like that of Kelsen's, is to negate that a person ("who wears the human face") exists outside of concrete legal or political organization. Law and political theory therefore counter each other both on the level of

---

[336] See also Kelsen, H. *Introduction to the Problems of Legal Theory*, Oxford: Oxford University Press, 1997. (My italics). For an analysis of the problems implicit in this position of the contemporary theory of human rights, see Habermas, J. *Between Facts and Norms:Contributions to a Discourse Theory of Law and Democracy*, Cambridge, MA: The MIT Press, 1998.

[337] Schmitt, C. *Constitutional Theory*, Durham, NC: Duke University Press, 2007, p. 257-258.

common usage and on the philosophical level in refuting any justification for the strictly human existence of "people." If Mauss wished to demonstrate that a person doesn't exist outside of institutions (first rituals, then religious, and finally social), modern law replies that a person does not exist except as a "total of norms" that define individual rights and responsibilities. We can translate these differing but convergent viewpoints of Kelsen and Schmitt in the following proposition: a person can exist socially only as a legal-political person, or only within "a system of rights and responsibilities" (Kelsen) or "as a subject of political organization" (Schmitt). Under this formulation, the significant differences are irrelevant between the two concepts of "inclusive system" of personhood—one based on a total of positive norms (Kelsen) and the other on the "person" as "a unity between governors and the governed" (Schmitt) as the fundamental expression of political organization. It is more important to note that in both cases, the person, or what "wears the human face" bounces from non-existence to existence based exclusively on positive laws. Both positions in their sincerity – or their brutality – have the merit of stripping away the frequently confused and misleading philosophical and theological definitions of "what is a human." Whatever the definition of human being may be, his or her existence is connected to the internal (or external) position to a concrete organization.

The implications of the juridical-positive (and therefore ultimately political) nature of "person" is evident. If it is true that one of the victories of modern political order is that it has conferred "rights" only upon those who are completely incorporated into the organizations, whomever is excluded from them *non habet personam,* and therefore is a person on in the biological not the social sense. Citizenship – that totality of rights belonging to those who are legitimately included in the organization[338] – is therefore the exclusive

---

[338] Due to limits of space, in this chapter I can only refer in passing to the vast debate about conferring citizenship on foreigners. To summarize, granting civil and political rights depends upon the constitution of the modern nation state. Citizenship is probably the central political problem in formation of the contemporary state. At any rate, citizenship depends exclusively on belonging to a national state or conglomeration of national states (such as the EU). The issue of citizenship has become explosive due to the intersection of three factors: 1) the globalization of markets 2) the end of the post-war order and 3) the erosion of social citizenship in the so-called

condition of social personality, not the reverse, as is often asserted by common philosophical parlance or those international declarations and conventions that so often reaffirm the "universal rights of the individual and the person."[339] It is not my intention to suggest that the person, given its complex social valences, can be reduced to its juridical-political nature, but simply to note that belonging to an organization (or having national citizenship) is the exclusive condition of personhood.[340] This reality that is so easily forgotten these days, became obvious after the First World War when the European countries found themselves inundated by masses of "*apolidi*," or "individuals without a State," pushed westward by the Russian Revolution and the crisis of the Hapsburg Empire:

> The whole question of human rights, therefore, was quickly and inextricably blended with the question of national emancipation; only the emancipated sovereignty of the people, of one's own people, seemed to be able to insure them. As mankind, since the French Revolution, was conceived in the image of a family of nations, it gradually became self-evident that the people, and not the individual, was the image of man.
> The full implication of this identification of the rights of man with the rights of people in the European nation-state system came to light only when a growing

Northern societies of the world. New international migrations are both a consequence and a cause for the complexity of this situation. For an introduction to the problem, see Andrews, G., ed. *Citizenship.* London: Lawrence and Wishart, 1991; Barbalet, J.M. *Citizenship: Rights, Struggle and Class Inequality,* Minneapolis, MN: University of Minnesota Press, 1989; Aa. Vv. *Schwierige Fremdheit. Über Integration und Ausgrenzung in Einwanderungslädern.* Frankfurt a.M.: Fischer, 1993; Turner, B.S., ed. *Citizenship and Social Theory.* London: Sage, 1994; Nuhoglu Soysal, Y. *Limits of Citizenship. Migrants and Post-National Membership in Europe.* Chicago and London: University of Chicago Press, 1994; Zolo, D. *Cosmopolis: Prospects for World Government,* Cambridge: Polity, 1997; Held, D. "Democracy, the Nation-State and the Global System." *Political Theory Today.* Ed. D. Held. Cambridge: Polity Press, 1995.

[339] While I do not intend to dismiss the importance of international declarations that affirm basic human rights, especially after World War II, the problem is that many nations have not endorsed such declarations. (such as the United Nation's Universal Declaration on Human Rights from 1948) See Cassese, A. "Diritti dell'uomo." *Lessico della politica.* Ed. G. Zaccaria. Rome: Edizioni Lavoro, 1987. 184.

[340] See Ferrajoli, L. "Dai diritti del cittadino ai diritti della persona." *La cittadinanza. Appartenenza, identità, diritti.* Rome and Bari: Laterza, 1994, 288, which affirms that in our contemporary world, citizenship is the only privilege of status.

number of people and peoples suddenly appeared whose elementary rights were as little safeguarded by the ordinary functioning of nation-states in the middle of Europe as they would have been in the heart of Africa. The Rights of Man, after all, had been defined as "inalienable" because they were supposed to be independent of all governments; but it turned out that the moment human beings lacked their own government and had to fall back upon their minimum rights, no authority was left to protect them and no institution was willing to guarantee them.[341]

After World War II and the downfall of Nazifascism, the process of de-colonization and the same definition of new world order, with the formulation of the United Nations and other multinational organizations, for several decades created the illusion that human rights and the universal recognition of the value of the individual were a reality and not merely an affirmation of principle. (These processes were responsible for the broad rights to asylum included in the constitution of the German Democratic Republic, later repealed in 1993). The economic expansion and industrial development allowed former colonial powers to accept a high number of migrants coming from former colonies and to naturalize them, including them as citizens who could therefore enjoy the same rights as natives, at least on paper. During the Cold War, "human rights" including the right to flee a dictatorship, were made in favor of those who chose to escape from behind the iron curtain.

This favorable situation for a formal culture of human rights ended dramatically with two concomitant processes: 1) the end of communism in Russia and its satellite countries in Eastern Europe, and therefore the end of bipolarism, and 2) the beginning of economic competition between the huge areas developed by global capitalism. Beginning in 1991 with the war in ex-Yugoslavia, the conflicts following the crises in the Eastern European regimes created a fear that masses of refugees would flood into western Europe, just as masses of young people from the GDR flooded into the German Federal Republic in 1989. At the same time, fear of Islamic extremism after the Iranian

---

[341] Arendt, Hannah. *The Origins of Totalitarianism.* Cleveland: Meridian Books, 1958, 291-292.

Revolution and the outbreak of civil war in Algeria together with an increased intolerance for migrants coming from poorer countries prompted the countries of the European community to assume restrictive measures toward foreigners. The process of European economic integration and the first uncertain measures of political unification in these years did nothing to overcome nationalism, but, as events evidenced, new forms of local patriotisms developed, frequently fed by mistrust and irrational fears about foreigners.[342]

Now more than ever, the ones who enjoy personal rights are those citizens of national states that have developed a culture that makes legal guarantees to protect those individuals who legitimately belong to the juridical-political order. Of course, by juridical-political I refer to a condition that goes beyond the mere letter of the law. Regulations that are formally different can still be in agreement with each other in extending the status of "person" to their respective citizens, based on obvious considerations. So the status of an American, or Japanese, or a Swiss citizen in the European Community is only formally that of an "*extracomunitario*," and is therefore non comparable to the status of a Moroccan, Albanian, or Senegalese. Political systems take different factors into account, economic first of all, in determining who is allowed to be recognized completely as a person.[343]

To think that depersonalizing certain categories of human beings is impossible in our humanistic, rational society is a dangerous illusion (when it is not the effect of an actual repression of history). The juridical-political processes that allow it are various and diffused but can be attributed to one common denominator: the existence of a legal double standard that operates one way for those who are

---

[342] See the studies collected in Jenkins, B. and S.A. Sofos, eds. *Nation & Identity in Contemporary Europe*. London and New York: Routledge, 1996.

[343] Clearly, belonging to a national or international order includes material distinctions, such as "poverty," "underdevelopment," etc. The Schengen accords for the regulation and delineation of European space does not involve "*extracommunitari*" such as Swiss, Americans, or Japanese. Thus, "racism" is not a process linked exclusively to racial discrimination but to the synthesis of multiple discriminations and inferiorizations. On this point, see Balibar, E. and I. Wallerstein. *Race, Nation, Class: Ambiguous Identities*, Brooklyn, NY: Verso, 1992.

included and another way for those who are excluded.[344] Empirically this type of legal situation exists when the regulations valid in one determinate territory are not applicable to certain categories of individuals either because they are foreigners or because they are subjects without civil rights. The condition of African slaves in the United States before the Civil War is an obvious example. The progressive removal of the civil rights of the German Jews before their extermination is the most relevant example, at least in the last century.[345] The truth is that even western democracies have established a double standard for foreigners and for their own citizens with foreign origins: consider the internment of the Americans of German descent during World War I, or of Japanese-Americans during World War II. Obviously, these are limited cases. But as has been recently observed, in all these cases, political supremacy appears in its naked reality, though it refers to legal provisions adopted according to the legislation in force or with adaptations that do not violate it. It is also true that nothing prevents a double legislative standard in our democratic and universalistic societies from distinguishing certain categories as foreigners, immigrants, or gypsies.[346] Under Italian legislation, a double juridical standard was instituted for the first time after the fall of Fascism under the Dini decree on immigration and consolidated with successive immigration legislation. Regulations on expulsions and the establishment of *"centri di permanenza temporanea"* both introduce an inequality in the treatment given to Italian citizens and foreign citizens. This inequality, which denies some foreigners fundamental

---

[344] This fundamental concept has been ably explained in Fraenkel, E. *The Dual State: A Contribution To The Theory Of Dictatorship*, Clark, NJ: Lawbook Exchange, 2006.

[345] Hilberg, R. *The Destruction of the European Jews, 3 Volume Set*, New Haven, CT: Yale University Press, 3rd Edition, 2003. For a reconstruction of the legal and political pretexts for the extermination, see Mommsen, H. "Die Realisierung des Utopischen: die 'Endlosung der Judenfragen' im Dritten Reich." *Geschichte und Gesellschaft* 9 (1983).

[346] I refer here to Agamben, G. *Homo Sacer: Sovereign Power and Bare Life*, Palo Alto, CA: Stanford University Press, 1998, and *Means Without End: Notes on Politics*, Minneapolis, MN: University of Minnesota Press, 2000. Agamben sees the concentration camp not as an irrational deviation from European democratic order but rather the basis of political sovereignty. I would only point that this applies as well to the tendencies to eliminate foreigners, and reduce them to impersonal entities which occurs in those states dealing with migration problems.

civil rights, is potentially the initiation of a process that reduces human beings into non-persons.

If it is true that a human being is or may become a "person" only inasmuch as he or she is a citizen, the philosophical debate about the Other or the foreigner ceases to be a mere verbal exercise if we approach the question of their legal-political condition from the point of one's relationship with some one like him or herself. It is not "the face of the Other," nor a symmetry based on an abstract pretext of common, universal roots that establishes a concrete relationship between us and another, but the exclusive condition of "recognizing the faces of others" in terms of a shared juridical-political space. A philosophical condition that moves away from this problem is condemned to being reductive. For example, using the seemingly intimate designation, "guest," setting aside the obvious submission of the guest to the host, removes the juridical-political problem of the personness of the foreigner and therefore depersonalizes the foreigner and renders him or her a non-person, regardless of any terminological contortion. Analogously, the notion of friendship is apolitical if it refers to individual foreigners, because it ignores the fundamental equality in status, citizenship, general condition, upon which any relation is based between people regardless of the favorite philosophical metaphors.[347]

---

[347] See particularly Derrida's discussion of such terms as "democracy," "friend" and "enemy" as applied to political theory, in *The Politics of Friendship*, Brooklyn, NY: Verso, 2006. Derrida attempted to deal with the issue of foreigners and especially the right to exile in Derrida, J. *Cosmopoliti di tutti i paesi ancora una sforzo!* Naples: Cronopio, 1997. Julia Kristeva, in *Strangers to Ourselves*, Irvington, NY: Columbia University Press, 1994, correctly identifies the "unsettling foreignness" of the other, but rather than seeing this as an effect of a multiplicity of exclusions, she connects this to the removal of the foreigner within us. Thus the foreigner remains a projection of some dark side of us. To bypass these false problems, one would need to consider not the Foreigner but many "foreigners" in their concrete individuality and the attendant political problems. One of the few contemporary theorists who deals with the issue of individuals foreigners created by borders rather than a metaphysical "Other" is Bauman, Z. *Life in Fragments. Essays in Postmodern Morality.* Oxford: Blackwell, 1997.

4 On the Margins of Rights

In determining the immediate consequence of foreigners' virtual condition as non-persons, I do not intend to interpret their status in a formal way. A legal system is series of conventions that can be modified legally with input from the political system, input that is relative to the solutions for different social conflicts and interests. The fact remains that the result of these processes once it has been codified can redefine and redirect different social and cultural relations between us and foreigners, migrants and destination society, between who is on the outside and who is on the inside. Ultimately, it's of no great importance that for years Italian legislation has lacked clear norms on the status of foreigners, or that the decrees regarding foreigners during the last decade have often been contradictory. The real importance is that every time these regulations and decrees reopen the possibility for foreigners to access our legitimate space, they allow foreigners to validate (or not) their actual social situation, extending or restricting the possibility for them to become "persons," or if they already were, it allows them to either remain as such or transform into non-persons. In other words, what matters here are the different social processes ultimately codified by law through which humans are deprived of their humanity and transformed into something else, a different name or identity from how they expect to be recognized or else transformed into a complete negation – non-persons – or simply disappear from relationships with those around them. These are essentially different processes in terms of their typology (legal, bureaucratic, social, cultural, cognitive processes), and are different in their effects upon the human beings subject to them. However, all these processes have one decisive factor in common: because of them, some one who normally expects to exist socially will see this expectation frustrated and will cease to exist.[348]

---

[348] One specific case would obviously be the left-wing opponents of the dictatorship in Argentina, the *desaparecidos* who were tortured and eliminated by the regime between 1976 and 1986. The Alfonsin and Menem administrations granted amnesty to the generals and officials. See Benedetti, M. "The Triumph of Memory." *NACLA Report on the Americas* XXIX 3 (1995).

A foreigner who is "illegal" or "illegitimate" does not exist socially or rather exists in a state of limbo where he or she is tolerated or invisible but at any moment can be sent away or made to disappear. Based on legislation currently in force, in Italy and other countries, an *immigrato clandestino* or *irregolare* literally can be captured at any moment by police authorities, imprisoned indefinitely and expelled from the country, from the society in which he or she was living. A gypsy with or without nationality has no right to live where and how he or she wishes, and several different local and national authorities, both administrative and political, have the power to remove these individuals, escort them to the border, which is to say, make those individuals disappear and reappear where the authority wishes.[349] A foreigner socially recognized as dangerous and guilty of a minor offence can be removed permanently from the country, left without any possibility of being tried or making an appeal, what our Constitution refers to as "Nature's judge." Thus the individual is distanced from the legal system with which it came in contact.[350] My purpose here is not to comment on the ethical significance of these disappearances nor am I comparing their consequences to the kinds of internment used by totalitarian institutions. The consequences for individual human beings can be commensurate or not, the social outcome for a foreigner who is expelled from the country can be comparable to the foreigner who has been interred, but in any case, the objects of the processes of disappearances are characterized exclusively by the fact that they no longer exist. I maintain that the common belief according to which a human being exists inasmuch as he or she is alive biologically is fundamentally flawed. It is necessary not to extend the category of human beings capable of disappearing to all subjects who endure different forms of social exclusion: the

---

[349] Consider the requirement that gypsies live outside of city limits. Particular forms of discrimination are aimed at gypsies. The most dramatic case of disappearances of the gypsies was their removal from historical memory in the Nazi extermination camps. See Hilberg, R. *The Destruction of the European Jews*, New Haven, CT: Yale University Press (3rd Edition), 2003.

[350] For a list of Italian legislation relative to foreigners, see Pastore, M. "Produzione normative e costruzione sociale della devianza e criminalità tra gli immigrati." *Quaderni ISMU* 9 (1994).

homeless, drug addicts, the impoverished, etc.[351] Though their conditions could be similarly terrible in terms of quality of life to the conditions of those foreigners who live in the limbo of society's margins, the former are still legitimate subjects and therefore even if they disappear socially, the retain the civil rights accorded to persons. The former can be aided, assisted, nourished, housed, treated, and informed of their legal rights.

Consider instead the condition of those foreigners who try to enter this or another country clandestinely. After having been registered and refreshed, they are interred in camps that elude the control of the courts and public opinion, then loaded onto a boat or airplane and sent back to their own country. Thus they can be made to disappear with a simple police procedure. Capable as they are of being made to disappear, *clandestini* have no other rights beyond their own physical integrity. These are difficult rights to violate in our "humanized" societies. But as *clandestini*, they are legitimately detained, removed, exiled, and made to disappear even through deception. The case of the Albanians who reached Italy in 1991 and were confined to the Bari stadium, then dispersed to different Italian cities with the promise of jobs and legal status before being expelled sufficiently illustrates how *clandestini* can be removed from any socially legitimate form of existence.

Paradoxically, the fact that a foreigner is not punishable even if convicted when expelled before serving prison time demonstrates how the social need for disappearance exceeds the social need for formal rights. A human being judged for a crime enters a certain juridical space and therefore enters into the society for which that space represents a formal expression. This means that the individual can and must be defended, heard, has rights, and exists. By expelling such an individual before or after the verdict, the society thus makes him or her disappear, demonstrating that the universality of legal norms proclaimed in the Constitution itself is useless in the face of the fixed necessity of making these

---

[351] The distinction I propose between "non-persons" and "sub-persons" is not merely rhetorical, but refers to the divergent fates of the two groups. For a complex analysis of the connotations implied by these two terms, see Bourdieu, P., *The Weight of the World: Social Suffering in Contemporary Society*, Palo Alto, CA: Stanford University Press, 2000.

individuals disappear. Their only recognized form of existence is that of a physical body that needs to be fed, controlled or detained. Hannah Arendt highlighted the paradoxical connection between the condition of non-person and the individual who is denied the right to be tried for a crime. The following excerpt, while written over 50 years ago, perfectly describes the condition of the "expellable" foreigner suspected of a crime and who is judged without a jury or the chance for an appeal:

> The best criterion by which to decide whether someone has been forced outside the pale of the law is to ask if he would benefit by committing a crime. If a small burglary is likely to improve his legal position, at least temporarily, one may be sure he has been deprived of human rights. For then a criminal offense becomes the best opportunity to regain some kind of human equality, even if it be as a recognized exception to the norm. The one important fact is that this exception is provided for by law. As a criminal even a stateless person will not be treated worse than another criminal, that is, he will be treated like everybody else. Only as an offender against the law can he gain protection from it. As long as his trial and his sentence last, he will be safe from that arbitrary police rule against which there are no lawyers and no appeals. The same man who was in jail yesterday because of his mere presence in this world, who had no rights whatsoever and lived under threat of deportation, or who was dispatched without sentence and without trial to some kind of internment because he had tried to work and make a living, may become almost a full-fledged citizen because of a little theft. Even if he is penniless he can now get a lawyer, complain about his jailers, and he will be listened to respectfully. He is no longer the scum of the earth but important enough to be informed of all the details of the law under which he will be tried. He has become a respectable person.[352]

The Foucauldian concept of "illegalism" cannot be applied to the expulsion procedures of foreigners from the system of juridical guarantees. These procedures themselves interfere at times with the very constitutional principles that ought to govern a system of rights. When foreigners deal with the legal system of another country, I would use the term *a-legalism*. Rights cease for

[352] Arendt, Hannah. *The Origins of Totalitarianism.* Cleveland: Meridian Books, 1958. 286-7.

the foreigner in the sense that foreigners are excluded from the environment of law. Foreigners are legally made to disappear from the legal environment in the name of a higher need (i.e. social alarm, "they are dangerous"). Or else the law decrees their non-existence when it decides they can't live among us because they are *clandestini*.[353] In any complex society it is possible to escaped the institution's requirement to disappear by deception, and deciding to disappear or hide before being forced to disappear, different states of limbo or hiding places where foreigners can exist in a state of suspension. These situations have historical precedence, for example, the condition of refugees from Eastern countries between World War I and II, and these situations serve definite social and economic functions.[354] It is telling to note that the legal system itself operates in a state of "a-legality" in regards to these situations. When the legal system concerns itself with *clandestini* or illegal foreigners, it extracts them from a condition of "a-legality" merely to complete their non-existence by expelling them. Paradoxically, the reluctance for granting a *permesso di soggiorno* reveals the legal-juridical system's preference for keeping foreigners in that a-legal condition.[355]

---

[353] As always when the issue is rights, terminology holds sway. Every unplanned arrival of foreigners heats up the debate over their public definition: are they to be considered "refugees" or "*clandestini*?" See the case of the arrival of 800 Kurds in Calabria as reported in the Italian newspapers from 29 December 1997.

[354] Migrants and refugees increase the illegal labor force and not only in those countries in which the unregulated economy plays a significant role. See Morice, A. "Les travailleurs étrangers aux avant-postes de la precarité." *Le Monde Diplomatique.* January 1997: 18-19.

[355] The advantages our society reaps from real or virtual disappearances are all too evident. An illegal immigrant hiding in the interstices of the economy constitutes an excellent economic resource as a worker without rights, a semi-slave, or as back up labor. It is no coincidence that the spokespersons for industry in Europe and America from Bill Gates to George Soros tend to be far more flexible toward immigrants than social and political forces from the left and right that call for the expulsion of migrants in the name of social order. On this typically post-industrial dialectic, see Moulier-Boutang, Y. *Le salariat bridé, Origines de la politique migratory, constitution du salariat et contrôle de la mobilité du travail.* Paris: Doctorate Thesis from University FNSP-IEP, 1997.

5 **Disappearances**

As the epigraph from Ellison at this chapter's opening indicates, the illegal foreigners – migrants, refugees, gypsies – are wrapped in a veil of invisibility in our world. Their irritating, inconvenient, disturbing, bothersome, extreme visibility is nothing more than the effect of what our world projects onto this veil: the image of the criminal, the impoverished, the illegal, the nomad, the "foreign," who demands the right to live among us and therefore must be expelled. Their radical foreignness to the world of persons is evident in the fate of those who perished as *clandestini*, drowning in our sea. According to reliable sources, the number of foreigners that has drowned in Italian territorial waters since 1992 is in the several hundreds.[356] Taking into consideration the number of drownings in Spanish waters and international waters about which information continues to surface, it would not be an exaggeration to suggest that the western Mediterranean in the 1990s became the cemetery for thousands of migrants. Even in a society that has difficulty dealing with the issue of migration, these disappearances present a problem. Perhaps this is why any situation can offer a good excuse for transforming this shadowy humanity into a threat, for transforming real or potential drowning victims into enemies. A skirmish between a Tunisian navy patrol vessel and an Italian fishing boat is enough to evoke the threat of the Islamic enemy and more *clandestini*:

> For years Lampedusa has helped Muslims to show the world that Italy will smilingly put up with anything. From over there, they fire on our fishing boats, they detain them, they deposit *clandestini* on our shores (more Muslims) […]. Foreigners take advantage, they think we are a nation without self-respect. Heaven help us, they're right.[357]

Bearing in mind the undeniable fact that European countries north of the Mediterranean have dealt with boat-people, the strategy adopted by Europe can

---

[356] "Una lunghissima sequenza di tragedie evitabili." *Il Manifesto,* 3 August 1997: 19.
[357] Editorial by Segio Ricossa. *Il Giornale.* 1 August 1997.

only be called a form of censorship. As with the Albanian invasion, arrivals and drownings will be exclusively labelled the effect of a criminal strategy, the Albanian "mafia" that organizes the traffic in human flesh, the Tunisian traffickers, the boat captains with not morals, and so forth. At the same time, any evidence to the contrary will be denied when it surfaces without "real" proof. Obviously, those who drowned cannot be interviewed by the press, but also the survivors don't count, their testimonies are disqualified as the testimonies of *clandestini*, of non-persons. This strategy of suppression robs the drowned even of the chance to be remembered. If they were considered mere irritations, inconvenient bodies when alive, once dead they become simply cadavers with no history, identity, or biography.[358]

One of the most dramatic cases of foreigners' double disappearance came to light only after investigations made by several journalists when the ship *Yoham* went down, which was known for several months as "the ghost ship." Around Christmas of 1996, several short articles appeared in the Greek and Italian press about the presumed sinking of a ship of *clandestini* near Sicily with hundreds of victims. The articles reported the events with scepticism, and the events were not confirmed by Greek authorities, even though over 30 Indian and Pakistani survivors managed to reach Piraeus and insisted that they had been trying to reach Italy on the *Yoham* before it sunk. This testimonies where essentially dismissed. Only in the spring of 1997 did the Greek and Italian authorities confirm the sinking of the *Yoham* and the *deaths of nearly 300 Indian, Pakistani, and Singhalese passengers*, though without creating any particular emotional reaction. This is how *Le Monde* summarized the event before the sinking was officially confirmed:

Around 5 a.m. [December 24]. "It was still night, and we could see the lights along the coast," Singh Baldwinder remembers. It was at this moment that the collision occurred. "We had turned the *Yoham* around to prepare for docking. The two boats were side by side. Then suddenly, there was a huge collision," adds another young Indian man, crying. "I jumped into the water and managed to grab

[358] Quagliata, L. "Se la notizia non c'è." *Il Manifesto.* 27 December 1997: 17.

onto a rope. My cousin was right behind me. But I couldn't do anything to help him. I heard him screaming. Then, nothing." [...] Within minutes, the old tub fell to pieces.

Instead of helping those who were overboard, the *Yoham*, with the captain of the "Maltese" boat on board, moved away, leaving the unfortunate people to their fate. According to the survivors, 289 people died: 31 Pakistani, 166 Indian, and 92 Singhalese. Is it possible that the survivors lied, as the Minister of the Greek Merchant Marine suggests, that they invented the massacre to win the compassion of their country of destination? "I am convinced that the events occurred exactly as the survivors have related them," maintains journalist Panos Sobolos, who has been investigating the story since January 4 for the paper *Ethnos*. According to Sobolos, the silence surrounding the story reveals the latent racism in international public opinion. "If the passengers of the *Yoham* had been French, Greek, or Italians, can you imagine what kind of scandal would have erupted? No one would have bee satisfied with a little excursion by boat to search for the bodies."

Currently, sixteen people have been accused, all of them on the run from authorities, including the two captains and their staff. The various nationalities of the accused—Greek, Maltese, Syrian, Lebanese, give an idea of how far the slave-trading mafia has extended into Mediterranean waters.[359]

Stories such as the *Yoham's* are embarrassing. Not only because the victims were not all necessarily Muslims, but migrants from other parts of the world. These events took place in a neutral space, in international waters, since the victims didn't have the shrewdness to drown inside of Greek or Italian territorial waters. A neutral space in terms of communication, a space for which any particular emotional response or even media attention would be unsuitable, though the disappearance of a single participant in a transoceanic regatta or the Paris-Dakar rally or the kidnapping of a European by a sheik in Yemen would have found instant front-page coverage. This is a neutral space particularly in juridical terms. Who were the drowned, and who should be worried about them? The latent racism that the Greek journalist mentions is certainly in play here, but there is also an evident desire to abandon the survivors on the shore. True, there are "slave traders" who make a profit at the expense of migrants

[359] Simon, C. "Les naufragés du *Yoham'*." *Le Monde*. 2 February 1997.

and leave them to drown at the first sign of danger. It is equally true that "slave traders" and "traffickers in human flesh" are always referred to when discussing illegal immigration, as a comfortable alibi for avoiding any discussion of the meaning of those migrations. Thus, the entire issue can be resolved satisfactorily with accusations and arrests of the captains and the traffickers, when possible, but also by criminalizing the attempts to land, i.e. the migrants and the shipwrecked. Following is an explicit example of this criminalization, including a nod to the fiscal obsessions of "citizens" and an allusion to the traitorous competition among migrants:

> [Who makes money from trafficking in migrants?] In this gallery of winners, we find the very immigrants who, even with the heavy penalties imposed upon them from the illegal condition in the labor market, simply skip over those who are waiting in line, cross the borders of "wealth" to enjoy a situation of incomparable improvement. But who are the losers? First of all, the employers and the honest entrepreneurs ruined by the traitorous competition from those who use illegal labor to reduce their salary costs. Just after them, we find the less qualified national workers and the legal migrants. Last but not least are the taxpayers. And even if they are often ignored, the costs of illegal immigration affects the national budget [...][360]

Actually, prevalent public opinion cannot bring itself to admit that there is a *demand* for illegal labor that corresponds to the supply of criminal transport, and the foreigners for whatever reason chose to undertake this voyage to another part of the world. The hundreds or thousands of drowning victims not only lose their lives and their right to be remembered, but also that freedom of choice that progressive common belief considers natural to every human being. Why not recognize that these aliens have demonstrated, in accepting the risk involved with a voyage of hundreds or thousands of miles, a spirit of initiative and self-motivation that contemporary economic ideology should consider natural to humanity? The answer is only too easy, as becomes obvious when analyzing the Albanian story. That kind of "freedom" of choice is admissible, even sanctified, insofar as it is exercised within the borders of one's own

[360] Bolaffi, G. "L'affare clandestine." *La Repubblica.* 27 August 1998.

country (according to the unwritten but ironclad rules regarding international labor).[361] Isn't there despotism, dictatorship, famine, or necessity that justifies (in the eyes of international public opinion) the right to individual "secession," from the nation or national economic order, a right that was solemnly proclaimed over 50 years ago with the United Nation's Universal Declaration of Human Rights. Whoever tries to flee famine or the place that the geoeconomy has assigned, leaving his or her "own" national space therefore loses any rights, first of all the right to be considered or remembered as a person. The unfortunate risks disappearing into the sea, while the more fortunate risks a precarious existence in the hiding places of the rich northern and western parts of the world, self-satisfied in their culture of human rights. An inexistence in which migrants begin to be aware, as the following child's testimony reveals, that one does not complain about the deprivation of identity, but perhaps recognizes the profound sense of one's own existence:

> A child apparently between 8 and 10 years old was taken to the juvenile prison because he had been found on the streets, trying to sell something at an intersection and then had fled the police [...]. The child has no identification documents and cannot offer any credible name. First he said his name was Dumbo, then Mickey Mouse, then Donald Duck, then John: he says he's American, but he looks Arab, he said he was French but the prison workers said he could be Slavic. One time he said he was from Rome, then Switzerland, then America, finally according to prison workers, he began to rant: "I'm an extra-terrestrial, I come from outer space!" From then on, he continued to say that he was an extra-terrestrial. [...] One day he confided to the social worker that had become his friend, "Instead of saying I'm an *extracommunitario*, why can't I say I'm an extra-terrestrial?"[362]

---

[361] Forrester, V. *L'horreur economique*, Paris: Fayard, 1996.
[362] Cited in Palidda, S. "Verso il 'Fascismo democratico'? Note su emigrazione, immigrazione e società dominanti." *aut aut* 275 (1996): 146.

VIII Global Paradoxes

Emigration is born from the need to breathe.[363]

1 A World of Uncertainty

As the target of society's obsessions and as "legally non-existent" (i.e. excluded from the national juridical system), a migrant is a completely marginal human being. A migrant by definition is one who crosses boundaries, but the migrant also comes to constitute the boundaries or margins of a society.[364] More than a century ago, Durkheim observed that innovation is the function of those who violate a law and those who inhabit the margins generally.[365] In the ritual of ceremonial punishments, as in penal law, as well as in purely procedural processes such as public and medial stigmatization of "collective enemies," a society attempts incessantly to reconstruct its unity, or solidarity in the terminology of Durkheim,[366] yet attempting at the same time to extend its boundaries. The marginal, the liminal being, represents the vector of social change. Threadbare functionalistic terminology aside, is it possible to approach the position of migrants in the contemporary world in these terms?

---

[363] R.S. Matta Echaurren, cited in Eckmann, S. "Der Surrealismus im Exil. Reaktionen auf die Europäisches Zerschlagung der Humanität." *Exil. Flucht und Emigration europaischer Künstler.* Ed. S. Barron and S. Eckmann. München: Prestel, 1997. 176.
[364] Simmel, G. *The Sociology of Georg Simmel,* New York: Free Press, 1964.
[365] Durkheim, E. *Rules of Sociological Method,* New York: Free Press, 1982.
[366] Durkheim, E. *The Division of Labor in Society,* New York: Free Press, 1997.

Any reply calls into question the global dimension of contemporary societies. In the decade following the fall of the Berlin Wall, we discovered that any conceptualization employed for describing society – class, state, capitalism, market, culture, communication – had to be understood in the light of the global dimension. If in previous times only monotheistic religions could presume to be universal, now there is no aspect of collective life that is not interpreted in terms of a prospective that transcends the boundaries of local society. The entire world is now the field of action for business ventures, the natural realm of financial movements, the inevitable terrain of politics, the vector of mass communication. A crisis in a local economy instantaneously becomes a problem for the entire world. The fall of a dictator or a civil war in a country far from us produces effects that reverberate in every part of the globe. As the news reports remind us every day, the material existence of every inhabitant of the planet is directly or indirectly conditioned by what occurs contemporaneously in every part of the known world. A globalized world recognizes the supremacy of one law: movement. Movement through space as the reduction or elimination of economic and communication borders allows an ever wider and faster circulation of goods, symbols, and ideas. Movement through time because the assumed contemporaneousness of events creates an acceleration in decision-making time in the strategic areas of politics and finance.[367]

Movement in society is certainly not a new phenomenon. Marx associated it directly with the role of industry in the expansion of the global market.[368] Beginning with the transoceanic explorations at the end of the fifteenth century, European history has always been associated with movement. Individual and collective travel experiences aside (crusades, pilgrimages, missions, commercial ventures) that kept the lines of communication open with Africa and Asia during

---

[367] Robertson, R. "Glocalisation. Space, Time and Social Theory." *Journal of International Communication* 1 (1994).
[368] Marx, K. *Capital: A Critique of Political Economy,* Vol. 3, New York: Penguin Classics, 1993, Ch. 20, and *Grundrisse: Foundations of the Critique of Political Economy,* New York: Penguin Classics, 1993.

the Middle Ages,[369] the birth of modern Europe would have be inconceivable without the economic exchanges with the rest of the world. As scholars of the economic evolution of the world economy have pointed out, first European and then western capitalism has experienced ever-widening cycles of commercial and financial expansion, whose control rested with the dominant powers.[370] From the Mediterranean hegemony of the Genovese to the oceanic dominance of the Dutch and English, and then the arrival of "the American century," the history of western capitalism has been dictated by the capability of the global military powers, first naval, then aerial, and now communicative to establish commercial stations, control the lines and means of communications, obtain raw materials and labor at low cost, and subject peoples and kingdoms.[371]

The role of western states in sustaining the expansion of capitalism on a global scale, a role that has always contradicted the liberationist myths of the natural and peaceful development of capitalism, is too well-known to require illustrative examples. From the beginning, the capitalist system would be unthinkable without the support of legal and political formulations that are capable of defining the entire world as its natural territory of expansion. This tendency toward a juridical-political universalism is consistent with the subjugation and enslavement of "exotic" peoples, looting their resources and channelling them to Europe or to other markets controlled by European powers.[372] It suffices to remember that from the beginning of the sixteenth

[369] Leed, E.J. *The Mind of the Traveler: From Gilgamesh to Global Tourism*, New York: Basic Books, 1991: Il Mulino, 1995, and *Shores of Discovery: How Expeditionaries Have Constructed the World*, New York: Basic Books, 1995.

[370] Braudel, F. *Civilization and capitalism 15th-18th century*, New York: Collins,1982; Walerstein, I., *Unthinking Social Science: The Limits of Nineteenth-Century Paradigms*, Philadelphia, PA: Temple University Press, 2nd Edition, 2001. For a discussion of the different "datings" of globalization, see Pieterse, J.N. "Der Melange Effekt. Globalisierung im Plural." *Perspektiven der Weltgesellschaft*. Ed. U. Beck. Frankfurt a.M.: Suhrkamp, 1998.

[371] For a reading of this process from the viewpoint of the "right," that is from the perspective of continental minorities, see Schmitt, C. *Land and Sea*, Corvallis, OR: Plutarch Press, 1997.

[372] Wolf, E., Cit. Op.. My study cannot here deal with the issue of colonialism raised by P. Bairoch in *Economics and World History: Myths and Paradoxes*, Chicago: University Of

century, the era of the conquistadores, theologians and jurists alike vigorously justified the freedom to travel the world well-armed in search of riches:

In 1539 [...] Francisco De Vitoria reformulated the rules of legitimization for the conquest of America by the Spanish, establishing the foundation of modern international rights and at the same time, modern natural rights. These rules of legitimization were determined by De Vitoria from the "ius communicationis ac societas," [...] and in a series of other natural laws from which he derived corollaries such as: the "ius pregrinandi in illas provincias et illic degendi," the "ius commercii," the "ius praedicandi et annuntiandi Evangelium," the "ius migrandi" in countries in the new world and to "accipere domicilium in aliqua civitate illorum," and to complete the system, the "ius belli," in defense of these rights should they be opposed by the *indios*.[373]

According to this interpretation, capitalism has been "global" from the beginning, "global" in its Promethean nature, brilliantly described by Marx and Engels in the *Communist Manifesto,* and "global" in its capacity to produce universal cultural forms through the expansion of its markets. If "globalization" has been discussed incessantly for decades, that would not be because the nature of capitalism has changed or that it is entering a new, transformative phase, but because it has entered a dimension that is new, a dimension defined by its apparently limitless capacity to utilize the work force wherever that is available, and to generate profits in every corner of the world. In addition to this saturation of economic spaces, the cultural and political consensus on capitalism as the exclusive economic system of society seems to be absolute, unlike a not-so-distant past. The sudden ending of practiced socialism cleared the horizon of the world's capitalism from any form of official opposition.[374] With a spectacular reversal of those tendencies regarding the economic culture

Chicago Press, 1995 in regards to the role of colonialism in modern economic development, which Bairoch considers to be secondary.
[373] Ferrajoli, L. "Dai diritti del cittadino ai diritti della persona." *La cittadinanza. Appartenenza, identità, diritti.* Rome and Bari: Laterza, 1994. 290.
[374] Beck, U. *Was ist Globalisierung. Irrtümer des Globalismus-Antworten auf Globalisierung.* Frankfurt a.M.: Suhrkamp, 1997.

that had oriented the political public for nearly 50 years, from the New Deal to the Reagan administration, today the only form of economic thought accepted universally is the neoclassical support of the free market, to the point of diluting the traditional opposition between political right and left. The affirmation of this "unified thought,"[375] reflects nothing more than the homogenization of material cultural world-wide. The stage where globalization is currently played out visibly is in the homogenization of consumption: an ever-increasing number of material and non-material goods defines the uniform life style of a growing percentage of the world's population.[376]

Thus globalization constructs the horizon of current political and social transformations, a horizon that is mobile and above all, uncertain. Capitalist globalization has no corresponding tendency to "globalize" the management of economic crises, political conflicts, or the ecological problems that have skyrocketed due to the "new" global dimension.[377] At the beginning of the twentieth century, Max Weber was an insightful prophet when he sustained that the tendency for a violent rationalization of life would spark a perverse dialectic ultimately dominated by a "polytheistic" conflict of values. While Weber had western society in mind, now we should speak instead of the entire planet as the area of conflicts that are fuelled by various economic, political,

---

[375] Usually this expression is defined as the "philosophy" that orients the politics of national and international authorities in the area of economics (the flexibility of jobs, reduction of social benefits and public debt, etc.) Naturally, the term "unified belief" cannot take into account the different orientations of individual governments in terms of political economy. See also Strange, S. *The Retreat of the State: The Diffusion of Power in the World Economy*, Cambridge, MA: Cambridge Univerisy Press, 1989.

[376] Latouche, S. *La megamachine. Raison technoscientifique, raison economique et mythe du progrés. Essais à la memoire de Jacques Ellul*, Paris: La Decouverte, 1995; Giddens, A. *The Consequences of Modernity*, Palo Alto, CA: Stanford University Press, 1991; Gruppo di Lisbona. *I limiti della competitività*. Rome: Manifestolibri, 1995; Ritzer, G. *McDonaldization: The Reader*, Thousand Oaks, CA: Pine Forge Press, (2nd Edition), 2006; see also United Nations Develpoment Program. *Nono Rapporto sullo sviluppo umano*. Cited in M. Forti. "Consumi forzati molto ineguali." *Il Manifesto*. 10 September 1998: 8.

[377] Beck, U. *Risikogesellschaft. Auf dem Weg in eine andere Moderne*. Frankfurt a.M.: Suhrkamp, 1986; Altvater, E. and B. Mahnkopf. *Grenzen der Globalisierung. Ökonomie, Okologie und Politik in der Weltgellschaft*. Münster: Westfälisches Dampfboot, 1996.

and cultural motivations. The fall of the Berlin Wall, for example, was hailed as the beginning of a new era of peace and prosperity, but almost immediately the predictions of the "end of History" by ideologists and futurologists were proven wrong. The world-wide triumph of neoclassical support of the free market did not translate into an increase in wealth, as laissez-faire ideology would have it, but rather as the chronic uncertainty in the economic prospects of the developed world.[378] The fact that financial crises occur faster than the 1929 stock market crash make it possible for a prominent economist to speak about fear as a *stable* psychological condition in the contemporary economy.[379] At the same time, the disappearance of communism, which had served as the "global" enemy of the west par excellence for more than 40 years, rather than insuring peace, has not halted the proliferation of local wars that today involve the very heart of Europe.[380]

Accompanying this atmosphere of global uncertainty are profound changes in the economic and political structure of dominant societies whose consequences are difficult to predict. The ever-increasing move towards the transnationalization of business and markets deprives states of the autonomous capacity to control and regulate the economy, thus rendering obsolete the concept of a national economy.[381] National political authorities still demand intervention in terms of the variables of economic politics but only within rigid parameters set by political-financial authorities such as the International Monetary Fund, the World Bank, the World Trade Organization, and the European Union itself. And while individual states formally participate in the management of the resources controlled by these organizations based on their economic positions, the economies of weaker countries (particularly developing nations and those which

[378] Martin, H.-P. and H. Schuhmann. *Die Globalisierungsfalle. Der Angriff auf Demokratie und Wohlstand*, Reinbeck bei Hamburg: Rowohlt, 1999; Brecher, J. and T. Costello. *Global Village or Global Pillage: Economic Reconstruction From the Bottom Up*, Cambridge, MA: South End Press (2nd Edition), 1999.
[379] Krugman, P. *The Age of Diminished Expectations.* 3rd Ed. Cambridge, MA: The MIT Press, 1997.
[380] On the disappearance of the "global" enemy and the rise of new local hostilities, see Beck, U. *Die feindlose Demokratie. Ausgewählte Aufsätze.* Stuttgart: Reclam, 1995.
[381] Ada, J. *La mondialisation de l'economie. Problémes.* Vol. II. Paris: La Découverte, 1997.

have only recently converted to the open market) are completely dependent upon international authorities. The outlines for political and social economy imposed by the WTO on those countries in economic difficulty in exchange for loans or remission of debts often determines the conditions of the lives of that nation's inhabitants in catastrophic ways.[382] But even wealthy nations, with the exception of the USA, have seen a progressive decline in their economic and political-social sovereignty.[383]

The progressive disappearance of local and state restraints imposed upon the freedom of economic initiatives has worsened the quality of life for an increasing number of people both in developed economies as well as in poorer economies. The tendency to transfer the production of good to those areas where the labor costs are lower, the so-called "outsourcing" of businesses, is the root of the progressive de-industrialization of developed economies. It is this race to reduce costs and de-localize labor, and not just the development of informational technologies and the general labor-saving practices of industrial management that accounts for the employment crisis squeezing the developed economies in this post-Fordist era.[384] In the 1990s, unemployment in Europe became a mass phenomenon, affecting on average more than 10% of the population. In the USA, the unemployment level remained lower than in Europe, around 5 %, though this figure fails to reveal the steady decline of the average wage and the high frequency of temporary, unstable employment.[385]

Due to these complex developments, which the term "globalization" reflects only on a generic level, the very structure of developed societies is being

---

[382] As in Mexico in 1994 and Russia in 1998. For example, the social crises in Morocco in the early 1980s with its resultant bloody repression was sparked by a "recommended" increase in school fees.

[383] See Sassen, S. *Losing Control? Sovereignty in an Age of Globalization.* New York: Columbia University Press, 1996.

[384] For the attribution of the structural crises in the field of information technologies, see Rifkin, J. *The End of Work*, New York: Tarcher, updated edition, 2004.

[385] Adda, J. *La mondialisation de l'économie.* Vol II, p. 97; Wacquant, L.J.D. "La gènèralisation de l'insecurit'salariale en Amèrique. Restructuration d'enterprises et crise de reproduction sociale." *Actes de la recherche en sciences sociales* 115 (1996): 65.

altered. The end of the modern social contract, based in the contractualization of labor and a system of stable social guarantees for workers[386] renders material existence precarious for nearly half of the population of "wealthy" countries, according to Dahrendorf.[387] Those who, due to insufficient education or other "positional" disadvantages, can never aspire to becoming part of that group who "manipulates the symbols," that elite of post-industrial society who in essence direct the processes of globalization for their own advantage are condemned forever to repetitive tasks, and low-paying jobs that are not secure.[388] The inequality does not coincide exclusively with traditional class divisions, both because the role of blue-collar labor has been progressively diminished, at least in developed nations, and because the economic and social marginality involves segments of the population that were once referred to as "lower-middle class," i.e. civil servants, teachers, social workers, autonomous workers in the "symbolic economy."[389] Today, a fine and unclear line separates this wide social group from the most marginal and subordinate workers, such as those who serve others as domestic workers or attendants for the elderly, and all those whose jobs involve heavy, unskilled labor but whose positions are not secure.

The alteration of the "Fordist" social structure has brought about alterations in the urban environment, where just under 80% of the population of developed countries lives.[390] So while the elites reorganize their own material existence, they also modify the space of the city – which is a global city only because it is in the service of the globalized elite[391] – and half of the population sees a decrease in its quality of life from the combined effect of diminished social services (health care, transportation, social assistance) and increased instability of

---

[386] See Ewald, F. *L'Etat providence*. Paris: Grasset, 1989; Castel, R. *La metamorphose de la question sociale. Une chronique du salariat*. Paris: Fayard, 1995.

[387] Dahrendorf, R. Cit. Op.

[388] Reich, R. *The Work of Nations: Preparing Ourselves for 21st Century Capitalism*, London: Vintage, 1992.

[389] Bologna, S. and A. Fumagalli, *Il lavoro autonomo di seconda generazione*. Milan: Feltrinelli, 1997.

[390] World Bank. *Workers in an integrating World, World Development Report 1995*. New York: Oxford University Press, 1995.

[391] Sassen, S. *The Global City. New York, London, Tokyo*. Princeton: Princeton University Press, 1995.

employment. The shocking increase in the number of homeless in the United States and their European counterparts dramatically reveals the abyss that opened between the segment of the population with guaranteed securities and the segment of the population forced to slide into marginality. The burning of Los Angeles in 1992, together with the periodical riots in "global" cities like Paris and London, illustrate more than any other events of that decade the persistent and explosive social problem at the heart of the developed world. This is a problem that the elites in the global cities attempt vainly to remove by fortifying their residential areas, tightening up on repressing social deviance or, as occurs in Italy, the urban *maquillage*, forcing marginal people out of the historic city centers, and expelling gypsies, or starting crusades against prostitutes.[392]

This scene of precariousness and conflict is synonymous with the reduction of the binding social contract as a whole that nation-states had guaranteed to its citizens in the nineteenth century, a contract based in publicly regularizing labor relations and integrating the working classes. This reduction prejudices the cultural and ideological justification for the modern state. Aside from its traditional role of including the proletariat, the "nation," a complex of mythologies and secular rituals developed relatively recently in the history of Europe,[393] had the function of symbolically integrating the construction of enormous repressive apparatus and social control. According to the famous definition of Max Weber, states had the monopoly on the space left open by other states. The creation of a system of public education, the most vast state apparatus together with the repressive-military apparatus, created another great monopoly of the national state: the control of symbolic systems and their transmission. Now, with the exception of the repressive apparatus and to some degree, the administrative apparatus, the state monopolies are under attack on all sides, including the most recent – the channels of mass communication. To an

---

[392] On these tendencies, in addition to the works of M. Davis cited previously, see Christopherson, S. "The Fortress City: Privatized Spaces, Consumer Citizenship." *Post-Fordism. A Reader.* Ed. A. Amin. Oxford: Basil Blackwell, 1994. 409.
[393] See in particular Hobsbawm, E. and T. Ranger, eds. *The Invention of Tradition*, Cambridge, MA: Cambridge University press, 1992

ever greater degree, national states control the great apparatuses that reproduced and transmit culture: the educational systems and mass communication. Private, national, and international competition is increasingly fierce, and at the same time, national states have had to renounce their sovereignty of economic politics and international politics.

This doesn't mean, as has been casually proclaimed by some apologists for globalization, that nation-states are "over."[394] Rather it means that they must, together with the public discourses that justify them, adapt themselves to a complex global picture whose developments are in many ways incompre-hensible.[395] The ever-intensifying denationalization of the economy causes new areas of interest to form within states and between states, and consequently wealth and poverty no longer coincide with traditional political delineations, even in the developed world. The redefinition of economic power is not mechanically expressed in new stable forms of hegemony, but in a constellation of dimensions of power that interact and enter into conflict in a kind of controlled instability that is continually being negotiated.[396] Examples abound: Japan, which is a Titan in the world economy, is one of the biggest lenders, holding 40% of the U.S.A.'s public debt[397] but exerts a secondary influence in terms of international politics, not unlike Germany. On the other hand, the military hegemony of the United States and the Americanization of consumer goods world-wide – two dramatic forms of current globalization – do not correspond to a stable power on the planet. In other words, while the economy, or rather, global capitalism, carries out an incessant destabilization of international relations and continually diminishes the traditional political

---

[394] Ohmae, K. *The End of the Nation State: The Rise of Regional Economies*, New York: Free Press, 1996.

[395] Jessopp, B. "Die Zukunft des Nationalstaates. Erosion oder Reorganisation?" *Jenseits der Nationalonomie. Weltwirtschaft und Naionalstaat zwischen Globalisierung und Regionalisierung.* Eds. S. Becker, T. Sablowski, and W. Shumm. Berlin and Hamburg: Argument, 1997. 50-95.

[396] Hirst, P. And G. Thompson. "Globalisierung, Internationale Wirtschaftsbeziehungen, Nationalökonomien und die Formierung von Handelsblöcken." *Politik der Globalisierung.* Ed. U. Beck. Frankfurt a.M.: Suhrkamp, 1998. 85-133.

[397] Bertone, U. "Tokyo, La miseria virtuale dell'opulento Giappone." *La Stampa* 15 September 1998: 7.

prerogatives of the state, nevertheless nation states still remain the most relevant area of investment from a political point of view.

The contemporary state is a machine far to complicated and costly, and it carries out functions too specialized in maintaining lifestyle and mediating different interests for it to be weakened by the delegation of some if its key functions to other organizations. On the one hand, such delegation or limitation of sovereignty are merely the precursors in many cases to the actual period of globalization and the redefinition of world powers. Consider for example the military alliances such as NATO and the organizations that oversee and regulate financial transactions. On the other hand, what remains of nation states has to do with functions so specific that no transnational apparatus could easily take them over. "What remains of nation states" is mere euphemism. Apart from their limited sovereignty, from their actual or virtual subordination to the vastest transnational powers, the apparatuses of social control involve millions of individuals and manage immense resources. Now, while the private sector is waging a ferocious battle against social spending, and while the public sector is facing a general decline, the costs of maintaining the police, the military, the judicial system and other social apparatus generally remain uncontested. The enormity of the stakes involved explains the ferocity with which the different organizations defend their privileges, the abundance of resources destined for modernizing and innovating those apparatuses, and the ever-increasing tendency to interpret conflicts in contemporary society in terms of police or legal repression. "What remains of nation states" in this era of the limitation – not the end – of their powers is the nucleus of their strength. In "civil" states, the most brutal and corrupt means are used to combat religious minorities, regional demands, and "terrorism" in general (for example, the fight in Spain against the ETA, the British repression in Ireland, and the ways in which sects and movements are liquidated in the United States.)

Rather than being a grass-roots cultural process, the revival of nationalism manifest in different degrees across the developed world appears more an attempt on the part of the ruling elite from both the political right and left to justify their control of public apparatuses. It is an artificial but effective attempt that becomes evident in the reinvention of traditional mythologies and patriotism, in the ethnicization of conflicts, and above all, as my study contends, the reproduction and amplification of "the enemy" in politics and the media. True, intolerance toward foreigners exists widely on the grass-roots level in urban life and society at large, an intolerance clearly fuelled by the worsening conditions and insecurity. But this intolerance is directed by local and national cultural and political elites, and it is only due to their manipulation that the intolerance becomes publicly codified as creating "the enemy." Today this is a formidable symbolic resource that guarantees the control of society and the functioning of public apparatuses of control.

The rise of alternative nationalisms, which are the local political expressions of the new stakes in the territorial reorganization of the economy, conform to the same line of reasoning. The rather artificial attempt by the local elites to construct centers of alternative power and to justify their own legitimacy finds expression in a culture of hostility that is completely in keeping with traditional nationalisms. In other words, as the case of the Northern League shows, neonationalisms try to compete with national elites in exploiting a common resource, the demonization of the foreigner, the hostility towards immigrants and "*clandestini*." Patrols, crusades against scandalous prostitution, clean-up crews and local police, expulsions, and detention centers for immigrants do not alter in the least the reality of immigration that to a degree is inevitable, and which is actually accepted without any fuss when it swells the ranks of underpaid labor. It is redefined as a subordinate phenomenon, and immigrants are assigned an inferior and marginal role in the social hierarchy. The effect of what I defined earlier as a "double bind," the migrant is the contemporary *metoiko*, mere meat for the labor market, without a voice or visibility, and who becomes a public enemy if voluntarily or involuntarily, he or she demands existence.

A globalized society in the vast sense of the term is the inverse of a "rational" reality. Although economic changes and market forces outline that society's material structure, it still remains a kind of puzzle in which traditions and customs, institutions and social apparatus, constellations of old and new interests coexist in an unstable equilibrium which is always subject to the influence of factors that cannot always be controlled. Therefore, appealing to a comprehensive rationality is simply a conventional way of calling for a utopian stability. First of all, what today is called the economy is perhaps the most unpredictable and unstable dimension of society. Gone is any illusion of strategic control, rather the world-wide economy is more a battle in which the victors change constantly: the fate of the Southeast Asian economies, the so-called economic "tigers," as well as Japan, were referred to until recently as the new "Yellow Threat," which speaks volumes about the ephemeral nature of economic success, threatened daily by speculative movements, the fears of investors and the whims of consumers. The race for technological innovation and competition, which is perceived "by everyone" as the only road to economic survival, is another way of hiding the fundamental irrationality of the global market.

On the other hand, in the economic process we also find actors who are calculating and rational – as fashionable social-economic theorists would have it – as well as passive and conditioned consumers. The latter have no possibility of controlling the quality of available consumer goods (or their corresponding "needs" for those goods), but have only the choice among an array of products whose real meaning is external. The expansion of available information and mass communication corresponds to the "natural needs" of understanding and communication, or are those "needs" nothing more than the effect of consumption, of a capitalism that is increasingly innovative, imaginative, immaterial, able to exploit the wish to avoid the idiocy of daily life and offers the illusion of participating in a "global" cultural dimension? An economy so voracious for expansion is infinitely more capable than the economy of the past to commercialize and connect ideas and symbols, transforming them into needs. This is equally true for the construction and circulation of "identity," that social clothing that humans use as a form of protection and security blanket. Local, regional, and national identities, like any other merchandise, are goods that come and go with astonishing speed. And this produces effects that are perverse and uncontrollable. Subsuming every cultural content in the net of global markets renders identities more or less arbitrary, identities that were once bounded by local folklore impose themselves instantaneously empowered by immediate communication. The internet doesn't only offer information, commercial services, and discussion groups, but the propaganda of reactionary military groups in Montana, neo-Nazis, and Islamic fundamentalists.

However, aside from these limited cases, it is the average citizen, the consumer of symbolic and material goods who is left helpless in the storm of world-wide markets. Material existence won painstakingly is exposed to incomprehensible collapses in the perspective of daily life. Demographic variations over time which no one could have predicted are suddenly called up to justify the reduction in retirement benefits or cut in wages. An absurd sexual scandal that threatened the credibility of the president of the United States can be considered the cause for a financial crisis. The crash of a stock market that is twenty thousand miles away become the direct or indirect reason (depending on the financial public) for modifying the bank rate which then is reflected in the rate of savings, level of salaries, and retirement benefits. In other words, daily life, even in the wealthy sectors of the planet is subject to an insecurity that has no means of comfort if not the incessant production of public rhetorics by media mobilization.[398] Consider the monetary unification of western Europe. A political moment that consolidated consumption from the political and economic consequences that had long been unpredictable, became the occasion for the production of unreal rhetorics concentrating on "civilization," "solidarity," and European "identities."

The role of public rhetorics in directing general insecurity is particularly evident in the way in which political and media apparatuses treat the "risks" or threats to society. True, a category of risks to typical lifestyle has become more visible in the social transformations of the past decades. I am not referring to "global" risks, the ecological threats to the environment due to the parasitic exploitation of resources. I refer instead to the real or apparent risks, those associated with the decay of social relations. The reduction or destruction, depending on the case, of social welfare systems brings about an increase in

---

[398] For a discussion of these points, see Münch, R. *Globale Dynamik, lokale Lebenswelten. Derschwerige Weg in Die Weltgesellschaft.* Frankfurt a.M.: Suhrkamp, 1998.

micro-conflicts, particularly in the urban scene due to increased uncertainty and a decline in the conditions of daily life. The upheaval in Los Angeles was not fundamentally a "racial" protest, but primarily an attempt by tens of thousands of African-americans and Latinos, who had been excluded and unemployed, to directly appropriate the material goods that Reagan's social politics had divided from them. Aside from these dramatic cases, it is natural that the activity of microcriminality is wide-spread, now and in the past, among those considered "marginal," especially the younger generation. What sociology calls "predatory phenomena" (thefts, muggings, assault) is the consequence of a high number of positional disadvantages – economic, social, urban, and educational. To interpret this reality, whose quantitative expansion is controversial and cannot be demonstrated, simply in terms of "the market of opportunities," avoids seeing the circular dialectic that is established in every society between the reduction of social benefits and the repression of criminal activity. Besides "classic" microcriminality, what today is publicized as "risks" for our lifestyle (i.e. social deviance of every kind, drug selling and use, "hooliganism," etc.) are often desperate behaviours, individual protests or withdrawals from a social order that offers no possibilities except subordination and dead-ends. To therefore interpret microcriminality and deviance as a natural "predatory" tendency of certain individuals indicates a lack of understanding of the systematic decline of social relations.[399]

The fact remains that the prevalent risks between citizens are socially constructed as such. This occurs less for those privileged citizens who can reinforce their own protection, isolate themselves behind the fortresses of their own neighbourhoods, but rather for the vast majority who directly experience those significant urban changes. And it is against this majority, the group more exposed to every other social group on the insecure globe, that different institutions universally practice a mobilization against the "risks," and also leverage fear. Retirees, senior citizens, small business owners, middle-class

---

[399] A tendency that is evident in H. M. Enzesberger, *Aussichten auf den Bürgerkrieg*, Frankfurt a.M.: Suhrkamp, 1993, as well as in the "anthropology" of violence in Sofsky, W. *Saggio sulla violenza*. Turin: Einaudi, 1998.

workers are the natural terrain for exploiting social anxieties and directing them against the most visible targets. The increasingly rapid decline, which is the direct result of the disintegration of contracts in labor relations, union regulations, various associations, and political parties themselves isolates individuals in daily existence who were once part of discrete and clear categories, and who do not fit now in that complex of codes that interpret their position in the world. Senior citizens and retirees are left to themselves to await a solitary death, small business owners are obsessed with competing with big distributors, and all the other micro-categories no longer enjoy a prospective social and material security, but has become the group most likely to vent their fears at the most visible and readily available targets: foreigners, delinquents, drug addicts, prostitutes, squatters, and so forth. Of course, in opposing solid citizens with these threats to society ancient anthropological mechanisms come in to play that delineate the distinctions between pure and impure.[400] However, the administration of these mechanisms is not the prerogative of "natural" sociality, of ordering, but rather of the modern apparatuses of symbolic control.

The conscious or unconscious game that vast sectors of the political and media systems and the intellectual elite are playing in this daily ritual of "the threat of the plague-spreader" is decisive in the new and sinister construction of social solidarity. In fact, this game has become the prerogative of institutions and centers of power in our democratic society. Those institutions and power centers have found that manipulating these symbolic constructions offers obvious and concrete pay-offs. Reagan, Giuliani, and Blair have taught our government leaders that stoking the fire of daily fear maintains the social and political consensus. The appeal to a "hard-line" against deviance and petty criminals allows the redirection of resources to repressive apparatuses of social control, thus guaranteeing the political support of those who direct those apparatuses. The daily replaying of this *grand guignol* by the organs of mass communication inevitably captures readers and viewers. It is futile to ask if these economic and

---

[400] See Maranini, P. *Miseria dell'opulenza. Il sacro nella società della tecnica.* Bologna: Il Mulina, 1998, who develops several fundamental ideas from Douglas, M. *Natural Symbols*, London: Routledge, 2nd Edition, 1996.

political advantages are intentionally sought as the object of deliberate strategies. The individual institutional actors, both large and small, are knowingly ensnared in the circular, "autopoeitic" systems of the social production of fear analyzed in this text. In that sense, these systems are irrational and inertial just like those other economic and social systems with which they interact.

2 Goods, People, and Borders

In a market that is increasingly globalized, the tendency to lower labor costs no longer finds any real barriers on the face of the earth. If in the past, outsourcing the base of production could refer a region or even a state, today it includes virtually any part of the globe where available, cheap labor and minimal infrastructure makes that area attractive. Businesses have no particular interest in supporting their own national states, but prefer to base production where their own connections to the place are minimal. So if a computer is designed in Silicon Valley or Seattle, it could be produced in different Southeast Asian countries, assembled in Germany, and sold in Holland. On the other hand, the freedom to produce and sell on a global scale allows businesses to free themselves from local markets when those begin to require the investment of too many resources. Entire regions of the earth participate in the world economy with natural resources or available work force without receiving anything in return. The world economy is not the producer of equality, but of new and ferocious inequalities, as the statistics demonstrate that reveal the dividing line between the wealthy North and its satellites (such as Southeast Asia) from the rest of the world. For example, the 1 to 30 ratio that exists between the per capita GNP of a citizen in Mozambique and a citizen of the European Union, or the 1 to 6 ratio that exists between an individual in Malaysia and an individual in Italy.[401] Actually, the gulf between rich and poor widened in

---

[401] World Bank. *Workers in an integrating World, World Development Report 1995.* New York: Oxford University Press, 1995; Adda, J. *La mondialisation de l'économie.* Vol II; *The Economist.* "Il mondo in cifre 1998." Italian edition in *Internazionale.* Rome 1998.

the decades of globalization. In 1960, 20% of the poorest inhabitants of the planet owned 2.3% of the world's wealth, but by 1991 that had become 1.4% of the world's wealth, and in 1998, it had become 1.1%.[402]

The outsourcing of production, which reflects a decrease in industrial jobs in developed countries, does not bring an increase in wealth to those who are in the work force. In these countries (India, China, Brazil, Thailand), the possibility of attracting foreign investment is largely based in low wages, lack of regulations that control work conditions, and the use of child labor, that is, forms of labor that could all be termed, "forced."[403] The tendency to move a base of production is obviously greater when the available work force is near to border of a developed country. The use of information that is transferable in "real time" can be contracted to workers in Bangalore by an American company, and the dirty industrial production can be advantageously relocated just a few hundred miles from the mother company. This is the case with the steel industries in Eastern Europe or, to use an example that is closer to home, with the small manufacturers in Morocco and Tunis who work for the European tourist industry[404] or the factories in Albanian that produce the soles for shoes, but are controlled by companies in Puglia.[405] The most dramatic example is perhaps the phenomenon of the *maquilladoras*, the factories that have sprung up in Mexico directly along the borders reinforced by electric fences which were erected to prevent migration into the United States. In these factories, the wages for a day's work are about five dollars, less than one-tenth the pay of an American worker in Texas or California. No degree of imagination is necessary to understand the perverse

---

[402] I take these data from *Internazionale* 247 (1998): 20.

[403] Seventy per cent of the soccer balls used world-wide are sewn by Pakistani child laborers. See Piñol, A. "Pakistan, cuciti a un pallone." *Internazionale* 249 (1998): 54. In the spring of 1996, *The New York Times* reported the slave labor conditions of Malaysian workers for Nike. The Italian company Benetton which utilizes anti-racist advertisements use workers in Slovenia that are paid only 350,000 lire a month. See Nicotri, G. "Il boom del Nord-Est." *L'Espresso.* 14 November 1996: 80.

[404] See Grazzini, F. "Di là dal mare." *Diario della settimana* 32/33 (1998).

[405] Lerner, G. "La griffe italiana masce in Romania. Da Stefanel a Lotto: Il Nord-Est va all'estero." *La Stampa.* 2 October 1996: 13 and "Tirana, colonia del made in Italy. Dalla Puglia alla 'conquista' dell'Albania." *La Stampa.* 1 October 1996: 7.

connection between displacing production, blocking immigration, and the xenophobia in the borderlands of wealthy countries. A similar phenomenon occurred in Italy in March, 1997 with the "Albanian invasion."[406]

However, the proximity between the wealthy and the impoverished areas of the planet is no longer only a spatial relation. Numberless economic fluctuations and communication channels connect the developed parts of the globe with the underdeveloped parts. Industrial investments, financial fluctuations (with the immediate consequences that they cause in weak and unstable economies), the global expansion of networks of information and mass communication, the traffic in illegal goods, the one-way flow of tourism from rich to "exotic" countries involve the entire planet and create an artificial proximity between areas that are geographically distant.[407] This means that the division of the planet into different worlds that are inferior and superior is mere convention. In a certain sense, the *Third world as an economic and political category no longer exists.*[408] Rather, worlds exist that are integrated and at the same time, subordinate in a complex panorama of economic, political, and military means of inferiorization to the dominant economic power, subordinate to that power's cultural and media models, ideologies, repressions, and censoring.[409] The apparent unification of the planet is only logical in the sense of an ironclad hierarchization of markets, economies, and peripheral societies. At the top of this hierarchy, we find the systems of wealthy countries, a galaxy of

[406] Rotella, S. *Twilight on the Line. Underworlds and Politics at the U.S.-Mexico Border.* New York: Norton, 1998. Cited in Goytisolo, J. "La frontiera di cristallo." *Internazionale* 247 (1998). For a structural analysis of the creation of "new social and transnational spaces" determined by globalization, see Pries, L. "Transnationale soziale Räume. Theoretisch-empirisch Skizze am Beispiel der Arbeitswanderungen Mexico-USA." *Perspektiven der Weltgesellschaft.* Ed. U. Beck. Frankfurt a.M.: Suhrkamp, 1998.

[407] Mattelart, A. *Mapping World Communication: War, Progress, Culture*, Minneapolis, MN: University of Minnesota Press, 1994.

[408] Bayart, J.-F. "Finishing with the Idea of the Third World. The Concept of the Political Trajectory." *Rethinking Third World Politics.* Ed. J. Manor. London: Longman, 1991.

[409] This theme was discussed by P. Berger, *Pyramids of Sacrifice: Political Ethics and Social Change*, Jacksonville, FL: Anchor, 1976 before the discussions on globalization became part of daily parlance.

transnational companies and a collection of brand names that administer the economic segmenting of the planet. The ferocity of this hierarchy was demonstrated by the first global war in world history, the Gulf War, a conflict for the control of resources in a strategic area of the planet that culminated in the annihilation of the military forces of Iraq and the starvation of one of the most developed populations of the Near East. Military apparatuses that are increasing more sophisticated and more diffused are capable of constantly maintaining international order, that is, defending those borders that are most useful to the world's economic and political powers.

In this era of globalization, the world economy superimposes its language and culture on a Babel of languages, traditions, and cultural differences that intertwine across the world. Thus, no region can be immune to the enticements of the world market, its products and its icons. The forest of skyscrapers that form the skyline in Singapore, Abu Dabi, or Johannesburg, the McDonald's signs that loom over the panorama of Moscow, Mexico City, Peking, or Rabat represent the artificial unification of the world that is followed to the point of bipolarism. It should therefore come as no surprise if the inhabitants of areas less favored by global markets respond to the stimuli and messages that global culture pours over them. The desire or the illusion of escaping from the limits of local markets, poverty, a thousand forms of servitude or oppression in impoverished, marginal or totalitarian countries is the least that we can expect from the millions of humans who move within the interstices of the world system.[410]

This is the situation today from which the willingness is born to emigrate and become foreigners in the wealthy world. The new migrations are only one of the effects of the triumph of the world economy and the material culture that perpetuates it. One may emigrate to avoid a civil war or a famine, for "adventure," to increase personal income, or to put down roots in a new place, or to keep a family together by accepting a low-level job overseas (but which still represents a salary ten times higher than they would receive at home). This

---

[410] Latouche, S. *In the Wake of the Affluent Society: An Exploration of Post-Development*, London: Zed Books, 1993. For an intelligent analysis of the desperate consumerism in impoverished countries, see Cooper, M. "Cile 98. Falso miracolo." *Diario della settimana* 36 (1998): 20.

is why, contrary to common public opinion, both impoverished and the college-educated emigrate, both the skilled laborers and students. Migrants can be Latinos that crowd into the neo-industrial cities of northern Mexico and try to enter southern California, Albanians attracted to Italy from the example of Italian entrepreneurs that swarmed into Albania, Senegalese graduates who can't find work in their impoverished, arid country, Nigerians who flee a dictatorship, young Moroccans, Tunisians, and Egyptians who live on the edge of opulent Europe, or the Polish and Romanians who cannot find a position in the new marginal economy of the market.

This plurality of motivations and realities does not correspond to the often obsolete sociological categories of demography and migration. The distinction between migrants and refugees is purely conventional these days, given that nearly all countries of emigration are governed by the assent, if not the explicit conniving of wealthy democracies, dictatorships, or totalitarian regimes in which human rights are violated on a daily basis. Reducing the nexus of conditions and motivations for migration to the cliché of "invasion" is one symptom of the positivism prevalent today in social sciences. "Migrating" does not mean that "masses" of indigents empty one region in order to saturate another, as the science of population trends likes to describe, but rather a plurality of individuals possessing possibilities and different expectations are willing to seek opportunities for a different life where such chances are possible or promised. Migrations may be thus understood as transfers that are not necessarily permanent, partial life projects that take advantage of sudden openings and that clash against unforeseen barriers, a circulation of lives between diverse regions and borders, hoped-for returns and separations that are endured, experiences in which individuals carry with them or search for complex and plural identities. Migrants may be Muslims, but not fundamentalists, underprivileged but not uneducated, willing to live abroad for part of their lives but also wishing to return home, willing to move but not assimilate completely to the destination culture. In short, the condition of migration oscillates between necessity and freedom, need and desire, fragile security and the insecurity that also carries the possibility of a better life.

According to the statistics from the World Bank, there are now approximately 120 million migrants, about 2% of the world's population. Even if this figure represented 10% of the population of developed countries, less than a third comes from Europe or North America. In fact, the majority of migrants do not move from "North to South," as is commonly believed, but rather from "South to South" in other regions, within sub-Saharan Africa or toward the Middle East or Southeast Asia.[411] Actually, in strictly quantitative terms, the phenomenon of migration affects the same percentage of the European population as 25 years ago.[412] In fact, even during periods of high "pressure" from migration, the rate of migration is actually determined by the number of migrants who return to their homeland or by the high number of immigrants who leave the destination country. For example, the four million migrants who entered northern Europe during the second half of the 1980s was offset by the emigration of two and a half million other people.[413] The relative stability of migratory phenomena together with the symptoms of an inversion in the tendency toward an expanding world population (and not just in developed countries) should help to deflate the paranoid perception about migration phenomena that we have seen affirmed in Italy and Europe. *If not, that is because today migrants and refugees represent one of the greatest paradoxes, or rather, greatest conflicts of globalization.* The circulation of goods, merchandise, symbols, and even people which defines the globalized market is allowed to flow only in the direction that is controlled by wealthy countries and that serves their interests. The "right" to move that functionaries of individual states or international organizations, entrepreneurs, business people, travelers, and tourists all exercise freely in the peripheral parts of the world in great numbers is not challenged by anyone. As bearers of actual and virtual property, these individuals meet no impediments. It is the "poor" from the periphery, the people who only own their own bodies, who are subject

---

[411] Collinson, S. *Le migrazioni internazionali e l'Europa.* Bologna: Il Mulino, 1994. 40; World Bank, World Population Projections. Short and Long-term Estimates. Johns Hopkins University Press, 1990.
[412] Gambino, F. "Alcune aporie delle migrazioni internazionali." *aut aut* 275: 129-141.
[413] Sopemi. *Trends in International Migrations.* Paris: OECDE, 1991. Cited in Collinson, S. *Le migrazioni internazionali e l'Europa.* Bologna: Il Mulino, 1994. 39.

to restrictions and customs controls, who are excluded from circulating freely. In this sense, they are inevitably "*clandestini*," as soon as they attempt to escape from the bondage of the conditions of existence in their hierarchical society.

To see the problem of contemporary migration in terms of freedom of movement redefines the status of refugees. Nearly all wealthy status tend to restrict the right to asylum to the most extreme cases – those cases in which there has been some form of official mobilization or display of interest from the public – indifferent to the vast majority, that is, the "normal" violation of human rights in all those authoritarian states that surround Europe, the U.S.A. and Japan. Even if a "democratic" opinion deceives itself that it is managing the problem of migrants and refugees with unrealistic plans for co-operation with weaker economies, the reality of the relations between states in the North and South is far more mundane. In order to get rid of a few thousand migrants, Spain and Italy did not hesitate to align themselves with police regimes in Morocco, Tunis, and Turkey, throwing millions of euros at them and offering military and logistical assistance. Such is the fate of many "undesirables" (often of different nationalities) in countries that are famous for the actions of their police and the horrific conditions of their prisons. In the summer of 1998, numerous Italian newspapers documented the desperate status of *clandestini* and political refugees were they to be returned to the care of King Hassan's functionaries or to the Tunisian or Turkish governments. This justifies, together with the conditions in the camps for "*permanenza temporanea*" their protests and attempts to flee. The blindness of our democracies confirms what is occurring only miles from the borders of southern Europe, a blindness that is more explicit political conniving with regimes that maintain the economic and social order for rich or nouveau riche states and acts as a form of outsourcing of social conflicts in the contradictory panorama of global society.

3 Inside the Paradox

In this book I have attempted to show how the public exclusion of migrants is the result of perverse mechanisms that various social actors manage to exploit to their own advantage: entrepreneurs and *imprenditori morali*, neighborhood politicians, those who administer the systems of social control and the media. Against this interplay of general irrationality and "rational" limited practices, invoking migration's economic and demographic benefits to the state seems useless. Hypothetically, if Italy were to accept and legalize 10,000 migrants a year, they would hardly "saturate" the country, but would only help to offset the decline in population that demographers now regard as irreversible.[414] Any such move, however, would require the complete overturning of those political, social and media presuppositions of "the enemy," and the recognition first of all of the right of the work force to freely circulate transnationally. Above all, it would require the social and institutional mechanisms to offer migrants educational opportunities, protection in the work place, the right to housing, in a word, political, social, and civil equality with the autochthones. By granting them citizenship, the only way to remove them from the limbo of being non-persons, society would also remove the material and symbolic basis for the radical exclusion of migrants and social and urban micro-conflictuality.

If this does not occur, it is because their exclusion, which depends on their status as *clandestini*, has a decisive function in maintaining the current hierarchies of globalized society. The political and military barriers to migration force the poor of planet to accept salaries and living conditions that the global industry imposes on the peripheral labor markets with the blessing of their local governments. On the other hand, the condition of those migrants who manage to leak through the cracks in the fortress always oscillates between marginality and *clandestinità* making them workers essentially without any rights, subjected to the exploitation wages and work conditions that the autochthon entrepreneurs impose upon them. I am not only referring to industries and small companies, but also to those positions that employ mainly women both legally and illegally in

---

[414] See for example, ISTAT. *Rapporto sull'Italia*. Bologna: Il Mulino, 1996. The evaluation was published by *Corriere della Sera* on 15 September, 1998. The same day the government announced the plan to legalize 38,000 immigrants, a number that corresponded to the number of available jobs in industries. In other words, no professional ability is attributed to migrants beyond their potential as workers in industries.

domestic or "personal" services. Prostitution is a specific case of the absolute subordination of immigrant women workers, but with due acknowledgment of the differences, the same is true for domestic workers and attendants to the elderly. The official barriers to immigration render it impossible for migrants to escape from their condition of subordination that could last a lifetime. A migrant is deprived of rights and of a voice in the society that "welcomed" him or her, just as in the homeland which he or she left to emigrate.

The proliferation of the "glass borders" or "iron borders" raised in Europe and in the developed world in general do not lead to optimism. The recent evolution in European legislation regarding immigration and the rights of migrants demonstrates a progressive regulatory intensification. The "fear machines" are not extraneous to it, and consequently, the hostile attitudes toward foreigners increase, as surveys highlight. Even though in the debates over legal principles involved in the question of citizenship for migrants, the clear contradictions are becoming obvious between the rhetoric of universal rights widely employed in developed societies and the actual negation of migrants rights,[415] the same social and political theory cannot seem to get beyond generic appeals to tolerance or transnational and cosmopolitan forms of democracy to oppose the tendency toward neo-nationalistic barricading.[416] More importantly, even the "reasonable" proposals for inclusion never truly approach the political aspect of the issue, but focus on curtailing the flow of migrants, or are aimed at extending the rights of asylum, but are still more limited than the requests.

This could be expressed in a formula that recognizes how the freedom of movement and the circulation of migrants is a condition for the development and consolidation of democracy, and not the reverse. In other words, the assumption must be rejected that western democracies can only accept migrants and refugees by the dropperful in order not to threaten their fragile structures and

---

[415] Schwartz, W.F., ed. *Justice in Immigration*. Cambridge and New York: Cambridge University Press, 1995.
[416] Held, D. *Democracy and the Global Order. From the Modern State to the Cosmopoltian Governance*. 2nd Ed. Cambridge: Polity Press, 1997. Held's book contains an excellent synthesis on the prospects for democratic politics in the era of globalization.

not to arouse xenophobic reactions in the masses. At least two reasons exist that justify the "right to migrate." First is that human rights are not a condition of citizenship or inclusion, but are the only way to recognize the rights of the individual. And even if it is not accurate to speak of a "global" citizenship within the complex panorama of international politics, the total equality of rights is still feasible between nationals and foreigners who live in the territory of another national state. Only under this condition can the legal double standards, the detention centers, the mass deaths by drowning at sea, and the institutional violence against foreigners be eliminated that are currently tolerated in our democratic societies. It could also be added that the right to immigration in no way threatens democratic stability or "cultural unity" for the simple reason that now as in the past, migrations are fundamentally a circulation of the labor force and not the transfers of populations.

On the other hand, xenophobia is not opposed by accepting its premises, but by combating those very premises, returning when possible to that tradition of political and cultural debate and reopening the discussion and political work of the left that democratic politics in general have let languish in the west over the last several decades. This brings us to the second compelling reason for recognizing the right to immigration. When a contingent of the political left essentially underwrites the culture of hostility and the stereotype of "the enemy" regarding foreigners, the left contributes to and authorizes a disturbing version of the world, and not just for foreigners. The history of the first half of the twentieth century has clearly demonstrated how the left's refusal to defend the rights of the weak has favored an increase in xenophobia and reactionary populism which ultimately leads to the defeat of the very workers and autochthon citizens of the left. And while it is no longer in vogue these days to speak of the development of democracy and social conquests, allow me to conclude this text with a quotation that defines what the stakes are in recognizing the rights of migrants: "Labor cannot emancipate itself in the white skin where in the black it is branded."[417]

[417] Marx, K. *Capital: A Critique of Political Economy*, Vol. 1, New York: Penguin Classics, 1992.

Afterwords

The first edition of this book appeared in 1999, at the end of what could be termed the Clinton decade. During the 1990s, on both sides of the Atlantic center-left "progressive" governments were in power: Clinton, Blair, Prodi, Schroeder, and others, in apparent opposition to the aggressive conservatism of Regan, Thatcher, and Bush senior. The slogan of these new majorities was "the middle road," i.e. a moderate, enlightened, reasonable socialism, that was set to reconcile the new globalized capitalism with the needs of the less privileged members of society.[418] Within a few short years, their program revealed itself to be only a dream, and not only because the "progressives" were supplanted nearly everywhere by administrations that were motivated by an aggressive neo-conservatism. The supposed progressivism of Clinton appeared as a political version of the "new economy," i.e. a development linked to the greater diffusion of new technology and the consequent decrease of steady employment. The same could be said for European variations. The introduction of the euro was heralded by a rigidly orthodox belief in the free-market, founded on reduction in public spending and cutting the social state to its minimal form. The "middle way" showed itself to be only a slightly more

---

[418] The intellectual manifesto of this position is available in Giddens, A. *The Third Way: The Renewal of Social Democracy*, , Cambridge: Polity, 1999, which can be contrasted with the less conventional reflections of Bauman, Z. *Work, Consumerism and the New Poor*, Maidenhead: Open University Press (2nd Edition), 2004.

moderate version of Reaganist or Thatcheresque free-marketism. What this latter considered to be free trade, in the "middle way" appeared as a conversion to a network of capitalism, democratic in that anyone who wanted to, could make money by becoming an entrepreneur.

Naturally, any such program could not be painless. First of all, like the other programs of the preceding conservative governments, this necessitated the erosion of institutions that for more than 50 years had been the pillars that sustained the development of the west under the shadow of the historic conflict between liberal world and socialist states, i.e. government spending on social programs, public education, the health system, and other services that were free or at government expense. The state not only withdrew from the direct management of the economy but also from regulating basic social needs, allowing these to be "satisfied" by the workings of the free market. Thus, to give an example, the cost and quality of essential services for workers, such as public transportation, were no longer guaranteed by the state, but by those private companies who began to battle for a slice of the market. Consequently, in Blair's England, the country which put the "middle way" program into action most radically, the railway system underwent the same disastrous decline that the American airline companies experienced under the Reagan administration. Also, the "middle way" brought about a profound revision in what sociologists term the criteria of public prestige. When a political economy veers from the primacy of collective well being in favor of individual enterprise, then the value of the steady employee is diminished in favor of the independent free-lancer. Employment in a factory or a public office became unappealing, seen as the result of inadequate training, if not lack of intelligence. Whoever did not work independently was therefore subject to a process of continual re-qualification. This refocusing became the new credo of hyper-liberal "socialism," and is disturbing in that it points to an eternal relearning and thus infantilizes and subordinates the workforce both cognitively and morally.

That the "middle way" was naturally uncharitable or attentive to the needs of the poor was obvious in the politics of social control, particularly those aimed at the weakest of society: the marginal, the deviant, the poor, the imprisoned, and the immigrants. The exhortations of Clinton and Blair were eloquent: the former flew to Arkansas where he had previously been governor in order to witness the execution of a minor who had been condemned to death for murder, while the latter repeatedly spoke out in favor of tightening up school discipline, including the use of corporeal punishment for recalcitrant or unruly students. The Clinton decade, progressive and enlightened according its European apologists, saw the convergence of government and public opinion in the terrain of the battle against microcriminality, juvenile delinquency, and "incivility," i.e. all the behaviors that without being serious crimes would threaten the peace, security, and tranquility of its citizens. The rallying flag of "zero tolerance" held up by the republican mayor of New York City, Guiliani, was created by the progressive culture.[419] To justify this spectacular inversion of perspective, the image of a ubiquitous civil war was called into action, a war that was capable of spreading spontaneously, like an infection, from the smallest, unimportant details or minor factors: graffiti, decline in urban appearance, nightly ruckus, fights between young people, and so on. In a successful pamphlet, Han Magnus Enzensberger, at one time considered an insightful intellectual, identified hooligans, non-integrated immigrants, urban rebels, thugs or even rude, irresponsible youngsters acting intentionally or not, as the instigators of this general attack on our civilization.[420] While it seems committed to defending the majority of citizens from danger, "middle way" culture vindicates a new kind of progressiveness, one that has cast off what we in Italy term the traditional "kindliness" of the left.

That "kindliness," has all but disappeared; we have seen absolutely no traces of it except in disputations with the radical right, which has taken power now at the beginning of the third millennium more or less everywhere throughout

---

[419] For an analysis of prison politics and social control in the United States, see Parenti, C. *Lockdown America. Police and Prisons in the Age of Crisis.* London and New York: Verso, 2000. For an analysis of analogous tendencies in Europe and Italy see Anastasia, S. and P. Gonnella, eds. *Inchiesta sulle carceri italiane.* Rome: Carocci, 2002 which shows how the prison population doubled during the 1990s under the center-left government, and that foreigners represent nearly half of all inmates in Italian prisons.

[420] Enzensberger, H.M. *Civil Wars: From L.A. to Bosnia*, New York: New Press, 1995.

Europe and the United States. It was precisely this Clintonesque, progressive pseudo-kindliness that acted as the impetus for this study in order to explore how migrations in developed and dominant countries could be subject to a *double strategy*, at the same time repressive and paternalistic, strategies which we can typically define as neo-colonial. I refer principally to the *discrepancy* between the public rhetoric about immigration, expressed in terms such as "accepting," "multiculturalism," "intercultural," "integration," and so on, as opposed to the actual practices anchored to slogans such as, "public safety," "the war on illegal immigration," "controlling flows," etc. In other words, the 1990s saw the institution of a double regime, symbolic and practical, to deal with immigration. On the one hand, there was public and political adhesion to the diffused and politically correct view that migrants represent a valuable resource, they are the bearers of a culture that must be "respected," and "recognized," and on the other hand, legislative measures and practices of containment, repression, and expulsion were put in place to deal with the vast majority of migrants or refugees seeking asylum. This book has attempted to show how the poorest, the most desperate, the "*clandestini*," were treated as non-persons.

The main objective of this text was to open a discussion of the modalities by which the annulment of the *social personality* of migrants has been promoted by the political culture of our society. That society has portrayed various versions of migrants – as invaders, useful or not, as the bearers of germs that are culturally destructive, as needy individuals, or at least as a necessary work force, but never as *subjects* whose individuality, claims to equality and therefore claims to rights must be recognized. To document this thesis, this study did not investigate the "objective" situation of migrants, nor employ those statistics which the sciences that study migration unfailingly recount in order to justify their own rhetorics. Rather, this study attempts to deconstruct the objectivization that migrants undergo in our society, without contrasting the coarsest rhetorics (the specialty of the Northern League) with the more "refined" rhetorics employed by nearly all other political forces. In fact, in this book, both sides are seen as tactical variants of the same dominant strategic discourse which renders migrants social non-subjects. Because of this, even though earlier editions of this book were well-received, I have been accused by scholars of migration who frequently act as government consultants for the center-left, of assuming an "apocalyptic" position.[421]

Alas, having re-read this text, it is hardly apocalyptic. The facts supercede the analysis here of the tautological mechanisms of the social construction of the dangerous migrant, of security campaigns, the rush by noted intellectuals to demonize "aliens," the rhetorics of multiculturalism and hospitality used by government administrations that specialized in expelling migrants, the tragedies at sea that occurred after we blockaded our coasts, and the complete subordination of foreigners in social life. Shortly after the incidents in Genoa in July, 2001 revealed the true nature of the Berlusconi government, the electoral campaign on both the left and the right concluded with promises of "security in our cities," (promised by Rutelli) and "security for everyone," (promised by Berlusconi). Of course, with the new administration, the condition of migrants worsened considerably. The tragedy of the *Kater i Rades* was repeated off the coast of Sicily as other sinkings occurred. Umberto Bossi joined with the cannon blasts against the *clandestini* and together with Fini quickly launched an even more repressive law against migrants. Notice how the strategy of double-edged political correctness was appropriated by the political right – welcoming words of accepting multiculturalism for "good" migrants, and strict repressive measures for "bad" migrants – supplanting the progressives of the 1990s. That same spirit of "tolerance" is even in the programs of the Ulivo coalition, in Romano Prodi's electoral program, and in the "humanitarianism" of Casini, as well as in Fini's proposal from August, 2003 that the vote be given to good migrants. Apparently only a declining political movement like the Northern League needs to be insistent in its xenophobic demagoguery. It is not coincidental that one of the bones of contention wearing down the majority of the right in Italy is precisely this mocking proposition of granting voting rights to migrants, a proposal that would actually allow a few hundred thousand

---

[421] See Zincone, G. Ed. *Primo rapporto sull'integrazione degli immigrati in Italia.* Commissione per le politiche di integrazione degli immigrati. Bologna: Il Mulino, 2000. 178. This report, like the subsequent one, includes valuable articles, but lacks any broader political or cultural analysis.

migrants to vote for their desired Italian candidates, those migrants that are legalized and above all, within a given income bracket. On migration issues, the center-right and the center-left agree. We will now try to understand why.

Ultimately, wealthy countries need foreign labor. In Italy, as in other western countries, the development of the "new economy" in the services sector, both high-tech services and otherwise, left a high number of positions available, manual labor often completed under dangerous or difficult conditions, that the local work force has not been interested in for some time. The small factories or family businesses in the northeast, the construction business across Italy, the agricultural industry and seasonal agricultural labor, businesses that are still driving sectors in our languishing economy, would not survive more than a few weeks without the labor of foreigners: Senegalese in the iron and steel industry, Albanians and Romanians in construction, Moroccans and Albanians field workers. The same is true for the low-cost clothing and trinkets industries where foreign street salesmen work in the service of Italian wholesalers, or in the domestic service industry which employs many foreign women from South America and Eastern Europe, not to mention those positions for unskilled labor such as building maintenance, hand deliveries, or street cleaning. Foreign labor allows the reproduction of the material conditions of immaterial work, the physical, dirty, fatiguing basis of a development that is more and more orientated toward the production and global distribution of "ideas," such as brand-name clothing, software, cultural and technological innovations and in general, "intellectual" goods.

In the markets where foreigners work, a neo-Hobbesian form of labor relations dominates, based on the simple meeting between job and selling of labor. Increasingly in the non-regulated "informal" economy (which represents 30% of the entire Italian economy), the foreign work force is by definition outside of public control, and continues to vanish thanks to progressive deregulation in all sectors of the economy. The woman who keeps her live-in attendant locked inside for 16 hours a day, the foreman who hires his Albanian workers off the streets, the agricultural company that houses its field workers in a barn all support, leaving aside doctrinaire definitions, a form of pre-contractual *slave labor* that conform nicely to the general privatization of the market. The freedom of Italian entrepreneurs to engage in self-exploitation in positions that are more or less creative depends upon the servitude of foreigners. Naturally, this servitude is without territorial or national connections, and is therefore fluid, able to feed on the circulation of individuals that are without options, if not on the mere edge of survival. This servitude extends to forms of deviant labor as well, such as prostitution and petty drug dealing, jobs in which essentially the same relations of slave labor exist as those in private houses, fields, and construction sites.

It is not difficult to realize how the laws created since the middle of the 1990s, in a spirit of increasing paranoia about migrants (the Dini decree, the Turco-Napolitano law, the Bossi-Fini law) all had as the common objective of maintaining the under-the-table demand for unskilled labor. The truculent or legalistic rhetoric of the "war on illegal immigration" should deceive no one. As in every other aspect of life, prohibiting illegal markets moves toward their proliferation. The obsession with quotas for temporary entrance permits which are established by arbitrary or absurd criteria, together with aggressive norms such as identifying the employers or sponsors of foreigners, essentially makes only jobs available only to those migrants who are without means or who are *irregolari* and therefore willing to accept any situation that would allow them to remain in the country. The "*clandestinità*" nature of their labor has two faces: the foreigners who are hidden by the privacy of domestic life, such as the "attendants" to the elderly, or those who are visible in the unstable markets on the streets, such as manual day laborers or field hands. For the former, their "*clandestinità*" is swallowed up in the untouchable status of families while the latter is subject to the mechanism of fear. The very real risk of expulsion or internment in the "*centri di permanenza temporanei*" established by the Turco-Napolitano law translates into the invisibility of laborers and their total subjugation to the work conditions imposed by bosses and foremen. The abundant testimonies of foreign workers tell of 12–14 hour work days, complete lack of any safety measures, starvation wages (200–300 euros a month, in the best cases), delayed or halved salaries, and non-existent contracts. Only rarely can events such the killing of Romanian Ion Cazacu or the collapse at Genoa's port in November, 2003, reveal the reality of a situation that has become accepted as "normal." It is well-known that workers who are disabled or hurt on the job must seek out medical care privately to protect themselves from a law that does nothing to prevent illegal labor or work accidents, but periodically authorizes sweeps to arrest the "*clandestini*" in urban centers.

The Bossi-Fini law radicalizes the Turco-Napolitano law, not only because it provides for officially deploying the coast guard to "push back" any *clandestini*, and doubles the maximum period of internment in a *centro di permanenza temporanea* (foreigners can spend months from their first detainment being shuffled from prisons to police barracks and other structures), but also because it directly connects legalization, that is, temporary residency, to a "contract for residency." This means subordinating legalized workers to the absolute will of the employer. This norm, vigorously supported by the Northern League, allows for the total subjugation in the workplace and obviously reduces the possibility for workers to organize resistance, which is already inherently difficult for obvious reasons (isolation, fear, personal prejudices, etc.) Organizing would also render the situation even more precarious for those who have already been expelled from the work force and have not been able to return. The tightening of the screws in recent years against foreigners in the name of increasing the safety of our citizens or initiatives against urban decline closes impoverished migrants in a vice, individuals who came to societies defined as "accepting," a term that would be comic if it weren't so sinister.

The rhetoric of "multiculturalism" or acceptance of diversity acts as a means of cultural legitimization for the progressive enslavement of foreigners. Just as "humanitarian" wars during the 1990s (before September 11, 2001) justified the reassertion of western hegemony, multicultural rhetoric disguises the problem of migration (and more generally in our relations with the less-developed areas of the world) in ethnic, cultural, or religious terms. Foreigners lose their connotation of subjects seeking a chance for a better life in a global economy and instead acquire the status of proponents of other cultures or believers of other faiths. This allows a powerful political force to confront the question of migration on every level except on the level of rights. In other words, *not in terms of equality, but in terms of diversity.* A worker at the mercy of his or her employer (especially if he or she cannot repatriate at the time, but perhaps could in exchange for some government aid from his country of origin), seems to be the perfect reflection of those propositions by the center-right, center-left (in only superficially different language), and ultimately even the Northern League when they suggest that the west helps the Third World so that foreigners will stay in their own countries.

In this sense, we can define the dominant strategy of migration as neo-colonialist. A consistent quota, even if it represents the minority of humanity, is taken into consideration only if it subordinates itself to the reasoning of the dominant world, either at home or abroad. Colonialism does not define itself as such – it even employs a rhetoric of human rights – but it is based in the radical distinction between the rich and the poor, between who offers work, and who requires it. This is a distinction that until recently applied to a vast part of Eastern Europe, but now tends to fall down along the borders that separate the East and West, the North and the South of the world, between Europe on one side and Asia and Africa on the other, between North America and South America. In other words, between the west who has restructured global economy and the periphery of the world that continues to suffer globalization.

War, that unforeseen institution of western culture that has returned powerfully to the forefront of our world, redefines international migrations within a clear and sinister frame. Only impoverished academic convention would refer to only those who were fleeing the desolation of war as migrants. Kurds of Turkish and Iranian nationality, Afghanis and Pakistanis, Tamil and Liberians, Albanians and Algerians, Nigerians and Eritreans, Guatemalans, Bosnians, and Rom all elude the categories that the science of migration would impose. In the Mediterranean, in the rain forests, or in the deserts of the American Southwest, it is not demographic factors of attraction and expulsion that are at work so much as the results of wars. Entire populations such as the Palestinians ejected from Saudi Arabia and Kuwait in 1991 become the hostages, the coins of exchange or victims of retaliation either directly or indirectly due to conflicts in which the western world is involved. Or they become the strategic targets of destabilization, as occurred with the entire Iraqi population as it was subjected to an embargo from 1991 to 2003 that can only be considered a form of indirect genocide. Millions of people join those who flee poverty in vast areas of Africa and Asia, or civil conflicts and repressive regimes. One hundred twenty million migrants in the mid-1990s, probably over one hundred fifty million now. Humanity is adrift, and aboard the same lifeboat, young Maghrebi or Senegalese seeking their fortune or exiles from half the world could easily be found.[422]

To that section of humanity that manages to flee, the west only knows how to offer unstable, semi-subservient jobs while to the rest of that population, the west offers a multitude of new borders, roadblocks, and hurdles, and a shocking chain of detention camps from Australia to the eastern coast of Europe, in Thailand, and in America, the barrier between those who speak Spanish and those who speak English. The 1990s saw a definite externalization of detention. Regimes that until recently were considered oppressive, such as Libya, or of doubtful reputation in human rights, such as Morocco, Tunis, and Thailand are offered millions of dollars and millions of euros so that they will control and inter their own migrants and those from other countries. The war against the *clandestini* increases the regulations controlling individuals in a world that is already paranoid about terrorism. While the free circulation of material and non-material goods floods the world with typically western consumer goods, the efforts of a small percentage of dispossessed humanity to gain access to the wealthy world leads more and more people to drown at sea, or in less fortunate cases, to the other side of a barbed wire fence.

Postulating similarities between detainment camps for migrants and the Guantanamo prison is not arbitrary. In both cases, rights have been suspended,

---

[422] For an analysis of the strategy that has dominated the so-called "new wars," since 1991, see Joxe, A. *Empire of Disorder*, Cambridge, MA: Semiotext(e), 2002.

or better, they reveal the true character of those citizens with "full human rights," those who belong to our world. The fundamental principles of juridical institutions that the west has painstakingly established over centuries do not apply to foreigners: habeas corpus for *clandestini*, the simple rule of law for combatants in a conflict (the one between "civilization" and terrorism) whose logic and forms western countries do not seem to understand. We know nothing, or rather, we have only hints and clues, all terrible, about the condition of Chechen prisoners in Russia. We know virtually nothing about the condition of prisoners in Afghanistan and Iraq, but we do know of at least one case in which hundreds, if not thousands, of Taliban prisoners were eliminated by the Northern Alliance while the indifferent American military looked on. We do know that it has been officially admitted that "non-lethal" torture has been used at Guantanamo and probably in other secret American camps throughout the world. In other words, we know that the principles upon which the supremacy of the West claims to be based, firstly the respect for elementary human rights, are violated in the name of conflicts that would oppose us to "other" parts of the world. "Objective" violations, as in the case of foreigners seeking their fortune or refuge, violations that are limited and yet deliberate and impassive, as in the case of a war on terrorism that actually seems implacable and interminable. The occupation of Iraq and the destabilization of the entire Middle East show that we are only at the beginning. The regression toward the neo-slavery of labor in our territory corresponds to the regression of our right to the rest of the world. As if in some third great accumulation, after the first at the dawn of the industrial age, and the more recent one in the era of colonialism, now the whip and the gallows have again become the main disciplinary tools of humanity.

Apocalyptic? I conclude these pages one day after an encounter in which twenty Italian soldiers stationed in Iraq were killed. No sorrow for their deaths, unless in the name of some morbid, anachronistic patriotism, can in any way obliterate the enormous destruction of human lives that George W. Bush's adventure in Iraq has provoked, a country that had been prostrated by two and a half decades of wars and embargos. It is impossible to suppress the question that spontaneously comes to anyone who opposes this war. What are we doing there? It is a form of peace keeping, as the neutralizing terminology of western hegemony would have us believe, or were they trying to patch up a failing neo-imperialist or neo-colonial strategy? And above all, how do we not see that the deployment of armed forces, especially for a small country like Italy, is aimed at controlling the population of impoverished countries? A global social conflict, not a conflict of cultures but of interests, begins to set the wealthy world against the majority of humanity. The collapse of regimes that the West had long coddled in the name of fighting Communism and Islamic fundamentalism, the religious translation of frustration and poverty that incites the peripheral masses in many areas, in the wars the west becomes involved in incessantly, these same absurd forms of the same conflict. But in the politics of repressing foreigners, the denseness of our own political culture becomes evident in the face of dealing with the problems created by globalization. Instead of aiding migrants to find the chance of making a decent living, which would be infinitely easier than the reigning political credo of Europe would have us believe, we throw them into the sea, in an unpublished version of gunboat diplomacy. Or we force them to live in the dregs in the society of the market.

The conflict of cultures is little more than a gloomy fantasy of neo-conservatism. Unless it can give form to, for us and the rest of the world, the claims of the excluded and their anxiety of exploitation. As historians never tire of telling us, Islam lived more or less peacefully alongside other religions even after the conquest of the majority of the Mediterranean world. It was only the insane massacre at the conquest of Jerusalem during the first crusade that bred the hatred for the Franks, as the crusaders were called. Once again, history seems to repeat itself in the form of farce.

Books to know, to understand, to compare, to improve our world
www.ipocpress.com

Luciano De Angelis, *That One Peculiar Year*
Luciano De Angelis, *That One Peculiar Year* Large Print
Romano Màdera, Luigi Vero Tarca, *Philosophy as Life Path*
Paolo Aite, *Landscapes of the Psyche Sandplay in Jungian Analysis*
Paolo Aite, *Landscapes of the Psyche* FIGURE
Tiziana Rocca, *Communicating Success Public Relations with an Italian Flair*
Marianella Sclavi, *An Italian Lady Goes to the Bronx*
Valeria Fraccari, *Sheltered by Enchantments A Diary*
Harold DeRienzo, *The Concept of Community: Lessons from the Bronx*
Lydia Dovera, *My Stomaco Hurts! A Journey toward a Different Kind of School*
Expert Group, *Science & Governance Taking European Knowledge Society Seriously*
Raffaele Mantegazza, *The Smell of Smoke Auschwitz and the Pedagogy of Annihilation*
Emilio Gabbrielli, *Polenta and Goanna*
Nicolas Lewkowicz, *The German Question and the Originis of the Cold War*
Anna Marina Mariani, *Parenting: A Necessity and a Utopia*
Mariano Gonzáles Campo, *Guta saga (Historia de los gotlandeses)*
Sergio Corbino, *The Naples Chef Cooks. Pasta & First Courses:51 Italian Recipes*
Stanislao Nievo, *Beyond*
Fabrizio Elefante, *Faith in Democracy*
Ida Magli, *Taboo and Transgression: Jesus of Nazareth*
Christiana Langenberg, *Half of What I Know*

Pietro Condemi, *La rosa di Jericho Il paradigma olivettiano per una nuova cultura della formazione*
Paolo Bove, *Il Teatromusicale Un'esperienza interdisciplinare*
Diego Napolitani, *Individualità e gruppalità*
Diego Napolitani, *Di palo in frasca*
Lydia Dovera, *Mi fa male lo stomach! In viaggio verso una scuola diversa*
Lydia Dovera, *L'isolachec'è*
Bruno De Maria, *Un'aria d'ombre*
Fabrizio Elefante, *La fiducia nella democrazia*
Pasquale D'Ascola, *Il pieno è il vuoto? Imparare con il teatro Manuale per pedagogisti*
Roberto Bianchi, *C'era una volta la favola*
Ornella Azzarà, *Bambi 116*

Printed in the United Kingdom by
Lightning Source UK Ltd., Milton Keynes
137376UK00002B/52-60/P